The Cloud-Based Demand-Driven Supply Chain

Wiley & SAS Business Series

The Wiley & SAS Business Series presents books that help senior-level managers with their critical management decisions.

Titles in the Wiley & SAS Business Series include:

The Analytic Hospitality Executive by Kelly A. McGuire

Analytics: The Agile Way by Phil Simon

Analytics in a Big Data World: The Essential Guide to Data Science and Its Applications by Bart Baesens

A Practical Guide to Analytics for Governments: Using Big Data for Good by Marie Lowman

Bank Fraud: Using Technology to Combat Losses by Revathi Subramanian

Big Data Analytics: Turning Big Data into Big Money by Frank Ohlhorst

Big Data, Big Innovation: Enabling Competitive Differentiation through Business Analytics by Evan Stubbs

Business Analytics for Customer Intelligence by Gert Laursen

Business Intelligence Applied: Implementing an Effective Information and Communications Technology Infrastructure by Michael Gendron

Business Intelligence and the Cloud: Strategic Implementation Guide by Michael S. Gendron

Business Transformation: A Roadmap for Maximizing Organizational Insights by Aiman Zeid

Connecting Organizational Silos: Taking Knowledge Flow Management to the Next Level with Social Media by Frank Leistner

Data-Driven Healthcare: How Analytics and BI Are Transforming the Industry by Laura Madsen

Delivering Business Analytics: Practical Guidelines for Best Practice by Evan Stubbs

Demand-Driven Forecasting: A Structured Approach to Forecasting, Second Edition by Charles Chase

Demand-Driven Inventory Optimization and Replenishment: Creating a More Efficient Supply Chain by Robert A. Davis

Developing Human Capital: Using Analytics to Plan and Optimize Your Learning and Development Investments by Gene Pease, Barbara Beresford, and Lew Walker

Economic and Business Forecasting: Analyzing and Interpreting Econometric Results by John Silvia, Azhar Iqbal, Kaylyn Swankoski, Sarah Watt, and Sam Bullard

Economic Modeling in the Post Great Recession Era: Incomplete Data, Imperfect Markets by John Silvia, Azhar Iqbal, and Sarah Watt House

Enhance Oil & Gas Exploration with Data Driven Geophysical and Petrophysical Models by Keith Holdaway and Duncan Irving

The Executive's Guide to Enterprise Social Media Strategy: How Social Networks Are Radically Transforming Your Business by David Thomas and Mike Barlow

Foreign Currency Financial Reporting from Euros to Yen to Yuan: A Guide to Fundamental Concepts and Practical Applications by Robert Rowan

Harness Oil and Gas Big Data with Analytics: Optimize Exploration and Production with Data Driven Models by Keith Holdaway

Health Analytics: Gaining the Insights to Transform Health Care by Jason Burke

Heuristics in Analytics: A Practical Perspective of What Influences Our Analytical World by Carlos Andre Reis Pinheiro and Fiona McNeill

Human Capital Analytics: How to Harness the Potential of Your Organization's Greatest Asset by Gene Pease, Boyce Byerly, and Jac Fitz-enz

Implement, Improve and Expand Your Statewide Longitudinal Data System: Creating a Culture of Data in Education by Jamie McQuiggan and Armistead Sapp

Intelligent Credit Scoring: Building and Implementing Better Credit Risk Scorecards, Second Edition by Naeem Siddiqi

JMP Connections by John Wubbel

Killer Analytics: Top 20 Metrics Missing from Your Balance Sheet by Mark Brown

Machine Learning for Marketers: Hold the Math by Jim Sterne

On-Camera Coach: Tools and Techniques for Business Professionals in a Video-Driven World by Karin Reed

Predictive Analytics for Human Resources by Jac Fitz-enz and John Mattox II

Predictive Business Analytics: Forward-Looking Capabilities to Improve Business Performance by Lawrence Maisel and Gary Cokins

Profit Driven Business Analytics: A Practitioner's Guide to Transforming Big Data into Added Value by Wouter Verbeke, Cristian Bravo, and Bart Baesens

Retail Analytics: The Secret Weapon by Emmett Cox

Social Network Analysis in Telecommunications by Carlos Andre Reis Pinheiro

Statistical Thinking: Improving Business Performance, Second Edition by Roger W. Hoerl and Ronald D. Snee

Strategies in Biomedical Data Science: Driving Force for Innovation by Jay Etchings

Style & Statistic: The Art of Retail Analytics by Brittany Bullard

Taming the Big Data Tidal Wave: Finding Opportunities in Huge Data Streams with Advanced Analytics by Bill Franks

Too Big to Ignore: The Business Case for Big Data by Phil Simon

Using Big Data Analytics: Turning Big Data into Big Money by Jared Dean

The Value of Business Analytics: Identifying the Path to Profitability by Evan Stubbs

The Visual Organization: Data Visualization, Big Data, and the Quest for Better Decisions by Phil Simon

Win with Advanced Business Analytics: Creating Business Value from Your Data by Jean Paul Isson and Jesse Harriott

For more information on any of the above titles, please visit www.wiley.com.

The Cloud-Based Demand-Driven Supply Chain

Vinit Sharma

WILEY

Published by John Wiley & Sons, Inc., Hoboken, New Jersey.
Published simultaneously in Canada.

For general information on our other products and services or for technical support, please contact our Customer Care Department within the United States at (800) 762-2974, outside the United States at (317) 572-3993, or fax (317) 572-4002.

Wiley publishes in a variety of print and electronic formats and by print-on-demand. Some material included with standard print versions of this book may not be included in e-books or in print-on-demand. If this book refers to media such as a CD or DVD that is not included in the version you purchased, you may download this material at http://booksupport.wiley.com. For more information about Wiley products, visit www.wiley.com.

Library of Congress Cataloging-in-Publication Data:

Names: Sharma, Vinit, 1974- author.
Title: The cloud-based demand-driven supply chain / Vinit Sharma.
Description: Hoboken, New Jersey : John Wiley & Sons, 2019. | Series: Wiley & SAS business series | Includes index. |
Identifiers: LCCN 2018029740 (print) | LCCN 2018041782 (ebook) | ISBN 9781119477808 (Adobe PDF) | ISBN 9781119477815 (ePub) | ISBN 9781119477334 (hardcover)
Subjects: LCSH: Business logistics. | Supply and demand—Management. | Cloud computing—Industrial applications.
Classification: LCC HD38.5 (ebook) | LCC HD38.5 .S544 2019 (print) | DDC 658.70285/46782—dc23
LC record available at https://lccn.loc.gov/2018029740

Cover Design: Wiley
Cover Image: © Fly_Studio/Shutterstock

Printed in the United States of America

V10004919_101118

To my parents and grandparents
for their lifelong love and support

Contents

List of Figures   xi

List of Tables   xv

Preface   xvii

Acknowledgments   xix

Chapter 1   Demand-Driven Forecasting in the Supply Chain   1

Chapter 2   Introduction to Cloud Computing   43

Chapter 3   Migrating to the Cloud   91

Chapter 4   Amazon Web Services and Microsoft Azure   117

Chapter 5   Case Studies of Demand-Driven Forecasting in AWS   221

Chapter 6   Summary   237

Glossary   253

References   255

About the Author   291

Index   293

List of Figures

Figure 1	Push and Pull—Sales and Operations Process	4
Figure 2	Digital Supply Chain—Interconnected	5
Figure 3	Supply Chain Control Tower	7
Figure 4	MHI 2018 Survey Results: Company Challenges	8
Figure 5	Example: Product Dimension Hierarchy	10
Figure 6	Example: Star Schema - Forecast Dimensions	12
Figure 7	Traditional Data Flow—Supply Chain Analytics	12
Figure 8	Data Lake - Data for Demand Forecasting	17
Figure 9	High-level Lambda Architecture Design	18
Figure 10	Hybrid Modern Data Flow—Supply Chain Analytics	20
Figure 11	DDPP Model—Types and Maturity of Analytics	22
Figure 12	Microsoft AI Example—High Level	24
Figure 13	Microsoft AI Services Example	25
Figure 14	Demand-Driven Forecasting and IoT	28
Figure 15	Demand Shaping—Personalized Recommendations	29
Figure 16	DDSC Benefits All Participants—BCG, 2012	30
Figure 17	Databerg and Dark Data	32
Figure 18	Random Walk Forecast Example	34
Figure 19	Sales and Seasonal Random Walk Forecast Example	35
Figure 20	SAS Demand-Driven Planning and Optimization Example	37
Figure 21	Combining Cloud + Data + Advanced Analytics	39
Figure 22	Benefits of Demand-Driven Supply Chain	40
Figure 23	Time Line for Cloud Computing—Part 1	45
Figure 24	Time Line for Cloud Computing—Part 2	46
Figure 25	Traditional Server and Server Virtualization	48
Figure 26	Data Center Virtualization—Transformation	49
Figure 27	Virtual Machines Compared to Containers	50
Figure 28	Data Stored in Data Centers, 2016–2021, Cisco GCI	53

Figure 29   IT Systems to Benefit from Big Data   54

Figure 30   Big Data—Open Source Ecosystem   55

Figure 31   Cloud Computing—Five Characteristics   62

Figure 32   Black Friday—Traditional and Cloud   66

Figure 33   Cloud Price Index—451 Research Group   70

Figure 34   The Three Cloud Service Models   71

Figure 35   AWS Shared Responsibility Model   72

Figure 36   Microsoft Azure Portal Screenshot—IaaS Example   73

Figure 37   Microsoft Azure Portal Screenshot—PaaS   74

Figure 38   Cloud Service Model Growth 2016–2021   75

Figure 39   Enterprise SaaS Growth and Market Leaders,
            Q2 2017   76

Figure 40   Four Cloud Deployment Models   77

Figure 41   Cisco Global Cloud Index 2016–2021   78

Figure 42   Public versus Private Cloud   80

Figure 43   Cisco Global Cloud Index—Private versus Public
            Cloud   80

Figure 44   Top IaaS Platforms—Public Cloud   81

Figure 45   Importance of Cloud Benefits   82

Figure 46   Cloud Benefits 2017 versus 2016   83

Figure 47   Cloud Challenges 2017 versus 2016   85

Figure 48   Challenges Decrease with Cloud Maturity   87

Figure 49   IT Benefits of Cloud Computing   87

Figure 50   Costs and Benefits to Cloud Users   89

Figure 51   Five Steps to the Cloud   93

Figure 52   Factors Preventing Enterprises' Use of Cloud   95

Figure 53   Economic impact of Cloud Computing in Europe   95

Figure 54   ISG Cloud Readiness Results Example   98

Figure 55   Example R Framework Migrating to Cloud   100

Figure 56   AWS Cloud Migration—6Rs   102

Figure 57   Considerations for Cloud Migration Examples   106

Figure 58   Cloud Migration Factory Approach   108

Figure 59   Cloud Vendor Benchmark 2016—Germany   112

Figure 60   The Race for Public Cloud Leadership   112

Figure 61 Cloud Migration Factory Methodology   114
Figure 62 AWS Cloud Portfolio Categories   119
Figure 63 AWS EC2 On-Demand Pricing Examples   121
Figure 64 AWS Global Regions for Public Cloud   125
Figure 65 Industrial Internet Economic Potential   156
Figure 66 AWS Cloud Service Portfolio   159
Figure 67 Microsoft Azure Cloud Portfolio Categories   161
Figure 68 Column Family Data Model Example   189
Figure 69 Data Flow Example   195
Figure 70 Industrial Internet Data Loop   204
Figure 71 Microsoft Demand Forecasting Example   217
Figure 72 Example Methodology—Solution Assessment for
           Cloud   226
Figure 73 Supply Chain Optimization Solution Suite   232
Figure 74 Case Study—Deployment Example   233
Figure 75 Connected Supply Chain Management   243
Figure 76 Demand-Driven Supply Chain—Integration and
           Technologies   245
Figure 77 Modern Supply Chain and Technologies   250
Figure 78 Road to Modern Supply Chain Management   251

List of Tables

Table 1   AWS Cost Calculation Example   69
Table 2   Percentage of Companies Adopting at Least One
          Cloud Solution by Industry Sector 2013–2015   85
Table 3   Revenue Growth Attributed to Cloud Adoption   88
Table 4   Cloud Readiness Check Example (ISG)   97
Table 5   AWS Cloud Adoption Framework   103
Table 6   Respondents' Views on Which Cloud Services Gave
          the Best Economic Return   109
Table 7   Preferred Choice of Cloud Services Provider   110
Table 8   Main Choice Factor for Cloud Service Provider   111
Table 9   Market Comparison of Top 25 to 100 Vendors
          by Origin   111
Table 10 Estimated EU Market Shares of Top 25 Public
          Cloud Service Providers   113
Table 11 Key-Value Data Store Example   188
Table 12 Document Data Model Example   190

Preface

It's time to get your head in the cloud!

In today's business environment, more and more people are requesting cloud-based solutions to help solve their business challenges. So how can you not only anticipate your clients' needs but also keep ahead of the curve to ensure their goals stay on track?

With the help of this accessible book, you'll get a clear sense of cloud computing and understand how to communicate the benefits, drawbacks, and options to your clients so they can make the best choices for their unique needs. Plus, case studies give you the opportunity to relate real-life examples of how the latest technologies are giving organizations worldwide the chance to thrive as supply chain solutions in the cloud.

What this book does:

- Demonstrates how improvements in forecasting, collaboration, and inventory optimization can lead to cost savings.
- Explores why cloud computing is becoming increasingly important.
- Takes a close look at the types of cloud computing.
- Makes sense of demand-driven forecasting using Amazon's cloud or Microsoft's cloud, Azure.

Whether you work in management, business, or information technology (IT), this will be the dog-eared reference you'll want to keep close by as you continue making sense of the cloud.

Acknowledgments

This book would not have been possible without the help and support from various colleagues, friends, and organizations. I would like to take this opportunity to thank Jack Zhang (SAS), Blanche Shelton (SAS), Bob Davis (SAS), and Stacey Hamilton (SAS) for supporting the idea and helping with moving it forward. A special thank you to Emily Paul (Wiley), Shek Cho (Wiley), Mike Henton (Wiley), and Lauree Shepard (SAS) for their help with turning the book into reality. Research from various organizations has been vital to the success of this book, and I would like to especially thank Carol Miller (MHI), Amy Sarosiek (GE), Emily Neuman (AWS), Frank Simorj (Microsoft), Heather Gallo (Synergy Research), Juergen Brettel (ISG Research), Kim Weins (RightScale), Michael Mentzel (Heise Medien), Owen Rogers (451 Research), and Suellen Bergman (BCG) for their help in including such content. Last, but not least, I would like to express a very special thank you to esteemed colleagues, supply chain gurus, and good friends Charles Chase (SAS) and Christoph Hartmann (SAS) for their expert help with this book.

A special thank you to the following organizations for their help: 451 Research, AWS, Boston Consulting Group, Cisco, European Commission, European Union, Experton Group, Gartner, GE, Heise Medien, IBF, ISG Research, McAfee, MHI, Microsoft, RightScale, SAS, Skyhigh, Supply Chain Insights, and Synergy Research.

The Cloud-Based Demand-Driven Supply Chain

CHAPTER 1

Demand-Driven Forecasting in the Supply Chain

The world is changing at an increasing pace. Consumers are becoming more demanding, and they expect products and services of high quality, value for their money, and timely availability. Organizations and industries across the globe are under pressure to produce products or provide services at the right time, quantity, price, and location. As global competition has increased, those organizations that fail to be proactive with information and business insights gained risk loss of sales and lower market share. Supply chain optimization—from forecasting and planning to execution point of view—is critical to success for organizations across industries and the world. The focus of this book is on demand-driven forecasting (using data as evidence to forecast demand for sales units) and how cloud computing can assist with computing and Big Data challenges faced by organizations today. From a demand-driven forecasting perspective, the context will be a business focus rather than a statistical point of view. For the purpose of this book, the emphasis will be on forecasting sales units, highlighting possible benefits of improved forecasts, and supply chain optimization.

Advancements in information technology (IT) and decreasing costs (e.g., data storage, computational resources) can provide opportunities for organizations needing to analyze lots of data. It is becoming easier and more cost-effective to capture, store, and gain insights from data. Organizations can then respond better and at a quicker pace, producing those products that are in high demand or providing the best value to the organization. Business insights can help organizations understand the sales demand for their products, the sentiment (e.g., like or dislike products) that customers have about their products, and which locations have the highest consumption. The business intelligence gained can help organizations understand what price sensitivity exists, whether there is effectiveness of events and promotions (e.g., influencing demand), what product attributes make the most consumer impact, and much more. IT can help organizations increase digitalization of their supply chains, and cloud computing can provide a scalable and cost-effective platform for organizations to capture, store, analyze, and consume (view and consequently act upon) large amounts of data.

This chapter aims to provide a brief context of demand-driven forecasting from a business perspective and sets the scene for subsequent chapters that focus on cloud computing and how the cloud as a platform can assist with demand-driven forecasting and related challenges. Personal experiences (drawing upon consultative supply chain projects at SAS) are interspersed throughout the chapters, though they have been anonymized to protect organizations worldwide. Viewpoints from several vendors are included to provide a broad and diverse vision of demand-driven forecasting and supply chain optimization, as well as cloud computing.

Forecasting of sales is generally used to help organizations predict the number of products to produce, ship, store, distribute, and ultimately sell to end consumers. There has been a shift away from a push philosophy (also known as inside-out approach) where organizations are sales driven and push products to end consumers. This philosophy has often resulted in overproduction, overstocks in all locations in the supply chain network, and incorrect understanding of consumer demand. Stores often have had to reduce prices to help lower inventory, and this has had a further impact on the profitability of organizations. Sales can be defined as shipments or sales orders. Demand can include point of sales (POS) data, syndicated scanner data, online or mobile sales, or demand data from a connected device (e.g., vending machine, retail stock shelves). A new demand-pull (also known as an outside-in approach) philosophy has gained momentum where organizations are learning to sense demand (also known as demand-sensing) of end consumers and to shift their supply chains to operate more effectively. Organizations that are changing their sales and operations planning (S&OP) process and moving to a demand-pull philosophy are said to be creating a demand-driven supply network (DDSN). (See Figure 1.)

The Boston Consulting Group (BCG) defines a demand-driven supply chain (DDSC) as a system of coordinated technologies and processes that senses and reacts to real-time demand signals across a network of customers, suppliers, and employees (Budd, Knizek, and Tevelson 2012, 3). For an organization to be genuinely demand-driven, it should aim for an advanced supply chain (i.e., supply chain 2.0) that seamlessly integrates customer expectations into

Driven by Sales Forecast ————————————————————————▶ PUSH

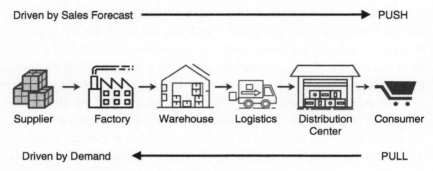

Supplier   Factory   Warehouse   Logistics   Distribution   Consumer
                                                  Center

Driven by Demand ◀———————————————————————————— PULL

Figure 1 Push and Pull—Sales and Operations Process

its fulfillment model (Joss et al. 2016, 19). Demand-driven supply chain management focuses on the stability of individual value chain activities, as well as the agility to autonomously respond to changing demands immediately without prior thought or preparation (Eagle 2017, 22). Organizations that transition to a demand-driven supply chain are adopting the demand-pull philosophy mentioned earlier. In today's fast-moving world, the supply chain is moving away from an analog and linear model to a digital and multidimensional model—an interconnected neural model (many connected nodes in a mesh, as shown in Figure 2). Information between nodes is of various types, and flows at different times, volumes, and velocities. Organizations must be able to ingest, sense (analyze), and proactively act upon insights promptly to be successful. According to an MHI survey that was published (Batty et al. 2017, 3), 80 percent of respondents believe a digital supply chain will prevail by the year 2022. The amount of adoption of a digital supply chain transformation varies across organizations, industries, and countries.

It has become generally accepted that those organizations that use business intelligence and data-driven insights outperform those organizations that do not. Top-performing organizations realize the value of leveraging data (Curran et al. 2015, 2–21). Using business intelligence (BI) with analytics built upon quality data (relevant and complete data) allows organizations to sense demand, spot trends, and be more proactive. The spectrum of data is also changing with the digitalization of the supply chain. Recent enhancements in technologies and economies of

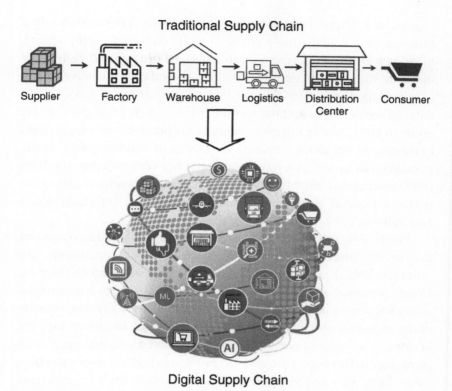

Figure 2 Digital Supply Chain—Interconnected

scale have made it possible to capture data from countless sources and at faster rates (e.g., near real time or regular ingress intervals) than previously possible. Data no longer must be limited to sales demand only, and can include other sources such as weather, economic events and trends, social media data (e.g., useful for product sentiment analysis), traffic data, and more.

Capturing data faster (e.g., near real time via connected devices) and capturing larger volumes of data (e.g., several years of historical data of many variables) have now become more accessible and more affordable than ever before. One of the main philosophies of Big Data is to capture and store all types of data now and worry about figuring out the questions to ask of the data later. There are opportunities for organizations to leverage technologies in computing, analytics, data capture and storage, and the Internet of Things (IoT) to transform their business to a digital supply chain (a well-connected supply chain). Such data and analytics can lead to improved insights and visibility of an entire supply chain network. The end-to-end supply chain visibility of information and material flow enables organizations to make holistic data-driven decisions optimal for their businesses (Muthukrishnan and Sullivan 2012, 2). Organizations wishing to optimize their supply chain management are moving toward an intelligent and integrated supply management model that has high supply network visibility and high integration of systems, processes, and people of the entire supply chain network internal and external to the organization (Muthukrishnan and Sullivan 2012, 2–5).

The holistic and real-time data coupled with advanced analytics can help organizations make optimal decisions, streamline operations, and minimize risk through a comprehensive risk management program (Muthukrishnan and Sullivan 2012, 5). The value of data is maximized when it is acted upon at the right time (Barlow 2015, 22). The benefits of the increased visibility and transparency include improved supplier performance, reduced operational costs, improved sales and operations planning (S&OP) outcomes, and increased supply chain responsiveness (Muthukrishnan and Sullivan 2012, 6). Implementing a supply chain with high visibility and integration provides benefits such as increased sales through faster responses and decision making, reduced inventory across the supply chain, reduced logistic and procurement costs, and improved service levels (Muthukrishnan and Sullivan 2012, 11).

The increasing needs for supply chain visibility are leading to the adoption of supply chain control towers (SCCTs), depicted in Figure 3. An organization could use an SCCT as a central hub to centralize and integrate required technologies, organizations (intranet and extranet supply chain network members), and processes to capture, analyze, and use the information to make holistic and data-driven decisions (Bhosle et al. 2011, 4). Using an SCCT can help with strategic, tactical, and operational-level control of a supply chain. Having a holistic view through an SCCT helps an organization and its supply chain network to become more agile (e.g., ability to change supply chain processes, partners, or facilities). It also helps increase resilience against unexpected events outside of the control of the supply chain network.

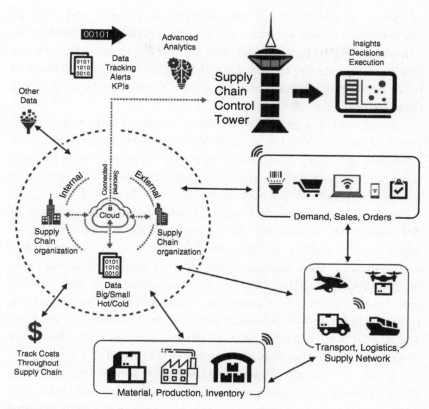

Figure 3 Supply Chain Control Tower

Reliability and supply chain effectiveness can be improved by meeting service levels, cost controls, availability, and quality targets (Bhosle et al. 2011, 4–6).

An SCCT can also help a supply chain network become more responsive to changes in demand, capacity, and other factors that could influence business (Bhosle et al. 2011, 6). There are three phases of maturity for implementing and executing such a supply chain control tower. The first phase typically focuses on operational visibility such as shipment and inventory status. Phase 2 is where the information flowing to the supply chain control tower is used to monitor the progress of shipments through the various network nodes of a supply chain and alert decision makers of any potential issues or events. In the third and most mature phase, data and artificial intelligence are used to predict the potential problems or bottlenecks (Bhosle et al. 2011, 5–8). The data captured and processed by the SCCT can provide the supply chain visibility and insights necessary to make appropriate decisions and to operate a customer-focused supply chain (Bhosle et al. 2011, 9).

Benefits of a supply chain control tower include lower costs, enriched decision-making capabilities, improved demand forecasts, optimized inventory levels, reduced buffer inventory, reduced cycle times, better scheduling and planning, improved transport and logistics, and higher service levels (Bhosle et al. 2011, 11).

One of the main challenges of the digital supply chain is demand-driven forecasting, and it is generally a top priority of organizations wishing to improve their business. Forecasting and Personalization were ranked as the top two needed analytical capabilities (Microsoft 2015, 14). The forecasting function was rated as either very challenging or somewhat challenging (39 and 36 percent, respectively) in an MHI Annual Industry Report (Batty et al. 2017, 9), and in a 2018 survey more than 50 percent of respondents noted the forecasting function as very challenging (see Figure 4).

There are distinct phases of maturity for forecasting, and such maturity levels vary significantly across organizations, industries, and countries. Unscientific forecasting and planning (e.g., using personal

Figure 4 MHI 2018 Survey Results: Company Challenges
Source: MHI Annual Industry Report, 2018, 8.

judgment versus statistical evidence) are still prevalent in many sectors, as shown in a survey by Blue Yonder (2016) in the grocery retail sector. The Blue Yonder report highlights the finding that 48 percent of those surveyed are still using manual processes and gut feeling to make choices, instead of using data-driven actions (Blue Yonder 2016, 25). There are many benefits of making a transition to a demand-driven supply chain. Research by BCG highlights that some companies carry 33 percent less inventory and improve delivery performance by 20 percent (Budd, Knizek, and Tevelson 2012, 3).

A strategy for improved forecasting needs to be holistic and to focus on multiple dimensions to be most effective. The journey toward improvement should include three key pillars:

1. Data
2. Analytics
3. Collaboration—people and processes using a collaborative approach

1. DATA

As mentioned earlier, data is the foundation for analytics, business intelligence, and insights to be gained. The famous "garbage in, garbage out" concept equally applies to today's challenges. Organizations must be able to capture and analyze data that is relevant to forecasts and supply chain optimizations. Having access to holistic data (e.g., historical demand data, data from other influencing factors) allows organizations to apply advanced analytics to help sense the demand for their products. Insights gained from analytics allows organizations to detect and shape demand—for example, the most demanded products at the right location, at the right time, at the right price, and with the right attributes. Leveraging data and advanced analytics allows organizations to understand correlations and the effect that influencing factors such as price, events, promotions, and the like have on the demand of sales units. As Marcos Borges of the Nestlé organization noted (SAS Institute press release, October 12, 2017), a differentiating benefit of advanced forecasting is the ability to analyze holistic data (multiple data variables) and identify factors influencing demand for each product throughout a product hierarchy. This process should be automated, and be able to handle large volumes (e.g., many transactions across many dimensions) with depth of data (e.g., a hierarchy of a product dimension).

Quality of data is an essential but often overlooked aspect of analytics. Generally, for a forecast to be meaningful, there should be access to at least two years of historical data at the granularity level of the required forecast (e.g., daily or weekly data for weekly forecasts). This data should be available for all hierarchy levels of the unit or metric of the time series. For example, a consumer packaged goods (CPG) company wishing to predict demand for chocolates would have a product dimension in its data mart for forecasting. This dimension would have a hierarchy with various categories and subcategories. Individual products are called leaf member nodes, and they belong to one hierarchy chain. Those products therefore have a direct and single relationship link rolling upward through the hierarchy. A leaf member can just roll up through one subcategory and category (see Figure 5). Ideally, data should be available for all relevant dimensions. Granular data for the levels of all dimensions should also be available. The combination of product dimension data in this example and time-series data (e.g., sales transactions) that is complete (e.g., sales transaction data across all levels of product hierarchy for at least two years) increases the accuracy of the forecast.

If data is available across all levels of the hierarchy of the dimension, then forecast reconciliation techniques (performed by software solutions) such as top-down, bottom-up, and middle-out forecasting

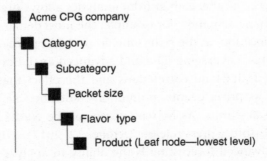

Figure 5   Example: Product Dimension Hierarchy

lead to more accurate results. Ideally, the system would highlight which levels of the hierarchy would provide the most substantial results. These reconciliation techniques aggregate data up or down a hierarchy, allowing forecasts to be consolidated and grouped at various levels. The aforementioned methods can help with demand planning (e.g., using the consolidated forecasted demand at a subcategory or category level). The more data there is available at the granular level (lower levels of the hierarchy of product dimension in this example) the more accurate the aggregation and proportioning can be. Using these methods, a demand planner can then view forecasts at a category level, store level, or regional level, for example.

Typically, other dimensions used in demand forecasting include store location and customers, and these are commonly represented in a star schema data model (see Figure 6). Such a design that separates data can help with the performance of the analytics process used for generating forecasts. The method of striking a balance between all data stored together and separating data is referred to normalization and denormalization of a data model. The data schema design has a profound impact on the analytic capabilities and the performance (speed of completion) of the computations. Therefore, it is equally important to collect the right data (data about metric to be forecasted, as well as data from causal variables), with data of at least two years' time horizon, and to organize the data appropriately (e.g., data marts, logical data schemas). Advancements in data storage and analytic technologies such as data lakes and Big Data can help provide more flexibility and agility for this design process and is elaborated on later in this section.

It is typical for individual analytical functions within supply chain optimization to have separate data marts. For example, data stored for demand forecasts can be stored in one data mart, whereas data related to inventory optimization or collaborative demand planning could each have separate data marts. Such data marts should have easy data integration and allow data flow between functions to enhance the usability of data and increase analytical value. This single or integrated set of data marts for the supply chain analytics is also referred to as a demand signal repository (DSR). (See Figure 7.)

The data model design of these data marts and their storage methods are well suited for advanced analytics (such that demand-driven

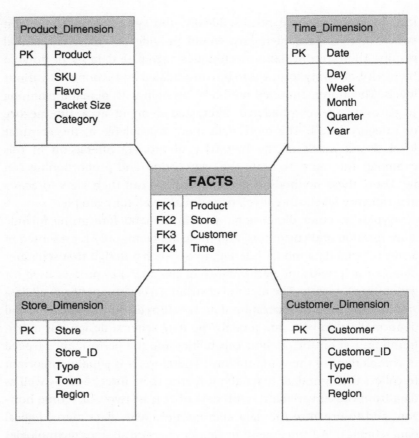

PK = Primary Key
FK = Foreign Key

Figure 6 Example: Star Schema - Forecast Dimensions

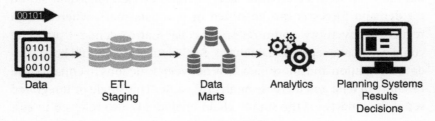

Figure 7 Traditional Data Flow—Supply Chain Analytics

forecasting uses). Business subject matter typically organizes data marts—for example, a data mart for forecasts, a data mart for inventory optimization, a data mart for finance, and so forth.

Slowly moving data (e.g., daily, weekly, or monthly ingress of data) is generally captured via traditional technologies such as databases or data warehouses. Such slowly moving data is also referred to as cold or warm data. Fast-moving data (e.g., per second, minute, hour, day) is captured with the help of connected devices (e.g., IoT), processing technologies such as event stream processing (ESP) that provide near real-time analytics, and advanced data storage (e.g., data lake) technologies and formats that focus on the rapid ingestion of data. This faster-moving data is also referred to as hot data. Real-time analytics with ESP will become a vital component of a connected supply chain in the future. Such data can flow into a supply chain control tower, and can help the organization gain insights from data and act upon it proactively—for example, analyzing data from logistic providers and demand data in real time, and reacting faster to changes in demand or logistics.

Organizations typically use a data mart purpose-built for analytics such as demand forecasting. Separation for a purpose generally increases performance (e.g., separating write operations into online transaction processing [OLTP], and read operations into online analytical processing [OLAP]). Such isolation also allows data management processes to be tailored to the types of data, as well as to the speed of data ingestion. The data storage types can help with analytical loads; for example, OLAP systems are purpose-built for analytics (e.g., searching through data, filtering, grouping, calculations, view multiple dimensions, etc.).

In a digital supply chain, there are many different data sources, which generate different types of data (e.g., point of sales data, retail sales data, online sales data, shipment data, logistical data, etc.). The volume, variety, and velocity of data challenge traditional systems and methods for storing and analyzing data. The data lake is a method to help with these challenges. Organizations can collect data from many sources and ingest these into their data lakes (on premises or in the cloud).

One of the differences of a data lake as opposed to a data warehouse or data mart is that with a data lake organizations initially do not have to worry about any particular data schema (organization of data), nor concern themselves with data transformations at the ingestion stage.

Traditional databases, data warehouses, and data marts follow a schema-on-write approach. Therefore data ingestion processes must extract, transform, and load (ETL) (the overall process is also referred to as data wrangling) the data to fit a predefined data schema. The data schema can include multiple databases or data marts but requires data to match definitions (e.g., data types, data lengths, data stored in appropriate tables). The ETL process is generally defined once or does not change that often, and is most likely scheduled after that. The method of data ingestion, staging data (importing into required formats, storing in a commonly accessible form and location), and ETL can take minutes or hours depending on the complexity of tasks and the volume of data. For example, forecasts at a weekly time granularity level often ingest incremental data at a weekly time interval. Forecasting systems often perform this data import process in batch jobs in nonbusiness hours (e.g., weekend or night time). The forecasting process can also be automated, as can the sharing of data with downstream planning systems. If a demand planning process involves human review and collaboration, then that process is included in a forecast cycle. Depending on the forecast horizon (e.g., time periods into the future) and other factors such as lead times (e.g., supplier, manufacturing) and speed of turnover of the products to be forecasted, the overall forecasting cycle can take hours, days, weeks, or longer.

A data lake follows a schema-on-read approach. In this case the data ingestion process extracts and loads data into a storage pool. Data transformations are performed at a later stage if required (ELT). The data remains in a data lake and can be accessed directly. It can also be transformed and copied to other data storage targets (e.g., databases, data marts), or accessed and leveraged via other means (e.g., data virtualization mechanisms). Such a data ingestion process via a data lake permits fast ingress of data and is typically aimed at fast-moving (hot) data. Analytics on such fast-moving data can occur as quickly as data is ingested. This process is often referred to as event stream processing (ESP) or streaming analytics and focuses on data that is moving in the second or minute time frames. Using the combination of a data lake and ESP, for example, it is possible to detect values near real time to trigger an event or to traffic light an anomaly.

Tamara Dull, director of emerging technologies at SAS, defines a data lake as follows: "A data lake is a storage repository that holds a vast amount of raw data in its native format, including structured, semi-structured, and unstructured data. The data structure and requirements are not defined until the data is needed" (Dull 2015). A data warehouse stores structured data, has a defined data model that information is molded to (also referred to as a schema-on-write concept), and is mature. This traditional method of ingesting, storing, and using data has a high consistency of data and is used by business professionals for deriving insights.

A data lake, in contrast, can be used to ingest and store structured, semistructured, and raw data. Structured data examples include comma-separated values (CSV) files with defined fields, data types, and order. Semistructured data examples include JavaScript Object Notation (JSON) file (defined fields, ordering, and data types can change). Raw or unstructured data examples include media files (e.g., JPEG, video), emails, documents, and the like. A data lake follows a schema-on-read method, eliminating the need for data wrangling and molding at ingestion time. A data lake is therefore well suited for fast ingestion of data from all types of sources (e.g., streaming, internet, connected devices, etc.). Data lakes are designed to be horizontally scalable, with commodity hardware providing an excellent cost-to-performance ratio for organizations. The maturity of data lake systems is steadily enhancing and, as the use by organizations worldwide and across industries increases, so do the solutions for easy access to data and analytics against such systems.

One of the standard technologies behind a data lake is the Hadoop distributed file system (HDFS) and the Hadoop framework. This technology allows storing any data type on an interconnected grid of computer nodes, leveraging cheaper local storage present in each node. The file system manages the complexity of distributing and managing data files, including redundant copies of each file for high availability (HA), disaster recovery (DR), and performance of computing and analysis (used with methods like MapReduce). The

Hadoop framework leverages cheaper commodity server hardware and scales out horizontally (adding more server nodes as storage or computing requirements dictate). This is a fundamental difference from the traditional framework of vertically scaling servers (increasing computing resources—central processing unit [CPU] and random-access memory [RAM]). The cost of vertically scaling is a lot higher, and, although advancements in computing are continuing, the vertical scale approach has a limit at some point, whereas in theory the horizontal scaling approach has no limit.

Another benefit of this horizontal scaling approach is that data and computing power can stay together on interconnected nodes. A big analytical processing job is broken down into smaller segments (referred to as the mapping phase) and each node in a Hadoop server farm (also called clusters) analyzes segments of that job, based on data that is available to its local storage. The results from each node are then consolidated into one result (this step is the reduce phase).

Once data has landed in a data lake, it can be analyzed, or processed further to be transferred into different formats and a data mart, for example. Simple MapReduce methods enable data to be mined on a large scale and at faster speeds than were previously possible. (See Figure 8.)

EXAMPLE

EXAMPLE

There are many data sets with patient records, and these data sets are distributed across many computer nodes. Typically, there are three copies of each data set, which are hosted on different nodes, assisting with disaster recovery goals. A user would like to report on the number of males per age group across all the data. The user submits a MapReduce job to filter for males per age group from each data set stored across the HDFS, and then consolidate the results. The inner workings of the MapReduce process and the Hadoop framework are out of scope for this book—the aim is to highlight the storage, processing, scalability, and speed (wall clock time) benefits of using a data lake and distributed computing power.

The technologies that enable a data lake, and a data lake itself, can help with the challenges of Big Data. The National Institute of

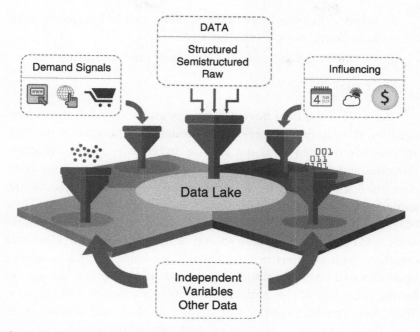

Figure 8 Data Lake - Data for Demand Forecasting

Standards and Technology (NIST) defines Big Data as follows: "Big Data consists of extensive datasets—primarily in the characteristics of volume, variety, velocity, and variability—that require a scalable architecture for efficient storage, manipulation, and analysis" (NIST.SP.1500-1). The Big Data concept can be broken down into two interrelated concepts that need to be addressed if organizations can successfully leverage such technologies. The first concept is the challenge of the data (also known as the 4-Vs). The second concept deals with a change in architecture to enable the 4-Vs of the data.

The 4-Vs of Big Data

1. Volume (i.e., the size of the data to be ingested—could be one or multiple data sets)
2. Variety (i.e., different data types, various data sources, different data domains)

3. Velocity (i.e., the speed of ingestion—could be in seconds, minutes, hours, days, weeks, etc.)

4. Variability (i.e., unexpected change in other characteristics)

Source: NIST.SP.1500-1.

The 4-Vs of Big Data have driven new architectural designs leveraged by IT systems to meet these modern challenges. A modern architecture referred to as the lambda architecture aims to separate functions and layers, enabling a scalable architecture with many components. Such components can perform tasks (e.g., storage, processing, analytics, presenting) on their own, in sequence, or in parallel. The building blocks of such an architecture depend on the software vendor and could be proprietary, open source, or a mixture of both. Extensive details of such architectures are beyond the scope for this book, but at an elevated level, the standard layers of an architecture design following principles of the lambda architecture are depicted in Figure 9. These layers enable ingestion of hot and cold (fast- and slow-moving) data. The processing of data can be sequential or in parallel.

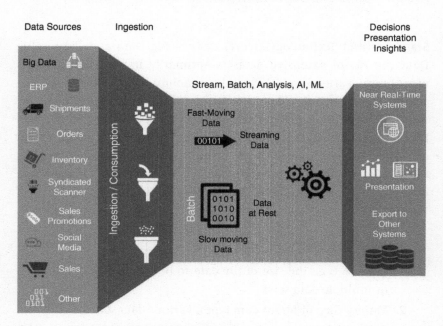

Figure 9 High-level Lambda Architecture Design

Data could be stored in a data lake or sent to different storage and analytics platforms such as databases, data warehouses, and data marts. The analytics layer can also be sequential and in parallel, and handle hot or cold data. The results can be shared with other targets, such as near real-time decision-making processes, different storage platforms, and different systems, or presented as results. This architecture is well suited for a hybrid approach of leveraging hot and cold in-streaming data, as well as already stored data. Analytical processes can combine newly ingested data with previously stored data to provide near real-time results or result sets for further analysis by other systems and processes. This hybrid approach assists with the challenges of the 4-Vs of Big Data. Data ingestion can follow schema-on-write or schema-on-read, leverage different storage systems and data types, and leverage distributed computational resources to provide results aiding data-driven insights promptly. The logical building blocks of a lambda architecture are depicted in Figure 9. Data sources are examples only, based on demand-driven supply chain needs.

Case Study: Leeds Teaching Hospital

To improve its hospital services, it was necessary for Leeds Teaching Hospital to identify trends through vast amounts of data. The primary challenge was the enormous volume of structured and unstructured data. One of the objectives of the health care provider was to detect possible outbreaks of infectious diseases as early as possible using data-driven insights and business intelligence. Previously such analysis relied on cold data that was already stored or archived, and hence out of date. There were enormous insights in text files from a mix of data sources such as unscheduled visits to the accident and emergency (A&E) rooms, retail drug sales, school attendance logs, and so on. Such data could help provide better data-driven insights near real time. The expected volume of data was half a million structured records and about one million unstructured data records. Leveraging data from various sources would provide better insights but would require a lot of computing power. It was not feasible to provision a server farm (lots of server computers) to handle such analysis. Costs, maintenance, and management of the computing environment would be too high a cost of ownership.

(Continued)

(*Continued*)

The health care provider decided to explore a cloud-based strategy. This would be cost-effective (the hospital would pay only for what it consumed) and would provide scalability and other benefits. Microsoft Azure cloud was chosen as it offered an integrated and seamless stack of solutions and components required (e.g., data ingestion, data lake, processing, business intelligence, presentation, and collaboration), and is one of the leading providers of public clouds in the world. This cloud environment enabled the on-demand processing of six years of data with millions of records. Using a combination of Microsoft's data platform technologies (i.e., SQL Server, HDInsight—a unique Hadoop framework), it was possible to process large volumes of structured and unstructured data. The integration of Microsoft business intelligence (BI) tools enabled a self-service approach to data-driven insights and evidence-based decisions. The digitalization of processes (e.g., data collection, coding, and entry into systems) saved time and reduced stationery and printing costs by a conservative estimate of £20,000 per year. The cloud platform and business model made it possible to spin up a Microsoft Azure HDInsight cluster to process six years' worth of data in just a few hours and shut down the cluster when the analytic job was complete.

Source: Microsoft (September 7, 2014)

In the context of demand-driven forecasting for a supply chain, a hybrid approach could help solve new challenges of the supply chain. Such an approach could combine features of data processing (hot, cold), data storage, analytics, and sending results to downstream systems for decisions near real time or at slower rates. (See Figure 10.)

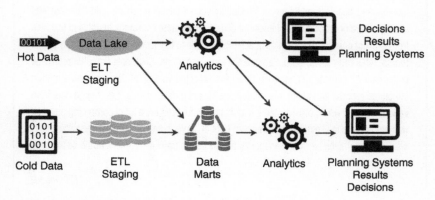

Figure 10 Hybrid Modern Data Flow—Supply Chain Analytics

Leveraging a mixture of data storage, databases, data marts, and analytical technologies is referred to as polyglot persistence. Data virtualization is also a useful technology for abstracting data sources and layers. Data remains at its location, and the data virtualization layer unifies and adds business-friendly access, metadata, and labels.

2. ANALYTICS

While data is an essential foundation toward the result, it is the analytics that provide the highest value for a demand-driven supply chain. Details of statistics, forecast models, and modeling are beyond the scope for this book. The aim is to highlight enhancements and possibilities made possible with cloud computing, and how the combination of disciplines can enhance value further. There are multiple challenges for the analytics of demand forecasting. First, there is the challenge of Big Data (the volume of data that needs to be ingested and analyzed at various speeds). Second, there is the challenge of multiple variables and identifying causal (influencing) variables. Third, there is the challenge of discovering patterns, trends, and links. Such analysis is helpful for detecting changes in consumer behavior and tastes. It is also useful to new product forecasting that can leverage patterns, and information about similar products to assimilate the demand for a new product based on similar attributes and possible tastes. Finally, there is the challenge of automation and leveraging a vast repository of forecasting models and modeling techniques to increase accuracy and value of forecasts. This becomes even more important with multiple dimensions and the depth of those dimensions (the depth of the hierarchy, e.g., tens or hundreds of thousands of products). All these computations must also be time relevant. This could mean near real time, or at least fast enough to fit into a demand forecasting and demand planning cycle and processes.

There are distinct phases of maturity when it comes to analytics, and the envisioned end state an organization wishes to be in will drive the state of advanced analytics leveraged. The four phases are depicted in Figure 11 and are also called the DDPP model, standing for descriptive, diagnostic, predictive, and prescriptive. The first type or maturity level of this DDPP model is descriptive analytics.

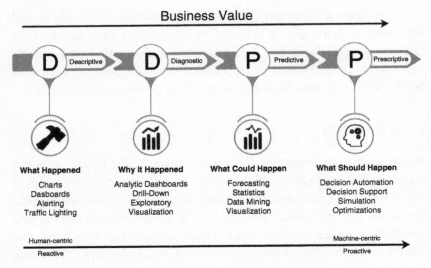

Figure 11 DDPP Model—Types and Maturity of Analytics

This is a reactive level and focuses on the past. In the context of a demand-driven supply chain, this type of analytics focuses on reporting on what has happened. Examples include charts, reports, business intelligence dashboards, alerting, and traffic lighting on key performance indicators (KPIs). Regarding sophistication and business value, this level of maturity and type of analytics provides the lowest benefit of the four levels.

The second level is diagnostic analytics. This type focuses on why something has happened. There are more interrelations between data, and reporting becomes more dynamic and interactive. Examples include interactive business intelligence dashboards with drill-down possibilities. These dashboards are more sophisticated and allow more exploration and visualization of data. The business value shifts to the right, providing more insights from the data.

Predictive analytics is the third level of maturity in the DDPP model. This type of analytics focuses on what could happen and leverages advanced analytics to provide possible outcomes. In the context of demand-driven forecasting, examples include forecasting demand for products based on demand signals. Multiple variables could be included in the analysis to identify possible links, correlations, and influencing factors, such as tastes, demographics, price, events, weather, location, and so on. Machine learning (ML) and artificial intelligence (AI) could be used to identify the most suitable statistical model to forecast a time series for different products throughout the hierarchy of a product dimension (see Figure 5). Identifying influencing factors and leveraging automated forecast model selection via ML and AI working together is a differentiating benefit of advanced forecasting. Demand signals will vary for different products, and applying the same forecasting models (e.g., autoregressive integrated moving average [ARIMA], exponential smoothing model) across all products will not be as useful as analyzing patterns, causal variables, and trends of the time series, and then applying a suitable forecast model. The computing platform must be intelligent to perform such analysis and have adequate compute (CPU+RAM) resources to complete the task in a time window that supports the business function (e.g., demand planning process cycle). Another example of utilizing ML and AI for demand forecasting could be clustering data from like products (also referred to as surrogate products) to help forecast demand for new products that may share similar traits or attributes. Only a machine could digest such vast amounts of data and spot commonalities and trends that could be applied to forecast products with no historical data. The business value of this level of analytics shifts further to the right.

The final level of maturity in the DDPP model is prescriptive analytics. This type of analytics focuses on providing decision support or automating decisions and providing input into downstream decision and supply chain planning systems. Advanced analytics with machine learning and artificial intelligence could be used to execute simulations and optimizations of possible outcomes and select the most appropriate decision based on data-driven analytics. The sophistication of advanced analysis using the scale and depth of data available, increased automation, and timely decisions all increase the business value to the highest possible in the DDPP model.

Business value through the DDPP types of analytics is further increased by leveraging a hybrid approach of data stores and technologies such as data lakes, databases, data marts, and so on, and then using cloud computing benefits (i.e., elastic scale, automation, ease of management, storage, processing, financial costs, etc.) to ingest and process hot and cold data in a timely manner. Such integration of components and technologies can lead to complex architecture designs and costs. However, one of the benefits of cloud computing is the ability to leverage specialized supply chain software solutions that are cloud aware (e.g., leverage fundamentals of the cloud computing paradigm). Another benefit is to utilize a platform as a service (PaaS) model in a cloud environment. Such a PaaS model makes it possible for organizations to extend on building blocks of software components and software stacks to address business challenges without having to worry about foundational elements. This could mean an organization could merely spin up a data lake environment or a data warehouse, leverage data ingestion technologies to process hot and cold data, and utilize tools for advanced analytics and visual reporting without having to worry about deployment, management, maintenance, or development of such components.

An example of a software solution stack to help organizations solve demand forecasting challenges through a cloud computing environment is depicted in Figures 12, 13, and 14. This example is based on Microsoft Azure Artificial Intelligence (AI). Azure is the name of the Microsoft cloud, which at the time of writing is one of the top two public cloud vendors in the world. At a high level, the AI services provide the advanced analytics and are the link between the data and presentation layer (see Figure 12). The underlying components required to ingest, store, analyze, and present data (to decision makers or decision systems) are included in the suite. There are multiple choices an organization can make depending on its need

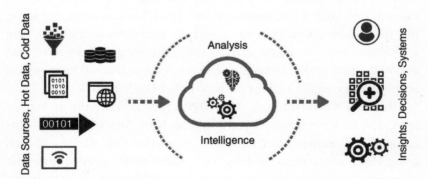

Figure 12 Microsoft AI Example—High Level

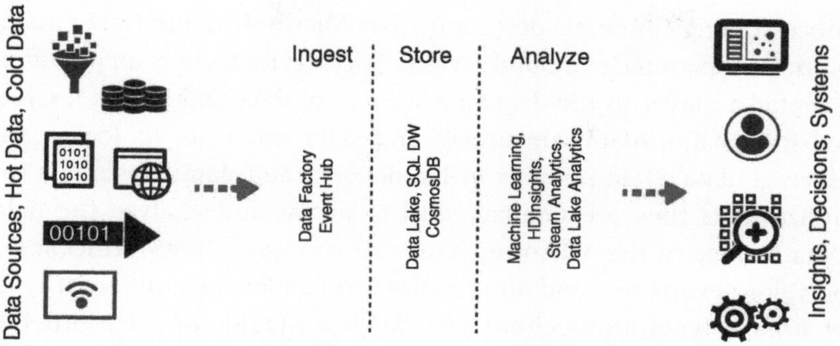

Figure 13 Microsoft AI Services Example

for data (e.g., hot, cold, structured, unstructured, etc.) ingestion and analysis. The design of the Microsoft AI suite has applied principles of the lambda architecture elaborated upon earlier. As depicted in all three diagrams (Figures 12, 13, and 14), data can be from a vast mixture of sources. There is support for hot (fast-moving) and cold (slowly moving) data. Data ingestion is handled by components listed under the Ingest category (see Figure 13). The Microsoft Azure Data Factory is a data ingestion service in the cloud that provides ETL/ELT tasks with automation and scheduling capabilities. Data sources could reside on an organization's premises, already be in the public cloud, or even be from other cloud services (e.g., software as a service [SaaS] applications). Back-end computing nodes are automatically scaled to support the data workloads. The Microsoft Azure Data Factory is a visual design tool used to build a digital data pipeline between data sources and data storage.

Microsoft Azure Event Hubs is also a cloud-based data ingestion service that focuses on hot data. It enables organizations to stream in data and log millions of events per second in near real time. A key use case is that of telemetry data (e.g., IoT devices). It is a cloud-managed service, meaning an organization does not have to worry about development, deployment, maintenance, and the like. These duties are the responsibility of the cloud vendor (in this example it is Microsoft). Event Hubs can be integrated with other cloud services of Microsoft, such as Stream Analytics. The Azure Event Hubs service focuses on near real-time analysis of the hot data being streamed into the cloud, and it can help with rapidly automated decision-making processes (e.g., anomaly detection). The Microsoft Azure Data Catalog is another example of a cloud service. This service focuses on providing a metadata layer to the disparate sources of data and makes it easier for information/data consumers and data scientists to locate and leverage data. Data remains in its location, and data consumers can utilize tools they are familiar with to access and analyze the data. Data storage in the Microsoft Azure AI services follows principles of polyglot persistence, and an organization can leverage different types of storage types and technologies. Such a hybrid approach provides flexibility and agility to store and later analyze cold and hot data. The decoupling of the data layer makes it possible to store, process, and analyze hot and cold data in parallel utilizing the most suitable data storage technologies for each task. Technologies included in the Microsoft Azure AI services include Data Lake, Microsoft SQL Server Data Warehouse, and a NoSQL database called Cosmos DB. These technologies are cloud services and managed by Microsoft.

The analytics layers (far right of Figure 13) are also cloud services. Included in the Microsoft Azure AI services are open-source technologies (e.g., Hadoop, Spark) and Microsoft technologies such as SQL Server. The back-end architecture scales elastically depending on the demand of the analytics. Management of these components is the responsibility of Microsoft (the public cloud vendor in this example). This makes it easy and financially viable to use these services, as they are all cloud-based. Spinning up and managing such environments on-premises would take days, if not weeks or even months, and would incur substantial up-front investments. Both hot and cold data can be analyzed via this platform. The Microsoft Azure Data Lake Analytics and Azure HDInsight cloud services focus more on cold data and are well suited for investigating unstructured or semistructured data. Microsoft Azure Stream Analytics focuses on hot data. In this context, it receives near real-time data from cloud services such as Microsoft Azure Event Hubs or Microsoft Azure IoT Hubs. Microsoft's Azure Stream Analytics is an example of serverless services as there are no servers or components to manage from an organization's point of view. The public cloud provider (i.e., Microsoft) manages the back end of this service, ensuring it provides the scale required for the analytics of an organization. An organization that consumes this service pays only for the processing and not for the infrastructure.

Applying such technologies and capabilities of these cloud services to the challenges of demand-driven forecasting can help organizations achieve improved forecast accuracy and business insights in less time, and more cost-effectively. Organizations taking advantage of such possibilities could improve their forecasts and demand planning process by sensing demand from downstream sources and adapting forecasts as new hot data is streamed and analyzed. Demand sensing uses granular downstream sales data (e.g., point of sales data, sales orders) with minimal latency to gain an insight into demand patterns and the impact of demand-shaping programs to refine short-term demand forecasts and inventory positioning to support supply plans of one to six weeks (Chase 2013, 24). An organization could also leverage near real-time data (e.g., online consumer shopping cart) and cold data (e.g., past historical shopping data of consumers) to provide a personalized shopping experience possibly leading to increased sales. Data, analytics, and intelligence are combined to improve demand-driven forecasts or shape demand. Two examples highlight these opportunities and possible benefits.

EXAMPLE 1: VENDING MACHINE—IoT DEMAND SENSING

In a simplified view (see Figure 14) in this example, connected (IoT) beverage devices could use telemetry to send near real-time demand signals upstream to demand planning and forecasting systems. Other data sources that are identified as causal factors (i.e., weather in this example) could also be sending hot data back to demand-driven forecast systems. Rolling forecasts could be updated based on newly arriving data. The time horizon of forecasts depends on each organization and the products sold. Perishable products, for example, would require a daily or even hourly forecast, whereas non-perishables (i.e., beverages in this example) could permit a weekly or monthly horizon. Improving the forecasts based on near real-time demand signals could help prevent stock-outs and lost sales. Improved forecast accuracy and timely insights could also assist with goals of preventing high inventory costs (supply exceeding demand).

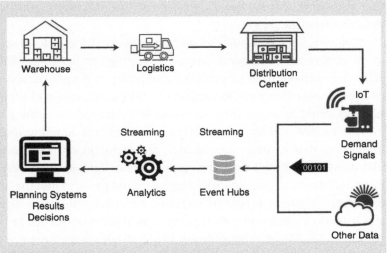

Figure 14 Demand-Driven Forecasting and IoT

EXAMPLE 2: ONLINE SHOPPING, DEMAND SHAPING, AND PERSONALIZED RECOMMENDATIONS

In this example, a consumer is shopping online. The surfing data of the current online session is streamed and analyzed in near real time with the help of weblogs. The consumer is a returning buyer, and data from previous purchases is available via cold storage. Advanced analytics is used to identify current shopping behavior and compare it with past actions. Analytics and intelligence (e.g., ML and AI) are used to map the consumer to similar consumers and what those people purchased (e.g., similar gender, age group, hobbies, tastes, etc.). Current inventory stock of the searched-for products as well as other related products is used as an input data variable for analysis.

The machine learning model is used to provide a specifically targeted recommendation to the online shopper. (See Figure 15.) Such a suggestion could take advantage of price sensitivity insights, add sale promotions for related or complementary products, or help reduce inventory overstock by discounting associated products. This provides a personalized shopping experience for consumers and can improve customer satisfaction, increase sale potential, and potentially lower inventory costs. Online stores like Amazon utilize similar strategies and technologies to help shape demand by using a data-driven approach. New technologies such as bots can take advantage of ML and AI and could provide a simulated human personal shopper experience (e.g., answering questions, providing suggestions) for online consumers. In summary, this example highlights benefits of operating a demand-driven supply chain, sensing demand, and using data and analytics to help shape demand (e.g., enticing consumer to act on purchases via targeted promotions and recommendations).

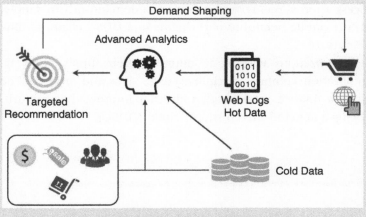

Figure 15 Demand Shaping—Personalized Recommendations

3. COLLABORATION—PEOPLE AND PROCESSES USING A COLLABORATIVE APPROACH

The previously mentioned technologies are powerful and necessary tools for organizations wishing to build and operate a digital supply chain. These technologies should be complemented by a collaboration of demand planners and forecasters. Good practices of forecasting and demand planning should be applied to utilize data insights, yet also leverage domain experience and knowledge. Machine-generated forecasts should not necessarily be overridden by human intervention, as the end result could be decreased forecast accuracy. Small adjustments, especially frequent ones, reduce forecast accuracy (Fildes et al. 2009, 3–23).

The optimal approach would use a blend between statistical demand-driven forecasts and collaboration between demand planners, as well as supply chain partners. Statistical forecasts can provide valuable decision support, but should not be used to automate the demand planning system completely. Automated decision systems will not be avoidable, but the human factor must remain an independent part of the demand planning process (Spitz 2017, 83). The benefits of improving supply chain management through advanced analytics, IT, process improvements, and becoming a demand-driven supply chain (DDSC) can be helpful to participants in a DDSC chain, as illustrated in Figure 16.

Organizations wishing to optimize their supply chain through digitalization combine disciplines (e.g., data and analytics, demand planners, finance, marketing), and aim to improve their maturity level of being a demand-driven supply chain (DDSC).

DDSCs Have the Potential to Deliver Benefits to All Supply-Chain Participants

	Raw Material Supplier	Manufacturer	Retailer	Consumer
Reducing inventory	✔	✔	✔	
Decreasing working capital	✔	✔	✔	
Improving forecasting accuracy	✔	✔	✔ (partial)	
Reducing transportation costs	✔	✔		
Optimizing infrastructure	✔	✔	✔ (partial)	
Decreasing order-expediting costs	✔	✔	✔	
Reducing other operating costs (such as handling and warehousing)	✔	✔	✔	
Reducing head count (such as planners and buyers)	✔	✔	✔	
Decreasing sales-planning and operations-planning time	✔	✔	✔ (partial)	
Reducing lost sales		✔ (partial)	✔	
Improving customer sell-through and satisfaction			✔	✔

✔ = Strong benefit ✔ (partial) = Partial benefit

Figure 16 DDSC Benefits All Participants—BCG, 2012

Sources: BCG analysis and case experience, and expert interviews.

There may be many advantages of becoming a DDSC, and some of these benefits of following such a strategy are the following (not an exhaustive list):

- Improved business insights
- Timely insights (information at the right time)
- Increased sales opportunities
- Higher sales revenue
- Lower inventory costs
- Better service levels
- Improved customer satisfaction (e.g., product availability, price)
- Omni-channel demand insights
- Possibly enhanced supply chain agility

There should not be an overdependence on IT and new possibilities such as machine learning. Benefits of leveraging such technologies are enormous, and ML accelerates time to business insights, but there is no magic one-button solution to all (Alexander et al. 2016, 10). Artificial intelligence and machine learning can support automation to a certain degree, and for essential parts of an organization's portfolio (e.g., high value, volatile demand) the statistical forecast can provide valuable decision support. It should not be used to automate the demand planning process completely. As mentioned previously, automated decision systems will not be avoidable, but the human factor must remain an independent part of the process (Spitz 2017, 83). The benefits come to organizations when they apply human knowledge and processes of demand planning (e.g., strategic choices, domain knowledge, and information about events), along with machine capabilities such as ML and AI, to computing an enormous size of data (Alexander et al. 2016, 5–10). Even though it is now possible to collect, store, and analyze vast amounts of data, companies must still formulate a strategy for data management (e.g., what and how to collect, store, analyze, and share). A recent survey of 1,500 companies across Europe, the Middle East, and Africa (EMEA) showed that a midsize company with 500 terabytes of data could be spending roughly US$1.5 million a year in storage and management costs of nonessential data (Alexander et al. 2016, 6).

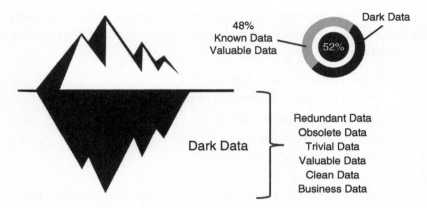

Figure 17 Databerg and Dark Data
Source: Data from Veritas (2016).

The Veritas Data Genomics Index highlights that over 40 percent of stored data has not been touched and leveraged in more than three years (Veritas 2016, 3). The Veritas Global Databerg Report identifies an average of 52 percent of stored data being "Dark Data," defined by Veritas as either being redundant, obsolete, or trivial (ROT), or being valuable clean business data (Veritas 2016, 3–5). (See Figure 17.) As there is more and more data, organizations need a good data management strategy to identify useful data, which could then be leveraged in the analytics process and assist with goals of being a demand-driven supply chain. The data value (value to the business, specifically to demand-driven forecasting) should be tested to ensure valuable data is ingested and analyzed. Such tests would probably be repeated over time to make sure an organization is aiming to be as data-smart as it can be.

When organizations transition along maturity models of analytics, Big Data, and digitalized supply chain, their needs and capabilities change over time, so it is important to have a process in place that reevaluates data, analytics, and operations. Demand planners have domain knowledge and can have an awareness of events outside of the digital network of data. For example, a purchaser has informed its supplying organization that it will place a large bulk order next month (e.g., lumpy demand), and this information has not yet been captured formally. A purely machine-driven demand forecasting process could be underestimating the actual demand in this example. Another example could be a demand planner knowing about a planned promotional event that could significantly influence demand. Forecasts could be skewed without such event data, and therefore it is essential to blend data and demand-driven forecasting with human demand planning inputs (achieved via a collaborative approach that seeks the consensus of the machine and the human inputs) to arrive at finalized demand plans.

A survey of forecasters highlighted that 55 percent of the respondents used a mixture of judgment and statistical forecasts, or a judgment-adjusted statistical forecast (Kolassa and Siemsen 2016; Fildes and Petropoulos 2015). Human judgment being widespread in organizational forecasting processes is due to domain-specific knowledge (Lawrence, O'Connor, and Edmundson 2000, 151–160). Domain knowledge and close collaboration across all functions are needed to make the most out of demand sensing and demand shaping (Chase 2013, 24). A two-by-two matrix for forecasting (Croxton et al. 2002, 51–55) helps to identify the type of forecast needed (e.g., data-driven forecast or people-driven forecast) based on the demand variability and demand volume. Demand Volume (Low and High) are mapped on the x-axis while Demand Variability (Low and High) are mapped on the y-axis. Low demand variability and low or high demand volume could use data-driven forecasts. High demand variability and low demand volume could use a make-to-order forecast, and high demand variability and high demand volume could use people-driven forecasts (Croxton et al. 2002, 51–66). Low demand variability and low and high demand volume could use statistical forecasts, high demand variability and low demand volume could use vendor-managed inventory and demand visibility, and high demand variability and high demand volume could use sales and operations planning (S&OP) with collaborative planning and forecast replenishment (Mendes 2011, 42–45). The forecast value added (FVA) metric is a useful tool to help highlight whether or not human judgment and overriding the statistical forecast are adding value. The FVA metric is used to evaluate the performance (positive or negative) of each step and participants in the forecasting process. In this evaluation process, a forecast performance metric is used as the baseline. Deviation from this baseline is then calculated as the forecast value added. If the FVA is positive, then there is a benefit of changing the statistical forecast. If the FVA is negative, then there is no value in altering the statistical forecasts, and it would have been better to leave the process untouched. The FVA analysis can thus be used to evaluate whether procedures and adjustments made to the statistical forecasts improved or decreased accuracy (Gilliland 2013, 14–18). One of the most common forecast performance metrics used is mean absolute percentage error (MAPE). The lower the MAPE value, the better is the forecast accuracy. Evaluating MAPE and the FVA will highlight when a demand planning process or participant improved the MAPE and added value in overriding a statistical forecast. These concepts are elaborated upon in the following example.

EXAMPLE: FORECAST VALUE ADDED (GILLILAND, 2015)

EXAMPLE

The first step in the forecast performance evaluation process is to use naive forecasts. A naive forecast is something that is simple to calculate, requires minimal effort, and is easy to understand. In this example, two frequently used naive models are used. The first model is the random walk model. This model uses the last actual value as the forecasted value. If actual units sold last week were 75, then the forecast for the following week would be 75 (see Figure 18). The second model used in this example is the seasonal random walk. This model uses the actual values from the same period a year ago. If actual units sold in January, February, and March last year were 90, 60, and 42, then the forecasts for January, February, and March for next year would be 90, 60, and 42, respectively (see Figure 19).

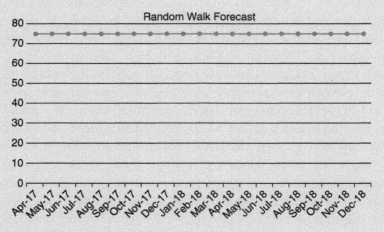

Figure 18 Random Walk Forecast Example

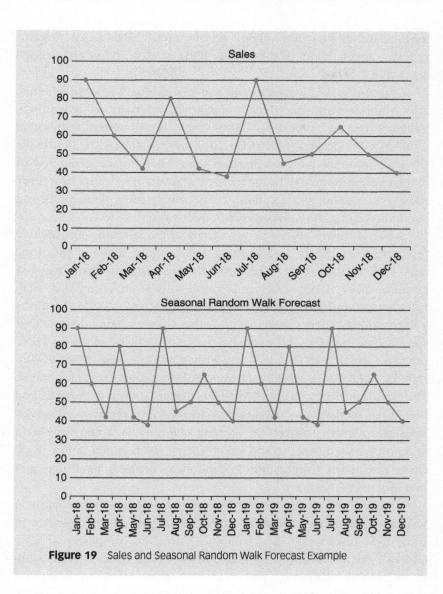

Figure 19 Sales and Seasonal Random Walk Forecast Example

Continuing with the example, the MAPE and FVA metrics are then compared to each other for evaluating the performance of the forecasts and any overrides. The lowest MAPE and highest positive FVA would provide the best business value. Organizations should assess forecasts and processes using a combination of forecast performance metrics, rather than just relying on one metric. Using FVA, organizations can evaluate whether overriding statistical forecasts added any value.

Organizations must decide on the significance of improvements, and whether using overrides and manual intervention is justified. Review cycles and forecast specialists cost time and money, so it is vital to balance the processes, overrides, and statistical forecasts to provide the most optimal forecasts/demand plans that can be generated in a relatively automated fashion. Such analysis must also bear time pressures in mind, as consumers are becoming more demanding and stress the supply chain in unprecedented ways.

Some software solutions for supply chain optimization include forecasting, inventory optimization, collaborative demand planning, and FVA functionality. The SAS Demand-Driven Planning and Optimization (DDPO) software solution suite is an example of such integration (see Figure 20). A demand signal repository (DSR) collects and consolidates demand signals and other relevant data into function-specific data marts. In this example, the DSR is a blend of the SAS proprietary format (SAS data sets) and a relational database (PostgreSQL). Data is molded into workbench-specific data models (data schemas). The results between business workbenches are shared seamlessly, and this fosters scenarios such as organizations performing demand-driven forecasting with collaborative demand planning, or forecasting with inventory replenishment and optimization, or a combination of all three disciplines (forecasting, collaborative demand planning, and inventory optimization).

An enterprise wishing to reap the most benefits of a demand-driven forecasting strategy should be exploiting advanced technologies in computing resources. Cloud computing provides computing at scale and can do so elastically, scaling out or scaling back in (increasing or decreasing computing power by adding or removing computer servers to process data in parallel). The unlimited computing power, increased agility, on-demand automation, and pay-as-you-go (PAYG) financial model in a cloud makes it very compelling for organizations to leverage such technologies for their demand-driven forecasting needs. Such possibilities and technologies are elaborated upon further in subsequent chapters. Organizations should also leverage capabilities

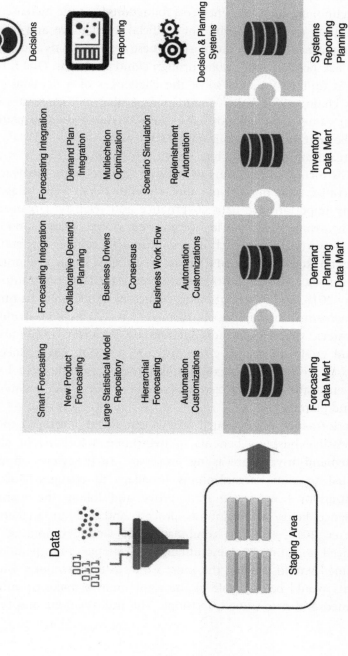

Data

Decisions

Reporting

Decision & Planning Systems

Smart Forecasting

New Product Forecasting

Large Statistical Model Repository

Hierarchial Forecasting

Automation Customizations

Forecasting Integration

Collaborative Demand Planning

Business Drivers

Consensus

Business Work Flow

Automation Customizations

Forecasting Integration

Demand Plan Integration

Multiechelon Optimization

Scenario Simulation

Replenishment Automation

Forecasting Data Mart

Demand Planning Data Mart

Inventory Data Mart

Systems Reporting Planning

Staging Area

Figure 20 SAS Demand-Driven Planning and Optimization Example

that allow the ingestion and storage of both hot and cold (fast- and slow-moving) data.

Technology advancements, cost reductions, and the increased ease of use now make it possible for artificial intelligence and machine learning to be utilized by the masses. These are all options and possibilities made possible and viable through cloud platforms. One function alone is unlikely to help solve the challenges of a demand-driven supply chain, and it is the combination of all areas that creates exponential value. Last, but not least, these technologies and platforms must be governed by organizational strategies.

Organizations should have a clear data management strategy, and this includes definitions of what to capture, store, analyze, and democratize. Data must be of value, and dark data should be avoided. Equally important are data governance and security. Organizations must be aware of what is being captured, stored, shared, and accessible. New regulations such as the European Union's General Data Protection Regulation (GDPR) must be adhered to, or else organizations can face substantial financial penalties. GDPR came into force in May 2018, and organizations in breach of GDPR could be fined up to 4 percent of annual global turnover, or €20 million (whichever is greater). GDPR does not differentiate between on-premises or a cloud environment, so clear structure, control, governance, and processes are needed. Organizations should select the right balance between statistically derived demand forecasts and collaborative demand planning.

Performance metrics such as FVA should be leveraged to identify possible business benefits of overriding a forecast or altering the demand-driven forecasting processes. Such reviews should be repeated to allow organizations to adapt to changes. Successful organizations keep trying to improve and follow the mantra of excellence being a continuous process and not an accident (BS Reporter 2013, 9). The combination of cloud computing, data, advanced analytics, business intelligence, people, and operations all combined would provide the most value to organizations. Business insights would be available at the right time to make or automate informed and data-driven decisions. The interrelations and benefits of using a cloud-based demand-driven supply chain (CBDDSC) are illustrated in Figure 21. Cloud concepts and advantages are explained in more detail in subsequent chapters. The combined value of cloud computing and a demand-driven supply chain is elaborated on in the following.

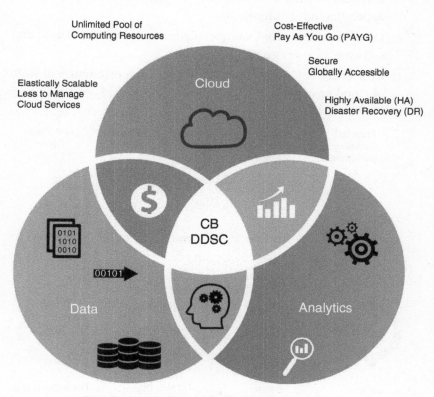

Figure 21 Combining Cloud + Data + Advanced Analytics

In the context of a cloud-based demand-driven supply chain, the following benefits can be gained by organizations:

Cloud

- A theoretically unlimited pool of computing resources can be utilized.
- Elastically scalable—use more or less computing resources depending on requirements.
- Less to manage—for example, platform as a service (PaaS) and software as a service (SaaS).
- Cost-effective - organizations can gain from economies of scale of cloud providers.

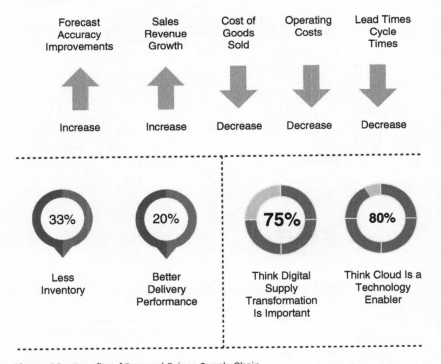

Figure 22 Benefits of Demand-Driven Supply Chain

Sources: (Top) Mendes (2011, 64–65); *(bottom left)* Budd, Knizek, and Tevelson (2012); *(bottom right)* Dougados and Felgendreher (2016).

- Pay-as-you-go (PAYG) financial models mean organizations pay for only what they use.
- Cloud data centers are secure, and cloud services are globally accessible.
- Cloud economies make it easier to be highly available and have disaster recovery options.

Data

- Ingest fast- and slow-moving data, and analyze hot or cold data in near real time or in batches.
- Big Data, data lakes, and operational databases.
- Data services scale with organizational needs.

Analytics

- Leverage machine learning and artificial intelligence for advanced analytics.
- Analyze hot data, Big Data, cold data, or a combination of all.
- Use analytics to provide personalized recommendations to downstream consumers.
- Leverage data + AI + ML to create data- and demand-driven insights.

The benefits for an organization digitalizing its supply chain and creating a demand-driven supply chain are illustrated in the infographic shown in Figure 22.

CHAPTER **2**

Introduction to
Cloud Computing

*C*loud or *cloud computing* is a term used to describe the use and outsourcing of information technology (IT). In such a usage model, organizations shift away from constructing and utilizing their data centers to leveraging services of a public cloud provider. There are instances where organizations will build and consume a private cloud, which is where IT resources are deployed internally and are available to only that organization. Cloud represents one of the most significant paradigm changes in recent computing history. Organizations that are leveraging this wave of technological advancements will have competitive advantages over those companies that choose not to leverage cloud. The first use of the term *cloud computing* is attributed to Professor Ramnath Chellapa, who described it as follows:

> Cloud-computing is a dynamic computing paradigm where the boundaries of computing are determined by rationale provided by technological, economic, organizational and security requirements. (Chellapa 1997)

Former United States Federal Chief Information Officer Vivek Kundra helped form a cloud-first strategy for reforming the U.S. federal government's use of IT, and he describes cloud computing as follows:

> For those of you not familiar with cloud computing, here is a brief explanation. There was a time when every household, town, or village had its own water well. Today, shared public utilities give us access to clean water by simply turning on the tap. Cloud computing works a lot like our shared public utilities. However, instead of water coming from a tap, users access computing power from a pool of shared resources. Just like the tap in your kitchen, cloud computing services can be turned on or off as needed, and, when the tap isn't on, not only can the water be used by someone else, but you aren't paying for resources that you don't use. Cloud computing is a new model for delivering computing resources—such as networks, servers, storage, or software applications. (Kundra 2010)

There are essential technologies that cloud computing builds on, and such technologies are highlighted throughout this chapter.

This chapter focuses on key reasons why customers should adopt cloud computing, and aims to introduce the types of clouds and cloud service models; it descibes the opportunities cloud computing can provide to various industries, and showcases the top vendors offering such technologies. Some of the critical milestones and technologies along the journey to cloud computing are depicted as time lines in Figures 23 and 24. These events are considered stepping-stones to cloud computing (Daconta 2013).

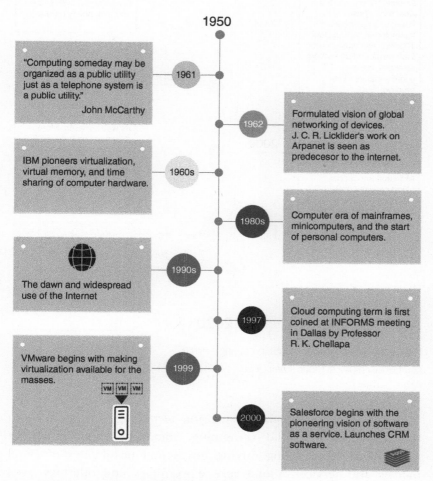

Figure 23　Time Line for Cloud Computing—Part 1

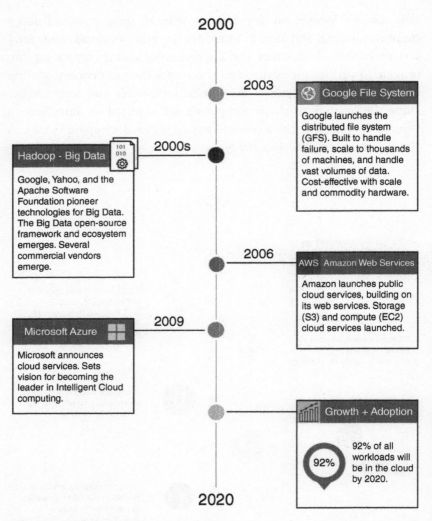

Figure 24 Time Line for Cloud Computing—Part 2
Source: Cisco Global Cloud Index (2016).

While there are many events and technologies from the past that have led to cloud computing, some are more important than others, accelerating driving forces and possibilities of cloud models and services. Cloud service examples and offerings from top-performing public vendors are showcased in Chapter 4. Details of such technologies are beyond the scope for this book, but this chapter will provide a brief insight into two key technology areas and accelerators for cloud computing:

1. Virtualization
2. Big Data

1. VIRTUALIZATION

There are different types of virtualization, such as server virtualization, desktop virtualization, and application virtualization. This section focuses only on server virtualization. Even though the pioneering work for virtualization is attributed to IBM as far back as the 1960s, it became a mainstream technology mainly through VMware (see Figure 23). Other software vendors such as Microsoft and Xen (open-source software) realized the market trend and adoption by organizations worldwide, and deliver virtualization software. Virtualization is recognized as the pre-version of a cloud. Server virtualization is a way of abstracting physical hardware of a server machine and creating virtual machines (VMs) that are hosted on a physical server machine. These virtual machines access only the abstracted hardware, and are unaware of other VMs running on the same physical computer (referred to as the host machine). A software layer called the hypervisor performs the hardware abstraction. Hardware that is abstracted includes CPU, RAM, storage, and network. This virtual hardware is differentiated by adding a "v" in front of the hardware type—for example, vCPU, vRAM, vHDD (hard disk drive), and vNet (networking). The hypervisor manages the access to this virtualized hardware and balances the load from multiple virtual machines that may reside (also referred to as hosted) on the same physical server machine.

Each VM has an operating system (OS) and can have applications within the virtual machine as if it were a regular operating system and computer. Hardware is presented virtually to the OS and applications within the VM, and instructions to this virtual hardware are as if it were native physical hardware. These abstraction features lead to broad compatibility of operating systems and applications within the VM. An operating system within a VM is referred to as a guest OS. The physical machine is referred to as the host or host machine, and the operating system on the host is known as the host OS. Depending on the virtualization vendor, this host OS can be thin (e.g., hypervisor only) or can be thick (include additional OS software). There are limits for the virtual hardware sizes (e.g., number of CPUs and amount of RAM), as these depend on the host machine and on support by the hypervisor from virtualization vendors. Should an application or operating system within a VM become rogue, then the other VMs on the host will still be unaffected, as the VMs are self-contained objects. VMs encapsulate the guest OS and applications (apps) within the VM. Encapsulation makes it easier to move VMs from host to host for performance balancing, for maintenance of hosts, or for disaster recovery with off-site storage. (See Figure 25.)

There are five key benefits of virtualization. The first benefit of hosting multiple virtual machines on physical server machines is cost savings. Through server virtualization, it is possible to host many virtual servers on fewer physical servers. The ratio of virtual machines to physical host machines is called the consolidation ratio. For example, if there are 40 VMs on one physical host machine, then the consolidation ratio would be 40:1. Cost savings are drastic in this example, as

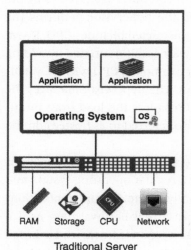 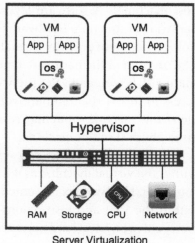

Figure 25 Traditional Server and Server Virtualization

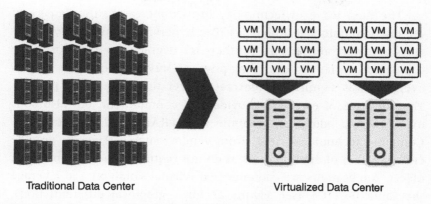

Traditional Data Center   Virtualized Data Center

Figure 26 Data Center Virtualization—Transformation

an organization would now only need to procure one physical server machine. The virtualization software would increase costs, of course, but in general the total cost of ownership would decrease, as less physical hardware would be needed, and consequently less data center space would be required.

Data center space and operation are very expensive (e.g., power, cooling, estate fees, manpower, etc.), so data center virtualization can lead to immense cost reduction (see Figure 26). A high consolidation ratio is also referred to as high density, meaning a higher number of VMs are squeezed onto a host machine. By virtualizing a data center, organizations can reduce IT costs tremendously. Processes such as procurement and deployment of servers are also transformed, as these would occur virtually. A VM can be deployed within minutes compared to procurement cycles and deployment processes that typically require several weeks. The capital and operational expenses that can be assigned to a virtual machine are much lower than similar costs for a physical server. As organizations in the early 2000s were struggling to do more with less and become more efficient, economical, and effective through IT, virtualization provided a solution. Virtual infrastructure (e.g., VMs, storage, and networking) led to increased automation and the rise of a software-defined data center (SDDC). The SSDC evolved further into private and public clouds, which will be defined and elaborated upon later in this chapter.

The next wave of technology further increasing the density of servers is container technologies. The hypervisor software layer provides hardware abstraction, but there is a degradation in performance compared to native (e.g., real physical server) performance. This overhead has significantly decreased over time but is still present. The guest OS of each VM provides self-containment, but also adds overhead and additional compute (CPU+RAM) and storage needs. Container technologies (e.g., from vendors such as Docker) provide encapsulation of applications but do not require a guest OS or a VM object. Applications are containerized (virtual sandbox) and leverage the same host OS (see Figure 27 for a graphical differentiation). There can only be one host OS, and applications must be supported by that host OS. Containers can be deployed on physical server machines, within VMs, or in a cloud. Such a containment technology further increases the density of physical hosts and improves agility. Applications are contained in virtual containers (i.e., acting as a virtual sandbox), and if one application becomes rogue, then other containers are not affected.

The second benefit of virtualization is isolation. VMs hosted on the same physical server machine do not affect each other. It is still

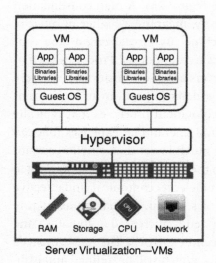
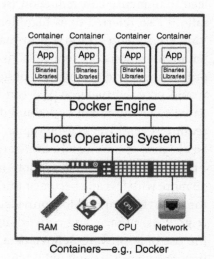

Figure 27 Virtual Machines Compared to Containers

possible to interconnect VMs to operate as groups (e.g., grid enabled applications, load balancing applications, sharing data, etc.), but the entity of one VM or a defined group of VMs does not affect other VMs.

The third benefit of virtualization is snapshotting or rapid build and deploy. It is possible to take a snapshot in time before an event (e.g., testing a software patch or upgrading software), and then decide whether to commit the changes if successful or revert to a snapshot before the event. IT development and deployment tools such as CHEF make the automation of creating and deploying a VM faster and easier. Testing processes and workflows therefore can be more efficient with VMs. Developers can create and deploy a VM, undertake testing, and then undeploy the VM, making the entire process more cost-effective. Configuration steps with the tool CHEF can be captured as "recipes," and these lead to increased standardization and reuse.

The fourth benefit of virtualization is the possibility of migrations. It is possible to move a VM while it is running (live) to another physical host machine. Such a move is also referred to as a hot migration. A cold migration is performed when the VM is not running (not switched on) and is possible due to the encapsulation of the VM. Both forms of movements provide possibilities that would be far harder to achieve with pure physical servers. VMs can be migrated to other host machines for performance reasons or maintenance reasons (e.g., maintenance of host machines). VMs may also be migrated to other data centers, and virtualization enables such possibilities. In 2014 Facebook migrated VMs from one data center to another without affecting the 200 million users of its Instagram service (Metz, 2014, June). It was an enormous undertaking, migrating the services and more than 20 billion photos, and this was made possible through virtualization technologies and more.

The fifth benefit of virtualization is improved high availability (HA) and disaster recovery (DR). Virtualization makes it easier to deploy VMs in parallel for service availability, or rapidly deploy a VM if needed. VMs can be migrated or stored at another location providing improved disaster recovery options and lower costs.

Cloud computing is more extensive than virtualization and is the evolutionary result of virtualization. The top-performing vendors of clouds are showcased later in this chapter. VMware and

Amazon Web Services (AWS) have a joint partnership to enable a hybrid cloud model—combining private clouds and VMs on-premises with the possibility to migrate or consolidate these with a public cloud environment. Microsoft can provide a hybrid option as the virtualization technologies, and cloud services are both owned and operated by the same vendor, making integration or migration seamless.

2. BIG DATA

The increase in data generation and data consumption has led to challenges and opportunities for organizations. There are three main challenges of this massive data increase. The first challenge is the ingestion of this data at scale for both hot (fast-moving) and cold (slowly moving) data. Challenge number two is the analysis and computation of this data, and challenge number three is the storage of this data. Google was a pioneer in trying to solve two of these challenges—computation and storage. Large server machines (vertically scaled with a high number of CPUs and RAM—memory) and network storage were the traditional means of solving such challenges, but these were very costly and could not keep up with the pace of data growth. Google and later the Hadoop framework addressed these problems by using a horizontally scalable architecture utilizing cheaper commodity server machines. The number of computer nodes in such a horizontal architecture could range from tens to thousands. Such an architecture increases the need for automation and ease of management. Organizations could deploy and manage such environments, or they could leverage a cloud service that provides easier and more cost-effective options for organizations. The financial models of cloud computing allow organizations to use and pay for resources (e.g., computing and storage) only when they are needed. As showcased in the Leeds Teaching Hospital case study (see Chapter 1), organizations could tap into the possibilities of cloud computing to capture, store, and analyze large volumes of data without having to worry about building such environments or managing the complexity of such solutions. (See Figure 28.)

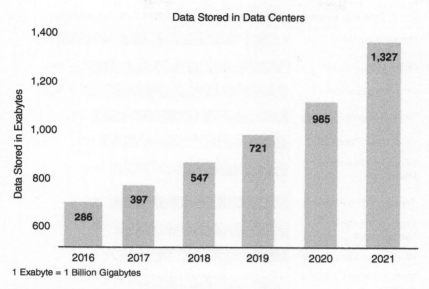

Figure 28 Data Stored in Data Centers, 2016–2021, Cisco GCI
Source: Cisco Global Cloud Index (2016–2021, 22).

As highlighted by Cecere (Cecere, 2013, p. 12), demand planning, order management, and price management are three of the top areas that would seem to benefit from Big Data (rated at the scale of 1 = No benefit, 7 = Great benefit), as shown in Figure 29.

A report by the European Commission (EC) projects that the insights gained by Big Data within the top 100 European Union (EU) manufacturers could lead to savings of €425 billion. The same report projects that by 2020 Big Data analytics could boost the EU economic growth by an additional 1.9 percent, leading to a gross domestic product (GDP) increase of €206 billion (European Commission 2016c, 4). Cloud vendors are supporting open-source software frameworks for Big Data as well as commercially extended software (e.g., features, support) solutions. Such broad offerings leverage fast-moving technologies, improve choice for organizations, and make it economically feasible to adopt. Detailed explanations of the Hadoop framework are beyond the scope for this book, but this chapter provides a high

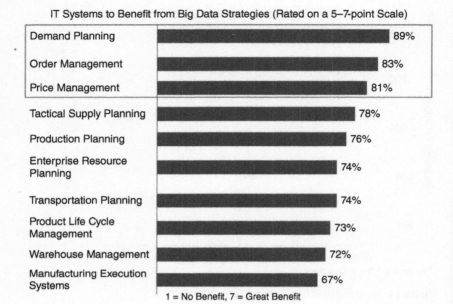

IT Systems to Benefit from Big Data Strategies (Rated on a 5–7-point Scale)

Demand Planning	89%
Order Management	83%
Price Management	81%
Tactical Supply Planning	78%
Production Planning	76%
Enterprise Resource Planning	74%
Transportation Planning	74%
Product Life Cycle Management	73%
Warehouse Management	72%
Manufacturing Execution Systems	67%

1 = No Benefit, 7 = Great Benefit

Figure 29   IT Systems to Benefit from Big Data
Source: Supply Chain Insights LLC (2013).

level of the ecosystem. Chapter 4 includes high-level showcases of the cloud offerings from the top two global public cloud providers (AWS and Microsoft). The deployment, orchestration, management, and use of such an ecosystem of technologies can be overwhelming for the organization, and this can become a hindrance to adopting a Big Data strategy. Cloud service providers can significantly reduce the time, effort, and complexity of deploying such ecosystems. Organizations leveraging such technologies can rest assured that open-source or compatible software is utilized, which provides choice and portability (e.g., code and programs can be reused across different environments). Big Data in a cloud can also reduce costs; for example, organizations can opt to pay for only the usage time (pay-as-you-go [PAYG] financial model of cloud) of such an environment. Virtualization could logically reduce efforts, time, and costs compared to pure physical environments, but the automation, scalability, expertise, and economies of scale make cloud-based Big Data strategies extremely

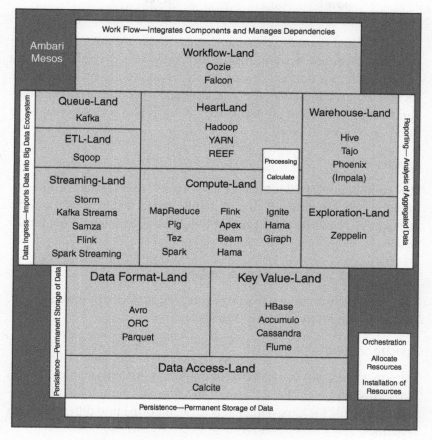

Figure 30 Big Data—Open Source Ecosystem

Source: Fischer and Winkler (2017), 66–70.

viable. Figure 30 illustrates some of the vast open source ecosystems of Big Data.

Software Tools and Components

Apache Ambari

Ambari has established itself as the standard tool for provisioning a Big Data ecosystem. The software can install the different components and manages dependencies.

Apache Mesos

The Mesos tool is used to manage clusters. Users see these highly scalable clusters as one system. Instead of having to worry about adding server nodes to a Hadoop cluster, Mesos allows the abstraction of the backbones, and administrators merely need to consider adding computational power to an environment. Mesos is also a tool leveraged in cloud orchestration work.

Apache Kafka

This component handles scalable data ingress of messages in queues. Receiving clients must be able to handle repeat delivery of the same message, as the technology provides "deliver-at-least-once" guarantee design.

Apache Kafka Streams and Apache Samza

These components allow analysis of streaming data in near real time. They are extensions of Kafka Queues.

Apache Squoop

Squoop is the go-to component for extract, transform, and load (ETL) that allows the ingestion of data in batch processing mode. This software is suitable for large data that is to be imported into different target systems.

Apache Storm

This component is purpose-built for streaming and can compute the incoming data very quickly. It leverages a lot of memory to do so, so systems must have adequate compute (CPU+RAM) resources.

Apache Flink

Flink provides a stream processing framework for applications that require high availability and high performance.

Apache Spark

Spark is a component that provides a fast and general engine for large-scale data processing. With Spark, it is possible to combine

Structured Query Language (SQL) with streaming and sophisticated analytics. Spark can leverage libraries that focus on SQL, streaming, machine learning, and graph algorithms.

Apache Oozie

This component is part of the Hadoop ecosystem and provides the capabilities of work flow scheduling specifically for Hadoop jobs.

Apache Falcon

Falcon provides feed processing and management on Hadoop clusters.

Apache Hadoop

This is a framework making it possible to process large data sets with the help of distributed clusters of machines. There can be single or thousands of machine nodes in such a Hadoop cluster, and each computer node in such a cluster provides local storage. This makes it easy to compute close to the data and allows for large-scale parallelism. Another benefit is the high availability of data, as redundant copies of data are copied to different nodes. Commodity hardware is used to reduce costs of such large networks, and hardware failure is expected. The Hadoop architecture design foresees such failovers and addresses this problem with cluster management and automated data copies across multiple nodes in a cluster.

Apache Avro

This component is a data serialization system. Data is serialized (translated into a format for storage) with an accompanying data schema.

Apache YARN

YARN stands for yet another resource negotiator. It is a framework for job scheduling and managing resources in a cluster.

Apache MapReduce

This component provides parallel processing capabilities of large data sets across a Hadoop cluster of server machines.

Apache Cassandra

Cassandra is a multimaster database that is scalable and has no single points of failure.

Apache HBase

This component provides capabilities of very large tables able to store billions of rows and millions of columns. It does so on clusters of computers that leverage commodity hardware. This HBase table is a nonrelational database, and very "performant" for random read or write access.

Apache Hive

The goal of this Apache project is to allow read and write access to data in a Hadoop ecosystem via friendly language such as SQL. Many data tools provide SQL features, and many data scientists and IT personas are familiar with SQL. This makes it easier to abstract data access, and makes the usage of data more accessible for many.

Apache Pig

Pig is a unique language aimed at making data analysis programs more natural to write and execute. An early version of the Hadoop framework required Java programming knowledge and code customization for each processing job. Pig aims to make it easier and faster to create data analysis jobs. Pig programs permit parallelization and hence make them ideal candidates for processing large data sets.

Apache Tez

Tez is a fundamental component for computation, but it is also flexible. It is typically used with other parts of the Hadoop ecosystem. It can provide data processing functions for batch processing as well as user interactive processing.

Apache Apex

This component relies on the YARN component and consolidates data from batch processing and stream processing. It is highly scalable, is distributed, provides required performance for Big Data, and is fault tolerant.

Apache Beam

Apache Beam is an abstraction layer for leveraging different execution engines and is platform neutral. It provides flexibility of programming languages to create jobs to process data in batch and streaming data.

Apache Hama

This component uses a bulk synchronous parallel (BSP) computing model. Hama can be used for large computational jobs that run in parallel against lots of data.

Apache Ignite

Ignite specializes in the processing of data in memory. Using memory is a lot faster than disk, so this component is very "performant." It includes a key-value and SQL engine, providing great flexibility.

Apache REEF

REEF stands for retainable evaluator execution framework. It aims to provide a library for developing portable applications to manage cluster resources.

Apache Calcite

This component provides a database based on industry standard SQL and uses a relational algebraic representation for SQL queries.

Apache Flume

Flume is a component in the Hadoop ecosystem that is built for capturing, aggregating, and moving large volumes of data contained in logs.

Apache Tajo

This component is aimed at providing a distributed data warehousing system for the Hadoop ecosystem. Tajo focuses on scalable ad hoc queries and ETL on large data sets stored in a Hadoop distributed file system (HDFS) upon which many data lakes are built. It also supports SQL standards, making it easy and flexible to access different data systems and sources.

Apache Zeppelin

This component is a web-oriented notebook providing capabilities for interactive user-driven data analytics. It can access data sources like HBase and allows users to select a programming language of their choice (e.g., Java, Scala, or Python).

Apache Accumulo

Accumulo is a component inspired by Google's BigTable. It is a key-value store and stores its data in HDFS. It also uses Apache Zookeeper.

Apache Zookeeper

This component is vital for successfully maintaining configuration information of a Hadoop ecosystem deployed, as distributed applications leveraging the Hadoop framework use such information.

Apache Phoenix

This component is used when applications require low latency in time. It provides capabilities of online transactional processing (OLTP) on Hadoop frameworks, leveraging the SQL standard. Apache Phoenix integrates with other components of the Hadoop ecosystem, such as Spark, Hive, Pig, Flume, or MapReduce.

Apache ORC

ORC stands for optimized row column. Data are stored in columnar stores, and Apache ORC has added unique indexes so that nonrelevant values within a column can be skipped during analysis. This feature combines the best of both row- and column-oriented storage worlds.

Apache Parquet

This component is also a columnar-store-oriented format, with subtle differences between it and Apache ORC. If there are nested attributes (e.g., similar to a tree structure) of data and dimensions, then Parquet is more suitable.

■ ■ ■

It may now be evident that such frameworks are complex and challenging to deploy, manage, and operate. Outsourcing these challenges to a cloud provider makes it much easier for organizations to leverage the technologies without having to worry about the back-end systems and components. Examples of cloud services by cloud providers Amazon Web Services (AWS) and Microsoft Azure are highlighted in Chapter 4. While the first section of this chapter focused on historical milestones and technologies leading to cloud computing, the remainder of this chapter will now focus on the definition and types of cloud computing, as well as some of the cloud service providers in the global market space.

There are different views and definitions of cloud computing, but probably the most generally accepted definition of cloud computing is that given by the U.S. National Institute of Standards and Technology (NIST). The NIST definition of a cloud computing is as follows:

> Cloud computing is a model for enabling ubiquitous,
> convenient, on-demand network access to a shared pool
> of configurable computing resources (e.g., networks,
> servers, storage, applications, and services) that can
> be rapidly provisioned and released with minimal
> management effort or service provider interaction. This
> cloud model is composed of five essential characteristics,
> three service models, and four deployment models. (NIST,
> 800-145, 2012)

Cloud Characeristics

The five essential characteristics of a cloud as defined by NIST that organizations see as standard requirements for cloud computing are as follows (see Figure 31):

1. On-demand self-service
2. Broad network access

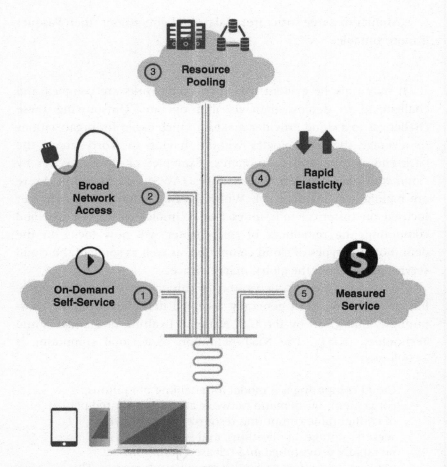

Figure 31   Cloud Computing—Five Characteristics

3. Resource pooling
4. Rapid elasticity
5. Measured service

1. On-Demand Self-Service

Organizations require self-service of cloud resources and therefore should be able to provision computing resources such as servers, virtual networks, and storage. Organizations should also be able to select and consume any of the cloud services available. Such selection can be user-driven, which typically occurs via a web portal interface. It is also possible to automate steps, deployment, and undeployment of resources and services via programmed access. Automation usually happens via vendor-specific application programming interfaces (APIs) that are made available to organizations and consumers of cloud resources and services. Such APIs enhance automation and ease of use (e.g., deploying tens, hundreds, or even thousands of virtual servers). These cloud-specific APIs can be surfaced via other tools and interfaces or can be included in scripted programs. One of the ordinary scripted methods is using Windows PowerShell (a programming language) and vendor-specific command-lets (cmdlet function-specific code blocks with parameters and logic), which substantially reduce any coding time and increase ease of use. The primary goal of this on-demand self-service requirement is not having to rely on cloud providers. Organizations should be able to use services when they so desire, 24/7, 365 days a year, without requiring external intervention that would slow the work flow process and agility granted by cloud computing. This can be compared to an analogy where people can walk to a food buffet table, select what they like, how much they want, and when they want without any intervention required from a waiter, and then just pay for what they selected and consumed.

2. Broad Network Access

Organizations may operate globally or have worldwide consumers, and therefore require resources in the cloud (e.g., storage, virtual servers) and cloud services (e.g., web hosting, databases, data warehouses, analytics, etc.) to be accessible to the organizations and their customers from anywhere in the world with computer networking access. Computer network access could be via physical (e.g., network cable) or wireless (e.g., Wi-Fi, mobile) interface. Consumers utilize thick clients (e.g., computer stations, laptops) and thin clients (e.g., tablets, mobile devices), and access to the cloud must be possible via any interface or device.

3. Resource Pooling

Organizations leverage economies of scale that cloud providers offer. Cloud providers deploy large data centers that house the physical resources of a cloud (e.g., host server machines, storage, network interfaces, etc.), and can gain economic benefits from bulk procurement of such supplies. These savings can consequently be passed on to consumers of the cloud. An example of this is when Microsoft, Facebook, Telefónica, and others joined forces to lay a large-capacity subsea cable with a length of 4,000 miles across the Atlantic (Microsoft Press 2017). Individual organizations would not be able to commit to such a massive undertaking, but as a cloud consumer, it is possible to benefit from such investments and back-end resources of cloud providers. Generally, a cloud resource pooling model means there is a multitenancy model in place. For example, virtual machines from organization A may be colocated on the same host or cluster of host machines as virtual machines from organization B. Virtual machines can be moved dynamically or through a schedule to avoid performance issues or avoid downtimes from scheduled maintenance of host machines. The end consumers or organizations leveraging the cloud are aware that the cloud is a multitenant environment and are not interested in or worried about where their virtual machines are located at a granular level (e.g., which host machine within a data center).

Cloud providers do provide options for consumers to pay a premium for dedicated resources (e.g., a host machine dedicated to virtual machines of organization A). The same applies to cloud services such as software as a service (SaaS). Such services are generally available to all cloud consumers utilizing a pool of resources in the back end. Microsoft Office 365 is an example of a software as a service offering where the back end is a pool of resources serving multiple users (also referred to as tenants). Cloud providers generally also make it possible for organizations to select high-level placement decisions (e.g., selecting the country, region (i.e., north, south), or data center from where they wish to consume cloud resources and services. Such flexibility enables organizations to have a choice, plan high availability and disaster recovery, and manage data protection laws.

For example, data in the European Union must be treated differently from data and information in the United States. Countries such as Germany require data to remain within the state. Cloud providers such as Microsoft have addressed such regulatory requirements and concerns of organizations by providing dedicated cloud environments in Germany. Public cloud providers have also addressed special needs of government departments by creating individual data centers that provide government-only clouds and cloud services. Commercial tenants are not permitted in such government or sovereign clouds. Location details of and access to such government clouds are even more strictly guarded than those of a commercial cloud data center, which are already very restrictive and secure.

4. Rapid Elasticity

One of the significant benefits of cloud computing for organizations is that they can leverage resources (e.g., computing, memory, storage) that expand or constrict depending on the demands of workloads. This feature dramatically increases efficiencies and cost benefits. In a traditional computing model such resources would have to be preplanned, procured, and deployed in advance. The additional capacity of computing resources may or may not be utilized, and the resources would be idle if the workload demand were not realized (see Figure 32). This scenario is optimized in a cloud, where resources can be added or decreased depending on the requirements. This can happen on a scheduled basis and can be completely automated. There is no need for intervention by system administrators. Applications that are aware of this elastic model can take advantage of the additional resources when needed, and there is no downtime or disruption. Organizations pay for only what they consume, and, as resources can be scaled back in, there is no wastage of resources or financials.

One typical example of such an elastic computing model is the Black Friday sales promotion event. Organizations typically expect additional demand during this time period. The organization's website may experience much higher traffic due to sales and marketing, and to avoid overloading the website (e.g., lengthy delays for visitors, and lost sales if visitors leave early) they could increase resources (e.g., adding

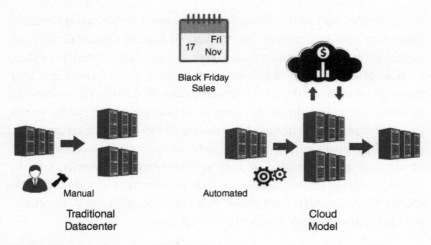

Figure 32 Black Friday—Traditional and Cloud

additional computer nodes to spread the load) during the Black Friday week and reduce resources back to normal afterward (see Figure 32). This operation can be completely automated without the need for downtime or installing or configuration of additional components. Many organizations choose to act proactively and schedule (again by automation) such elastic growth before a Black Friday event.

Case Study: Microsoft Social Experience Platform—SXP (2011)

The social experience platform (SXP) is a web service that provides conversation content to Microsoft.com. In this case example, the web traffic increase was caused by advertisements that were run for one or two days. Regular web traffic was around 100 percent. If computing resources had been inadequate, then the web service would not have been available, thus causing a negative user experience and lost sales opportunities. In a traditional data center model, such increases in traffic would have been serviced with increased computing capacity that would need to be purchased beforehand. The disadvantage of such a model is that the extra capacity would then remain idle for most of the time, as the regular demand was lower than the spike in demand. The general baseline demand in this case study is around the 100 percent line. Therefore, the traditional approach would be wasteful of resources and increase costs for an organization over a more extended period. Cloud automation was used to double the capacity of the back-end web service components.

> As the event of the advertisements was known, this increase in capacity was a proactively scheduled activity by the IT department responsible for ensuring the SXP platform would perform well. Resources were increased via automation technologies and cloud components of the Microsoft Azure cloud platform. The human time to accomplish this task (expanding the back-end capacity) was in minutes, and the overall time of completing the work (automated configuration of capacity components, etc.) was roughly 30 minutes. The IT team responsible for the SPX platform monitored the utilization of the platform, and when it saw demand reducing to normal levels again, it decided to cut the back-end capacity back to its usual level. This was still wholly automated and required minimal human intervention and time. The costs for this increase in size were recorded at US$70 (granularly metered consumption of cloud resources). Organizations can therefore benefit from the elasticity of cloud computing by expanding resources when required and reducing capacity when no longer needed. This increases cost efficiencies, and the automation possibilities increase flexibility and agility and reduce time and effort needed to respond to such challenges.
>
> *Source:* Bartr (2011).

5. Measured Service

Cloud vendors provide a level of abstraction (i.e., metrics) to meter the consumption of resources within the cloud. Such parameters indicate throughput, capacity, and performance for cloud consumers. Computing resources can be controlled by the organization, which has control over what and how much it wishes to consume. Monitoring and reporting capabilities provided to organizations utilizing the cloud increase transparency. Such information then permits organizations to base utilization decisions on cost information. Financial costs are a significant driver of user behavior, and in this context, the expenses influence planning decisions for organizations. Public cloud providers provide different cost models to assist organizations with judgments for different use cases. One of the most common cost models is pay as you go (PAYG). The model measures resources at granular levels, and organizations pay for only the number of resources (e.g., computing capacity) for the duration of time such resources are consumed (e.g., seconds, minutes, hours, days). The granularity of measurement and charging varies between vendors, but the most common granular models allow time intervals of minutes or hours. There can be different rates for cloud resources for different geographic regions and times of the day. Public cloud providers may also charge different prices for bursting capabilities (e.g., increase in computing resources for the temporary period). Depending on the cloud services consumed and the cloud vendor, the units of consumption and hence the charges will also vary. For example, serverless computing may charge for the processing of jobs rather than for servers, as the back end is wholly managed as a service.

Other cost models allow the use of the spare capacity of a public cloud provider at certain times (when overall total demand is low and the cloud vendor has ample additional capacities). This allows the cloud provider to charge for resources that would otherwise be idle. Customers gain from such models by leveraging lower-rate prices. The downside of such cost models is the unexpected price and time window available. Such resources may then be recaptured by the public cloud provider at any time (within a short warning time) to reallocate to premium usage cases of customers. Applications leveraging such unreliable short computing capacity must therefore be fault tolerant and be able to deal with and recover from resources being unavailable in the middle of a processing job. Amazon AWS refers to this cost model as "spot instances." Microsoft Azure refers to this cost model as "low-priority VMs."

Another cost model in the cloud is where an organization can foresee regular usage over a long time horizon (e.g., one to three years). Applications that would be heavily used on a daily basis may fit this scenario, and in such a case the PAYG cost model would be more expensive (although an organization may benefit from paying for cloud resources only during business hours on Monday to Friday, for example). To assist organizations in such scenarios, public cloud vendors provide a long-term cost model (e.g., over three years) with discounted prices. Organizations can then assess their usage of cloud resources and select the appropriate cost model. Amazon AWS or Microsoft Azure refers to the long-term cost model as "reserved instances (RI)."

Public cloud providers increase financial feasibility by generally offering four cost options for organizations:

1. Pay as you go (PAYG)
2. Spot instances (also known as low-priority VMs)
3. Reserved Instances
4. Discounted unit prices with increased usage

Table 1 AWS Cost Calculation Example

Description	# of Instances	Usage	Type	Billing Option	Monthly Cost
8 vCPUs 32GB RAM	1,000	75% utilization per month	Linux m4.2xlarge 8 vCPU 32GB RAM	On-demand PAYG	$219,600
8 vCPUs 32GB RAM	1,000	75% utilization per month	Linux m4.2xlarge 8 vCPU 32GB RAM	One-year partial up-front reserved	$ 86,140
8 vCPUs 32GB RAM	1,000	75% utilization per month	Linux m4.2xlarge 8 vCPU 32GB RAM	Three-year partial up-front reserved	$ 58,400

Source: https://calculator.s3.amazonaws.com/index.html (AWS, October 2017).

Amazon AWS provides an online calculator to estimate possible costs. A small example is depicted in Table 1.

Organizations that have useful information regarding their usage of servers can then select discounted pricing options over a more extended period (e.g., one to three years). Public cloud vendors provide opportunities not to commit any finances up front, or to only commit partial funding up front and pay as you go throughout the rest of the active period at the discounted rate. It is generally possible to alter such commitments throughout the cloud contract, but such flexibilities depend on the cloud vendor. For Azure pricing examples, visit the URL https://azure.microsoft.com/en-us/pricing/details/batch.

Costs of technology and hardware have decreased over time, and the decrease of the expenses over the past five years has led to increased adoption of cloud computing. The research and advisory company 451 Research produces a Cloud Price Index (CPI) encompassing 12 cloud services that include the most commonly used services by organizations, such as compute resources, storage resources, databases, serverless computing services, and more.

The standard and best price ranges are on a downward trend, with a decrease between 2 and 10 percent respectively, with the best price index being on a exponential reduction compared to a more slowly degrading of the standard price (see Figure 33). Increased competition

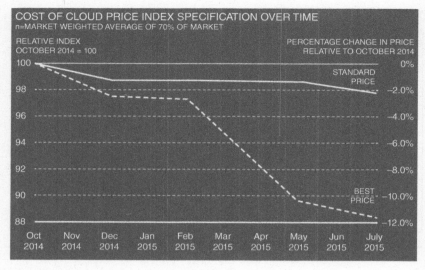

Figure 33 Cloud Price Index—451 Research Group
Source: Rogers, Fellows, and Atelsek (2016, 2).

between public cloud providers has led to price wars and increased services and value for money, and this benefits all organizations wishing to leverage cloud computing.

Service Models

The five characteristics of cloud (as defined by NIST, 800-145, 2012) have led to the three service models of a cloud, shown in Figure 34. Adoption of cloud computing by organizations mostly began with infrastructure as a service (IaaS), and companies worldwide are now consuming more of the platform as a service (PaaS) and software as a service (SaaS) service models.

1. Infrastructure as a Service (IaaS)

A cloud vendor provides the capabilities for organizations to self-provision compute resources, storage, virtual networks, and other resources that a company may require to deploy and run software applications. Organizations generally can select a virtual machine with

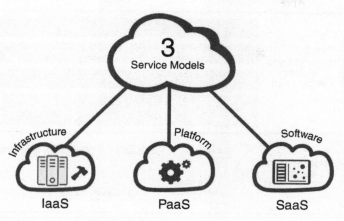

Figure 34 The Three Cloud Service Models

an operating system or can choose an empty virtual machine and use their own choice of operating systems and customizations. A cloud consumer does not access the actual hardware or anything physical at a cloud data center. Organizations that leverage infrastructure as a service (IaaS) have full control of the virtual machine, operating system, and applications within the virtual machine. Automation within a cloud to provision such resources is vital for large-scale self-service automation. Such data centers are also referred to as software-defined data centers (SDDCs). There are specific tasks and duties that the cloud vendor performs and is responsible for. These include maintaining and operating the data centers, and specific security (e.g., protection of physical resources, access to the estate). The organization consuming the cloud resources is responsible for patching and maintaining the operating system in a virtual machine, security access to the virtual machine, or the applications within the VMs. This balance of duties is called a "shared responsibility model."

In a shared responsibility cloud model the onus moves from a single responsibility (e.g., organization solely responsible for on-premises components) to a joint responsibility model where specific duties and responsibilities move to a cloud provider, but others are still the responsibility of the organization consuming cloud services. As an organization consumes more advanced cloud services (i.e., platform as a service [PaaS] or software as a service [SaaS]), the majority of

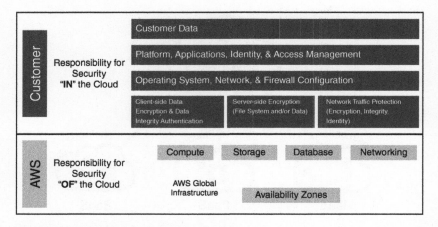

Figure 35   AWS Shared Responsibility Model

Source: https://aws.amazon.com/compliance/shared-responsibility-model/ (2017).

responsibilities shift to the cloud provider. An example of the joint responsibility model with AWS is depicted in Figure 35.

Amazon AWS defines its version of the shared responsibility model as responsibility "of the cloud" and responsibility "in the cloud." Organizations consuming cloud services are responsible for security "in the cloud." This would include being responsible for their data, operating systems (if using an IaaS cloud service), client-side access to resources, and more. AWS, in contrast, is responsible for security "of the cloud." This typically includes management of the cloud data centers, maintenance, and operation of hardware (e.g., compute, storage, and networking), and advanced cloud services should the organization choose to utilize them; for example, databases as a service (AWS) or cloud vendor would be responsible for smooth operation, performance, backups, high availability, disaster recovery, and more. (See Figure 36.)

2. Platform as a Service (PaaS)

The platform as a service is the next evolutionary step in adopting cloud services. It follows in the same footsteps as the IaaS, in that it allows self-service of resources, and there is also a shared responsibility model. In this PaaS cloud service model, there are more responsibilities that fall onto to the cloud provider. As an

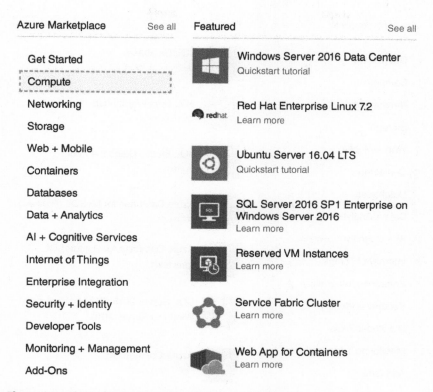

Figure 36 Microsoft Azure Portal Screenshot—IaaS Example

example, an organization could choose to select a preconfigured environment for storing transactional data in a database. In this scenario, the cloud-consuming organization could choose a PaaS option whereby there is already a virtual machine with a relational database installed and configured. Self-service and automation make the deployment of such environments very quick (typically within minutes) and easy. Continuing from the early example, the cloud provider would be responsible for the underlying cloud resources, the virtual machine, the operating system, and the relational database. It would also be the responsibility of the cloud provider that there is adequate performance of the database, database backups are performed in an automated manner, and there is high availability as well as ways to prevent or recover from disasters (e.g., hardware failure, power failure, entire data center failure). In contrast to the

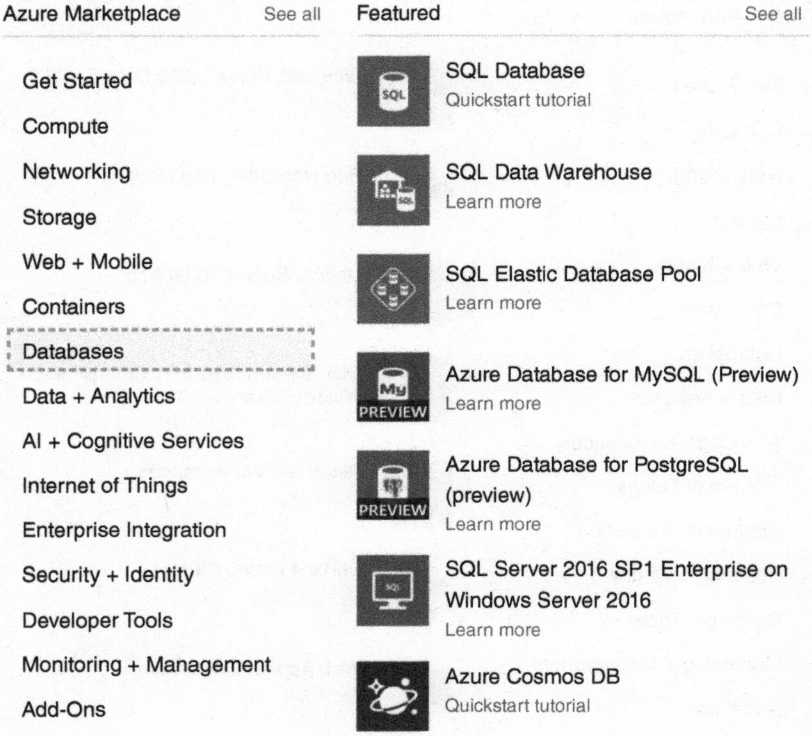

Azure Marketplace	See all	Featured	See all

Azure Marketplace   See all

Get Started

Compute

Networking

Storage

Web + Mobile

Containers

Databases

Data + Analytics

AI + Cognitive Services

Internet of Things

Enterprise Integration

Security + Identity

Developer Tools

Monitoring + Management

Add-Ons

Featured   See all

SQL Database
Quickstart tutorial

SQL Data Warehouse
Learn more

SQL Elastic Database Pool
Learn more

Azure Database for MySQL (Preview)
Learn more

Azure Database for PostgreSQL (preview)
Learn more

SQL Server 2016 SP1 Enterprise on Windows Server 2016
Learn more

Azure Cosmos DB
Quickstart tutorial

Figure 37   Microsoft Azure Portal Screenshot—PaaS

IaaS environment, the cloud-consuming organization does not have access to the virtual machine, the operating system, or administration of the database in this example. The cloud provider manages the underlying infrastructure, so the environment is tightly controlled. (See Figure 37.)

3. Software as a Service (SaaS)

Software as a service is the most advanced use of cloud services. Management and responsibilities mostly lie with the cloud provider. Organizations consume software application services without the need for deploying or managing anything. Probably one of the most famous examples of software as a service is Salesforce.com. Organizations consume the cloud-based application without needing to deploy, manage, or worry about any underlying infrastructure or the application. No development work is necessary, nor is there a need for integrating additional software components. Application maintenance and updates are the responsibility of the cloud provider. In an SaaS model, an organization pays a monthly or annual subscription for the use of software that is cloud-based. Another prominent example of software as a service is Microsoft Office 365. The Office suite is accessible via the internet and is maintained by Microsoft. A subscription-based licensing and cost model means consumers of this service receive constant updates and new features to the application. Software as a service is predicted to have the largest growth of the three cloud services (IaaS, PaaS, SaaS), as depicted in Figure 38.

Several leaders are establishing themselves in the software as a service market, as illustrated in Figure 39.

Deployment Models

The five characteristics flow into the three cloud service types that then flow into the four deployment models (NIST, 800-145, 2011). (See Figure 40.) As mentioned earlier, the cloud movement began

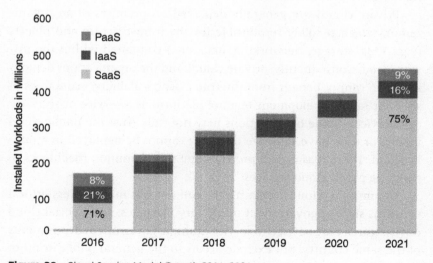

Figure 38 Cloud Service Model Growth 2016–2021
Source: Cisco Global Cloud Index (2016–2021) (2018, 18).

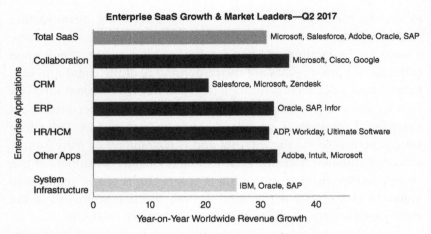

Figure 39 Enterprise SaaS Growth and Market Leaders, Q2 2017
Source: Synergy Research Group (2018).

with virtualization and then progressed to private clouds and later public clouds. Private clouds make use of automation and being a software-defined data center (SDDC). These private clouds provide a degree of self-service, agility, and flexibility, but not as high as when compared to public clouds.

Private clouds are generally deployed on-premises of an organization, which is solely responsible for the infrastructure and objects (e.g., VMs, storage, networking, data, etc.) contained within the private cloud. Consequently, private clouds and the organizations deploying them cannot benefit from the true elastic scalability, economies of scale, or rapid development (e.g., of platform as a service or software as a service). Some organizations may not fully trust the public cloud model, or they have sensitive data that cannot be deployed in a public cloud. These reasons are probably the most common roadblocks to adopting public cloud services.

Community clouds are a niche segment but may address critical concerns such as government or military use cases. One special cloud environment may be used to service multiple government departments of the same country, but exclude access to the general public or other nations. Data resides in the same country of residence. Public cloud vendors are addressing such sensitive needs by providing government

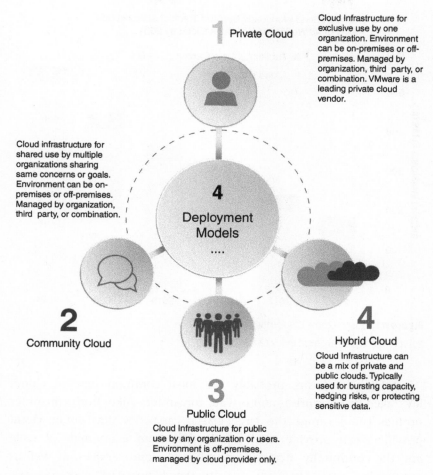

Figure 40 Four Cloud Deployment Models

clouds (also referred to as sovereign clouds). Another example is where local regulations and concerns require all data to reside in a local country. Germany, for example, needs data to remain in Germany whether the users of such cloud services are government or private organizations. Microsoft Azure has an example offering where the local cloud data center is managed by a partner (Germany's T-Systems), and no non-German citizen has access to this cloud environment in Germany.

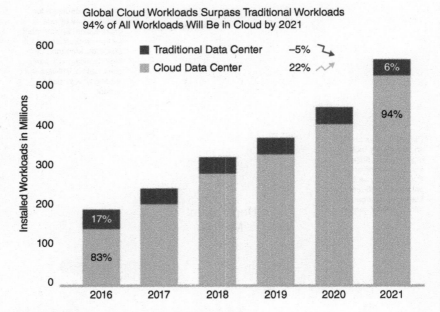

Figure 41 Cisco Global Cloud Index 2016–2021
Source: Cisco Global Cloud Index (2016–2021, 14).

Public clouds are probably the most common type of cloud, leveraged by enterprises and private consumers alike. Both consumer profiles can leverage the large elastic capacities that public cloud providers can provide, and can benefit from economies of scale and the continually increasing number of cloud services, as well as automation, ease of use, and security. (See Figure 41.)

Public cloud vendors are developing enhancements in security (e.g., encryption of data at rest, encryption of data in motion) that are providing more options for organizations to protect data. Through 2020, 95 percent of cloud security failures will be caused by customers (Skyhigh 2016, 3). Gartner, in its June 2017 Magic Quadrant for Cloud Infrastructure as a Service Worldwide Report, recognized AWS and Microsoft as a leader for cloud infrastructure as a service. Also recognized in the report are Alibaba Cloud, CenturyLink, Fujitsu, Google, IBM, Interroute, Joyent, NTT Communications, Oracle,

Rackspace, Skytap, and Virtustream. Note that the capabilities referred to in this magic quadrant report are those of cloud infrastructure as a service (IaaS).

Note: Gartner does not endorse any vendor, product, or service depicted in its research publications, and does not advise technology users to select only those vendors with the highest ratings or other designations. Gartner research publications consist of the opinions of Gartner's research organization and should not be construed as statements of fact. Gartner disclaims all warranties, expressed or implied, with respect to this research, including any warranties of merchantability or fitness for a particular purpose.

The fourth deployment type of cloud (NIST, 800-145, 2011) is the hybrid cloud model. This cloud model is typically used to balance the benefits and risks of a private cloud and a public cloud. Organizations can stretch or burst into capacity and services of public cloud providers when and where required. Microsoft can provide such a mixture via its on-premises virtualization (Hyper-V) capabilities or via technologies that are designed to leverage cloud services. The Microsoft SQL Server (a database technology platform) is such an example, where data can reside on-premises and stretch into a public cloud where required. This allows organizations to leverage elastic capacity when needed, or leverage an off-site disaster recovery option. The Microsoft SQL engines of on-premises and cloud are the same, enabling organizations to develop applications and workloads that seamlessly integrate and can be migrated when required with minimal effort.

Amazon AWS and VMware have formed a partnership to allow organizations to migrate on-premises virtual machines to the public cloud and back (Barr 2017). A survey conducted by RightScale highlights that 96 percent of the respondents are using cloud, whereby 71 percent are using a hybrid approach, 21 percent use public cloud only, and only 4 percent use private cloud only (RightScale 2018, 12) (see Figure 42). The Cisco Global Cloud Index (GCI) highlights that while private and public clouds continue to grow, use of private cloud will probably decrease to 27 percent by the year 2021 and use of

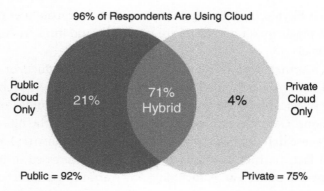

Figure 42 Public versus Private Cloud
Source: RightScale (2018, 12).

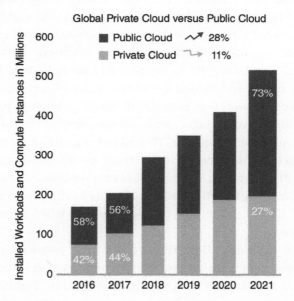

Figure 43 Cisco Global Cloud Index—Private versus Public Cloud
Source: Cisco Global Cloud Index (2016–2021, 27).

public cloud will likely increase to 73 percent (Cisco Global Cloud Index 2016–2021, 27) (see Figure 43). Private clouds will continue to exist in parallel, serving data-sensitive usage cases, as well as those having other reasons for utilizing a private cloud alongside a public cloud.

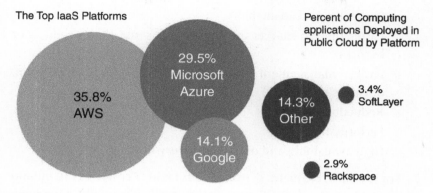

Figure 44 Top IaaS Platforms—Public Cloud
Source: Skyhigh (2016, 17).

Three main cloud providers (AWS, Azure, and Google) in the public cloud space have established themselves, with the top two public cloud vendors owning the majority of the market share (more than 65 percent), as shown in Figure 44. Two other vendors, SoftLayer and Rackspace, have negligible market shares of 3.4 percent and 2.9 percent, respectively (Skyhigh 2016, 17).

Cloud Benefits

The growth of cloud computing and related technologies is forecasted to continue well beyond 2020 (Manyika et al., 2013). Research studies have shown that a global cloud market growth of US$1.3 trillion is likely by 2018, and that the cloud market in the European Union is expected to be worth €44.8 billion, with a cumulative revenue benefit of €449 billion added to the gross domestic product of the EU member states (Wauters et al. 2016, ii, 52). Benefits and priorities may vary slightly across countries and industries and are driven by the nature of their business, regulation, and attitude. The most common benefits of adopting cloud computing are (not ranked by any priority):

- Reduction of information communication technology (ICT) costs
- The shift of IT costs from capital expenditure to operating expenditure

- Scalability and adaptability
- Faster time to market for organizations and their products or services
- Easier management (e.g., time efficiencies, automation, outsourcing of tasks)
- Reduction of costs
- Performance
- High availability and disaster recovery options

For example, estimates of overall savings in IT costs of €140 million across the UK, Germany, France, Italy, and Spain would have been realized by adopting cloud computing between 2010 and 2015. Similarly, IT operational expenditure (opex) and IT capital expenditure (capex) savings of €130 million and €154 million, respectively, were noted between 2010 and 2015 across the UK, Germany, France, Italy, and Spain. (Wauters et al. 2016, 87–88). (See Figure 45.)

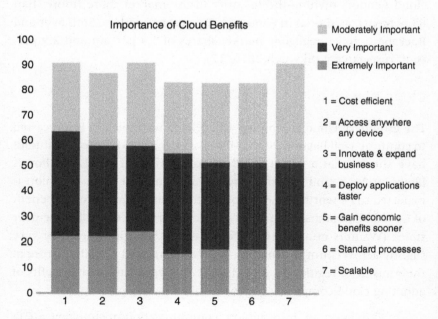

Figure 45 Importance of Cloud Benefits
Source: European Commission, (2014, 35).

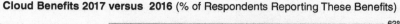

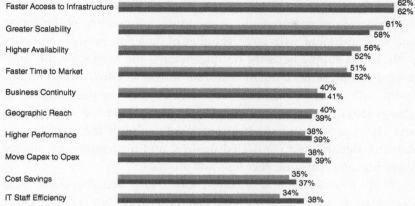

Figure 46 Cloud Benefits 2017 versus 2016
Source: RightScale (2017, 15).

Such benefits are shared across organizations and countries, as is highlighted by a survey from RightScale that reports the importance of benefits ranked by respondents. Cost savings and efficiencies were also noted as necessary, but are lower in the scale of importance compared to other benefits of cloud computing. As shown in Figure 46, faster access to infrastructure, greater scalability (e.g., compute and storage capacity), higher availability (e.g., uptime of services and applications), and faster time to market (e.g., application development, speedier product or service development accelerated by cloud computing) are ranked as the top four essential benefits of cloud. The top four priority areas have generally maintained their percentages of importance when comparing 2016 and 2017 results. Other priority areas have slightly diminished in importance (e.g., IT staff efficiency, cost savings) (RightScale 2017).

In the context of the supply chain, such benefits of cloud computing can help organizations with cost efficiencies by utilizing the cost models of cloud providers (e.g., PAYG or discounted reserved instances). The elasticity of computing resources would also provide benefits and flexibility to organizations. For example, an organization could scale out computing resources when analyzing large time series for demand-driven forecasts, or computing inventory optimization and replenishment with large volumes of data and multiple network paths in the supply network (multiechelon), and then scale the computing resources back down when no longer needed. Organizations could utilize new disruptive technologies such as the Internet of Things (IoT) through cloud computing. Leveraging IoT technologies and cloud services would help organizations with the collection of demand signals from connected devices, and processing and storing them for near real-time decisions and analysis.

High availability and business continuity benefits could help organizations with the highest possible uptime of their services. Large spikes of demand (e.g., during seasonal shopping) could be met via automation and elasticity of scaled-out resources. Business continuity could be increased by leveraging related services from cloud providers. For example, data could be seamlessly mirrored to different data centers or regions operated by a cloud provider. Depending on the design of the applications, it is also possible to have standby computer nodes for increased performance or for handling the failure of some nodes. For example, the web application and supporting back-end services for the online shopping web portal of a retailer could have several computer nodes that increase when there is increased demand (e.g., Black Friday, Christmas shopping time), or standby computer nodes could handle the demand node should a primary computer fail. Cloud vendors also make it possible to have such web applications globally available. This provides a fast and responsive experience for end consumers (e.g., a consumer in the UK accessing an instance of a retailer's online shopping portal that is located in Europe), as well as high-availability options should one region fail or be overloaded.

As mentioned earlier, the nature of the industry, local regulations, and local attitudes toward cloud computing all influence the rate of adoption of these platforms and technologies. (See Table 2.)

Challenges, fears, and reasons for not adopting cloud computing are dwindling over time. Data sensitivity, regulations, and risk averseness of organizations will significantly influence reasons for not adopting cloud. (See Figure 47.) Some of the most common reasons

Table 2 Percentage of Companies Adopting at Least One Cloud Solution by Industry Sector 2013–2015

Industry	At Least One Public Cloud Including Office/Collaborative		At Least One Public Cloud Excluding Office/Collaborative		At Least One Private Cloud Service	
	2013	2015	2013	2015	2013	2015
Finance	69.1%	76.4%	69.1%	76.4%	32.7%	43.8%
Manufacturing	55.0%	65.3%	54.5%	65.3%	20.3%	44.2%
Health Care/ Education	54.4%	65.7%	52.8%	64.2%	32.1%	49.2%
Distribution	68.8%	74.3%	68.8%	74.3%	20.3%	45.4%
Telecom/Media	71.2%	80.3%	79.8%	80.3%	31.1%	45.3%
Other Services	66.3%	75.9%	66.1%	75.9%	25.4%	52.2%
Total Business Sector	63.3%	72.4%	62.8%	72.2%	26.0%	47.7%
Government	53.0%	60.0%	52.7%	59.2%	27.7%	49.6%
Total EU	61.5%	70.3%	61.0%	69.9%	26.3%	48.0%

Source: European Commission, (2014, 21).

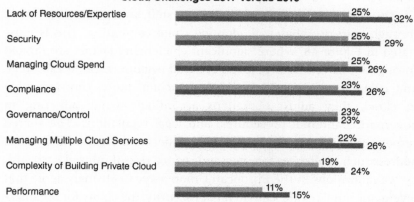

Cloud Challenges 2017 versus 2016

	2017	2016
Lack of Resources/Expertise	25%	32%
Security	25%	29%
Managing Cloud Spend	25%	26%
Compliance	23%	26%
Governance/Control	23%	23%
Managing Multiple Cloud Services	22%	26%
Complexity of Building Private Cloud	19%	24%
Performance	11%	15%

Figure 47 Cloud Challenges 2017 versus 2016
Source: RightScale (2017, 16).

for not adopting cloud or not adopting public cloud computing fast enough are (in no particular order):

- ▓ Security
- ▓ Lack of expertise (internal to the organization)

- Compliance
- Governance and control
- Cost management
- Control
- Compatibility (e.g., of applications)
- Vendor lock-in
- Performance

Security is ranked as the most critical risk factor of public cloud computing by most organizations. Approximately 63 percent of respondents of a cloud IaaS survey noted that they perceive the public cloud to be equally secure as or more secure than their own data center (Skyhigh 2017, 13). Organizations must modify their procedures and processes to adapt to a cloud platform. In a shared responsibility model of public cloud computing, organizations are responsible for their data, and the public cloud provider can provide options such as encryption of data at rest and in motion, secure access, and authentication.

The importance of these challenges shift as organizations move through maturity phases of adopting cloud computing. This is illustrated in Figure 48, where significant challenging factors are ranked throughout three maturity levels of cloud beginners, cloud explorers, and cloud focused. As organizations become more knowledgeable in cloud, they adjust operations accordingly while adhering to governance, internal procedures, and legal regulations. The shared responsibility model of public cloud providers and organizations helps address such challenges together and reduce risks if utilized correctly.

Organizations in the European Union agree or strongly agree that leveraging public cloud leads to higher security, the ability for organizations to leverage up-to-date IT technologies, and that the public cloud is more reliant and easier to use (see Figure 49). Revenue growth is also seen as an attributable benefit of adopting cloud computing, as shown in Table 3. Percentage of revenue growth as a result of leveraging cloud computing is evenly spread across small, medium, and large organizations (European Commission: 2014, 41). The research highlights that the majority of respondents estimate 5 to 19 percent revenue growth attributed to adopting cloud computing.

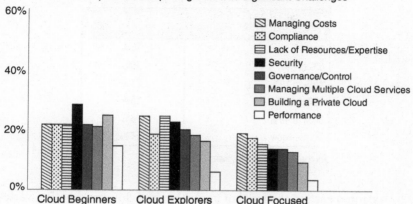

Figure 48 Challenges Decrease with Cloud Maturity
Source: RightScale (2017, 17).

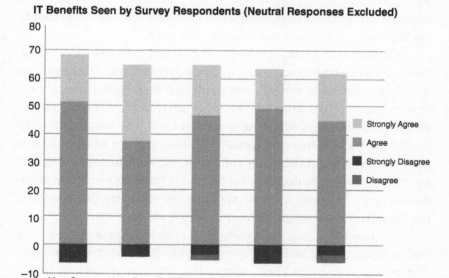

Figure 49 IT Benefits of Cloud Computing
Source: European Commission, (2014, 38).

Table 3 Revenue Growth Attributed to Cloud Adoption

Revenue Growth Attributed to Cloud Adoption	% of Respondents
1 to 4%	15%
5% to 9%	36%
10% to 19%	23%
20% to 29%	15%
30% to 49%	8%
Do not know	4%

Source: European Commission: (2014, 41).

As noted earlier, the level of importance of cloud computing varies across industries (e.g., Table 2). In the manufacturing sector, cloud computing is seen as a way of improving supply chain management, as well as improving inventory, orders, and distribution. Sixty percent of respondents of an Economist Intelligence Unit survey see cloud computing as a way of supporting production processes, and 54 percent of respondents see cloud computing as an enabler leading to better supply management (Economist Intelligence Unit 2016, 7).

As organizations adopt cloud computing and consume more public cloud services, the financial costs incurred also increase. Organizations must select the most suitable cost model for their business and must ensure that internal processes are adapted to a new way of operation with cloud. Such operating procedures will help organizations to ensure there are no cost wastages. Public cloud vendors assist with such goals by providing monitoring and reporting information, as well as methods to automate decisions for balancing business needs and costs. Even though expenses increase as organizations utilize the cloud, the net benefits still outweigh the costs. (See Figure 50.)

In summary, cloud computing has evolved into a mature and widely adopted platform. There were some pioneering technologies and events that led to cloud computing, and new emerging trends like Big Data and IoT continue to drive the need for public clouds. It is estimated that a "smart city" with connected devices (e.g., planes, cars, factories, buildings, hospitals, public safety, weather sensors, etc.) will generate 200 million gigabytes of data per day by the year

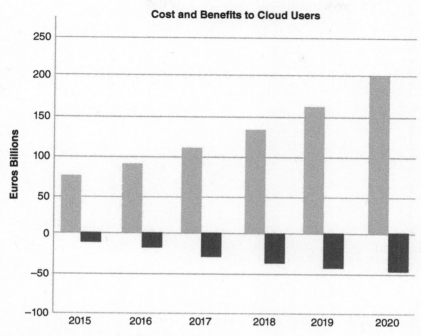

Figure 50   Costs and Benefits to Cloud Users
Source: Wauters et al. (2016, 104).

2020 (Cisco Global Cloud Index 2015–2020, 14). The number of cloud services to help organizations adapt to such new challenges is also set to increase. Adoption of the cloud by organizations is likely to rise further, with exponential growth predicted to continue over the next few years. Although private and hybrid clouds are expected to coexist for the foreseeable future, the majority of cloud usage will continue to be public clouds. Regulations, specific industry rules and needs, and organizational attitudes will continue to influence the rate of adoption of cloud computing. The next chapter will highlight possible options for organizations wishing to migrate to a cloud platform.

CHAPTER **3**

Migrating to the Cloud

igrating to the cloud requires a clearly defined strategy, and organizations should consider short- and long-term goals, a methodology, and careful planning. There are many options for an organization to consider before deciding on a cloud strategy and an approach to executing such a vision. This journey could be undertaken alone by an organization or with the help of specialist firms and cloud vendors. Specialist firms such as EY, KPMG, and McKinsey, for example, can help with the defining, planning, and execution phases. Cloud providers typically provide assessment tools and services to help identify suitable options balancing strategic, business, technical, and financial needs of organizations wanting to move to a cloud. Consulting services firms or branches of cloud vendors can provide the workforce to help with the execution of plans (e.g., IT tasks, project management tasks). Moving to the cloud (e.g., private, public, hybrid) and selecting the suitable service types (e.g., infrastructure as a service [IaaS], platform as a service [PaaS], software as a service [SaaS]) require a paradigm shift of operations, workflow, and design of IT, and should therefore be assessed with diligence. Selecting the right strategic partner(s) for this change and journey to the cloud can also make the difference between failure and success, so careful assessment should be undertaken, applying suitable criteria that are important to each organization. Organizations in different industries and geographic regions will have different priorities, and hence assessment criteria should reflect such differences.

This chapter aims to highlight common practices and methodologies for planning a move to the cloud. There are different methodologies that organizations can adopt, and a commonly accepted framework is the R-model. Amazon AWS cloud has a 6R framework, and this chapter will highlight both methodologies for migrating to the cloud. Cloud readiness checks are a useful step in the journey to cloud computing, and some examples of such tools are showcased throughout this chapter.

At a high level there are five possible steps in the journey to cloud computing (see Figure 51):

1. Identify business reasons for cloud.
2. Perform cloud readiness checks.

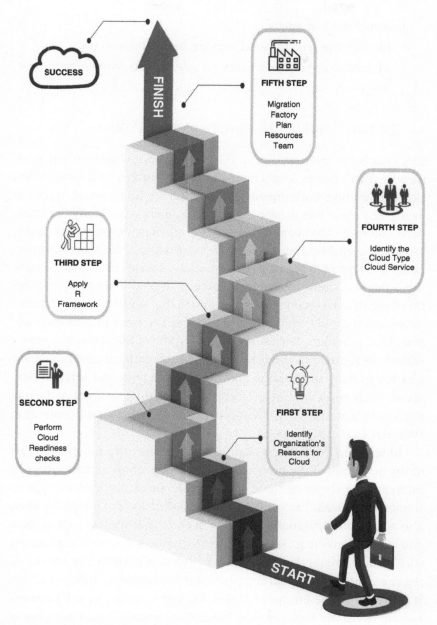

Figure 51 Five Steps to the Cloud

3. Apply the R-model.

4. Identify the type of cloud, service, and vendor to use.

5. Migration factory (resources, people, project management, testing, etc.).

1. IDENTIFY BUSINESS REASONS FOR CLOUD

This step is the most crucial step in the process. Organizations must identify their business challenges and viable justifications for adopting cloud computing. Each organization has its own problems and pressing needs, and these will dictate the decisions made later. Many organizations embrace cloud computing for cost efficiencies, increased agility, increased availability, and more (refer to Chapter 2 for more information). The type of industry an organization operates in will also dictate the uptake of cloud computing. There may be different risk perceptions, regulations, and geographic options that influence the decisions for adopting cloud computing and selecting the types of cloud services and cloud providers. For example, in a survey of European businesses (shown in Figure 52), the risks of a security breach, uncertainty about location of data, uncertainty about applicable laws and legal mechanisms, high costs, and insufficient knowledge were listed as factors preventing enterprises of different sizes from using cloud computing (Wauters et al. 2016, 41–45).

Identifying the business reasons will help identify suitable options in the next steps of the process. The risk profile of an organization will influence the choice of cloud (e.g., private, public, or hybrid), type of services (e.g., IaaS, PaaS, SaaS), and possible risks. Organizations must also adhere to regulations and laws in their industry, as well as local and regional laws (e.g., state, country, region specific). New regulations such as the General Data Protection Regulation (GDPR) add additional requirements for safeguarding data and information. This regulation is particular to the European Union, though it applies to any business (regardless of the location of its headquarters) that conducts business within the European Union.

Figure 53 highlights risk profiling and concerns across different industries by enterprises in the European Union. Identifying priorities,

Factors preventing enterprises using Cloud Computing (CC) - 2014

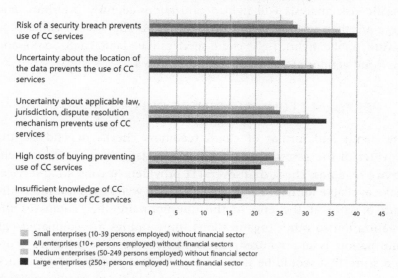

Figure 52 Factors Preventing Enterprises' Use of Cloud
Source: Wauters et al. (2016, 75).

Barrier — Sector / Use Case	Data Protection	Intellectual Property Rights	Confidential Information	Outdated Legacy Laws	Information Security Concerns	Supervision and Inspection	National Sovereignty	National Security	Jurisdiction Enforceability	Procurement Rules
Public Sector	X		X	X	X	X	X	X	X	X
Taxation and Social Security	X		X		X	X	X	X	X	
Health Care and Legal Services	X		X		X	X		X	X	
Media and Entertainment	X	X	X	X	X	X			X	
Financial Services	X		X	X	X	X		X	X	
National Archiving	X						X		X	
Manufacturing / Consumer		X			X					

Figure 53 Economic impact of Cloud Computing in Europe
Source: Wauters et al. (2016, 76).

conducting a cost-benefit analysis, and performing an organizational-specific risk analysis will help organizations identify priorities, and these are then used in step 4 of the process. The type of cloud (i.e., private, public, hybrid), the cloud services (i.e., IaaS, PaaS, SaaS), and the cloud vendor(s) are then selected in step 4.

2. PERFORM CLOUD READINESS CHECKS

The depth and format of cloud readiness checks depend on the provider of the assessment service. Organizations can utilize a self-service readiness check that several IT providers or consulting services make available for free. These are typically a web-based questionnaire with a score at the end of the questionnaire that compares the organization to other organizations (only ratings are compared—all information is anonymized) or compares the organization's score to a score that would be possible (see Table 4 and Figure 54). Such baseline scoring allows an organization to identify its starting position before adopting cloud computing and provides useful insights into what improvements are possible in which areas. Organizations can also choose to engage with consulting firms for a more in-depth and consultative assessment with a more tailored evaluation and specific recommendations that may result in a higher value of the exercise. This section showcases an example of such a cloud readiness check. Average responses were selected to simulate organizations that are at the beginning of the journey of fully adopting cloud computing.

EXAMPLE

EXAMPLE: CLOUD READINESS CHECK: ISG (GERMAN LANGUAGE VERSION)

URL: http://cloud-readiness-check.com/kalkulator

1 — 2 — 3 — 4 — 5 — 6 — ✓

Organization & Strategy | Portfolio | Technology Development | Infrastructure Operations | Marketing Distribution | Service & Support | Results

Table 4 Cloud Readiness Check Example (ISG)

Question	Response
How many employees does your organization employ?	5,000
What primary segment does your organization operate within?	Applications
What is your industry focus?	Large distribution/retail
What percentage of your revenue do you expect to save via replicated software solutions?	10%–20%
How much revenue was driven by software last year?	€5–10 million
What is your primary customer audience of applications?	Private consumers
What is your biggest challenge in the next few years?	Digital transformation
In what development phase of cloud computing is your organization?	Analysis and evaluation
What percentage of new business in the next three years would be attributed to cloud computing?	11%–20%
What type of software is developed and distributed in your organization?	Mobile apps
Will your business model process procurement specific customer data?	Yes
In which segment does your organization plan to use the cloud-based software?	E-commerce, e-shops, social media
What form of cloud portfolio is relevant to your customers?	Standard public cloud offering
What type of cost model do you plan to offer for your software?	Buy license, PAYG
What consulting services do you offer to your customers in combination with an IT solution?	Strategic advice
Does your application support multitenancy and can it be offered via the internet?	Yes
Is your application web-based or rather client-server based?	Web-based
Does your application follow a microservice platform design?	No
Which frameworks do you use to develop your software?	Node.js, Java, Python, .Net
Do your customers care where data is processed and stored? Do laws dictate where data is to be stored and processed?	Yes
Have you tested any cloud platforms?	Amazon AWS, Microsoft Azure
Do you operate any production environments in the cloud?	Not at the moment
Which cloud type do you plan to use in the future?	Public cloud
Do you plan to build your own operation or use a partner?	External operation, external data center
Where should the data centers be located?	Europe
Is your product distributed in Europe or also internationally?	Internationally

(*Continued*)

Table 4 *(Continued)*

Question	Response
Do you have international distribution resources?	Yes
Have you thought about a cloud-based distribution model?	No
Have you thought about a cloud-based marketing option?	No
Have you modified your internal processes to adapt to cloud computing?	No, but in planning
What support services do you plan to offer via cloud?	Email, web support, free phone support

Results

Category	Average Score	Your Score
Organization and Strategy	68%	24%
Portfolio and Services	55%	35%
Technology and Development	47%	30%
Infrastructure and Operations	41%	18%
Marketing and Distribution	61%	43%
Service and Support	57%	19%
Total Evaluation	39%	25%

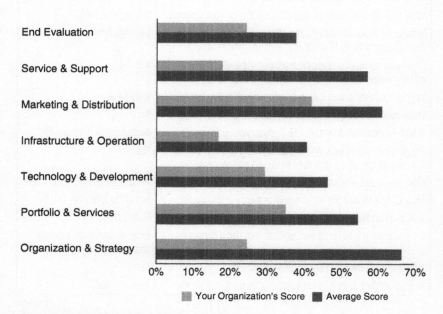

Figure 54 ISG Cloud Readiness Results Example

Cisco provides a similar readiness check tool and uses a spider graph to compare an organization's assessment with industry baselines. A digital score (out of 100) helps organizations compare its current state with the desired state. The closer the score is to 100, the better.

Cisco readiness tool URL: www.cisco.com/c/m/en_us/solutions/data-center/offers/Digital-Readiness-Assessment/index.html.

EMC also provides a simple tool for assessing the use of private or public cloud computing. This type of cloud readiness check is simpler than the previous examples and leads to consulting services for a more customized assessment. It is a good practice to use several readiness checks (many of them are free) to gain an understanding of the category areas and help build a baseline for an organization. Such assessment exercises should also try to ensure the advice is impartial.

EMC cloud readiness tool URL: https://www.emc.com/cloud/hybrid-cloud-computing/suitability/index.htm.

3. APPLY THE R FRAMEWORK

Probably one of the most common frameworks organizations adopt for migrating applications to the cloud is the R-model (see Figure 55). This framework provides five or six critical options for organizations, and these can be used in combination when migrating applications to the cloud. Using a combination of the five possibilities provides flexibility for organizations and can reduce risks as not all applications are forced into the same mold. There will be different technical, business, and licensing principles that govern the migration of applications to the cloud. The R-model framework can help to identify the beginning and end states of cloud computing maturity that an organization wishes to adopt, and different applications can move through this maturity model at different rates. Therefore organizations do not have to force a big bang approach (doing it all at once) and can move in stages.

The business and financial returns also increase in stages with such an approach, but the risks are reduced and spread across the different stages. Organizations can find the right sweet spot for their liking (e.g., which applications are suited for public cloud or private cloud, or which applications deserve a redesign, etc.) and can build the internal know-how, experience, and methodology required to execute

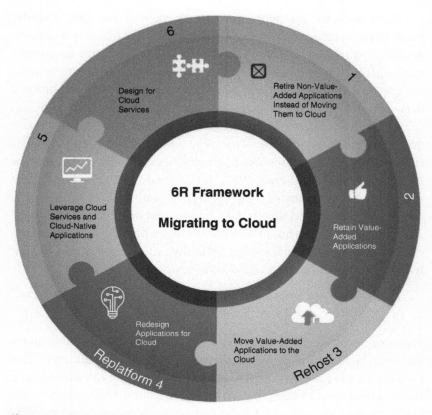

Figure 55 Example R Framework Migrating to Cloud

the strategies chosen. This execution phase is commonly referred to as a "migration factory" where the methodology consists of assessing applications to be migrated, migrating, and then testing the end result state. It is also a common practice to begin with the simple and easy applications first to test the processes and gain internal trust for the paradigm shift. The selection of simple and low-risk applications to test the approach and "factory"-style execution is usually referred to as selecting the low-hanging fruit.

The Amazon cloud (AWS) 6Rs are as follows:

1. Retire
2. Retain

3. Re-host

4. Re-platform

5. Re-purchase

6. Re-factor

The Amazon cloud (AWS) framework approach, referring to it as the 6R framework (Amazon Web Services 2015, 11), is depicted in Figure 56.

The decision tree in Figure 56 depicts the process of selecting the appropriate option from the framework. In this AWS R-model framework, different applications can be migrated via different "Rs"—there is no need to force all types of applications through one process. Organizations must identify suitable options (e.g., from the R frameworks) for different applications or categories of software applications to minimize risk and make the migration to the cloud successful. Amazon cloud (AWS) provides useful guidance via a framework called the AWS Cloud Adoption Framework (CAF).

This AWS CAF highlights different perspectives that an organization wishing to migrate to the cloud should consider early on in the planning process. There are seven critical perspectives in the AWS CAF model, and these are highlighted in Table 5.

Microsoft has a similar framework for helping an organization with its journey to the cloud. There are 5Rs in this Microsoft framework (Briggs and Kassner 2017, 17–20):

1. Retire

2. Replace

3. Retain and wrap

4. Re-host

5. Re-envision

1. Retire: Organizations should perform a cost-benefit analysis of applications. If an application is not providing business value or not used, then it could be a candidate for retiring. There would be no need to migrate such applications to the cloud. This option is also seen as an application consolidation option.

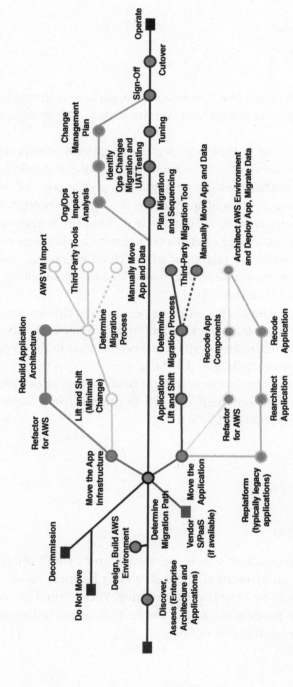

Figure 56 AWS Cloud Migration—6Rs
Source: Amazon Web Services (2015, 11).

Table 5 AWS Cloud Adoption Framework

Perspective	Area of Focus
Business Perspective	Identify business value of leveraging cloud technology services. This category helps an organization to ensure that there is an alignment of business and technology strategy, and that there is support from senior stakeholders.
Platform Perspective	Focus attention on the technologies and relationships with services in complex environments.
Maturity Perspective	The assessment of current state of maturity and organization's capabilities. Identify the future state that an organization is aiming at.
People Perspective	Identify baseline assessment of operations and processes; people resources, knowledge, and experience; and Center of Excellence, and perform a gap analysis to ensure people will be able to operate new cloud model.
Process Perspective	Identify the process, change programs, project management, and execution personas to ensure the business outcome is realized within time and budget.
Operations Perspective	Focus on change programs, adopting a new mode of operating in the cloud.
Security Perspective	Identify organization-specific needs of security, especially data security. Ensure industry and geographic laws are adhered to (e.g., finance, health care, U.S. regulations, and EU regulations).

Source: Amazon Web Services (2015, 4).

2. Replace: It may be possible to replace legacy applications with more modern applications to solve the same business challenges. Software as a service (SaaS) applications or other native cloud applications could be viable options for modernizing the application landscape within an organization.

3. Retain, wrap, and expand: Once the application has been classified as valuable to the organization's business, it is retained. One possible way of modernizing an application may be adding "wrappers" to older applications (e.g., via new application programming interface [API] management tools), or adding triggers and functions to integrate cloud services such as data, analytics, machine learning, and so on.

4. Re-host: This option will help organizations "lift and shift" existing applications to the cloud. Application servers can be virtualized and hosted in the cloud. If an organization is using virtual machines (VMs) on-premises, then those VMs can be imported into the cloud. There is no redesign or architectural change to applications when organizations use this option. It is a low-risk option, but does not provide the higher value possible from cloud computing, as the migration is simply a 1:1 lift and shift.

5. Re-envision: With this option, organizations identify applications that could benefit from modernization and becoming more cloud-aware (e.g., benefiting from elasticity). This option typically involves a redesign of the application and architecture. There are higher risks as the software application is redesigned, but the rewards are generally higher since modern applications can benefit from cloud technologies (e.g., integrating data flows from fast- and slow-moving streams, utilizing near real-time analytics, machine learning, etc.). Architectural changes typically involve applications being able to horizontally and vertically scale based on performance demand. A redesign may also include moving away from a monolithic design (e.g., client-server) to modernized microservices-based design. New technologies and development frameworks (e.g., DevOps) provide more agility and flexibility for the organization to adapt to new challenges. Cloud-aware applications can integrate with the ever-expanding list of services cloud vendors are offering, and so can continuously evolve with the organization's business requirements.

KPMG has identified 10 key considerations for helping decision makers migrate to the cloud (Heppenstall, Newcombe, and Clarke 2016, 28–29), and these are detailed as operational readiness, develop a cohesive and consistent approach, evaluate the data and service, determine the appropriate security wrap, evaluate the proposed cloud service, document responsibility splits, evaluate the service provider, evaluate the service terms, take the accountability test, and, last, make an informed decision.

An organization should have a change program and task force for migrating to the cloud. Such a task force would help define organizational goals and map these to a cloud strategy. In addition to technical changes, there are also process, administration, management, and cultural modifications that are required to move and use a public cloud successfully.

Such a change program should assess business, technical, and legal requirements to short-list the cloud providers, locations of data storage and processing, and types of cloud services to leverage. This will help with the next step of evaluating the short list (e.g., one to three vendors) of vendors. Identifying the types of cloud services needed to meet current business challenges and provide a platform for innovation for an organization would help with defining narrow sets of criteria for proof of concepts.

The organization should assess its cloud vendor of choice carefully. Essential criteria include market rating, financial stability, independent accreditation statements, and other independent checks. Some organizations may choose to split their risks and avoid vendor lock-in by utilizing multiple vendors. This allows hedging of risks, but may increase the complexity of a cloud strategy. Organizations should confirm that industry and other regulatory requirements are met when selecting a cloud provider. For example, organizations in Germany may be more inclined to choose a cloud provider that has cloud data centers located in Germany, thereby ensuring data is stored and processed in Germany only. Organizations should use assessment models such as the Gartner magic quadrant or other global and regional assessment models as inputs to their decision when selecting a cloud vendor.

The launch of the GDPR in May 2018 will mean heavy penalties for noncompliance, and therefore organizations must identify the data they would be storing and processing in a public cloud. Only relevant data should be kept, and only for as long as required. Data encryption technologies should be utilized (e.g., data encryption at rest and in motion), and organizations must remember that cloud computing follows a shared responsibility model.

Service-level agreements (SLAs), licensing structures, and support processes must also be carefully assessed by an organization contemplating moving to the cloud. This will help ensure an organization's cloud strategy is effective, efficient, and economical (also known as the 3-E test).

New models of operation, processes, and management should be tested and improved where possible and be practical. Training and documentation of such changes will help drive cultural and process changes in an organization, and it would therefore be more likely for the move to the cloud to be successful. In such an environment cloud computing would be embraced, allowing an organization to benefit from the change, innovation, and agility continuously, and move to the cloud. (See Figure 57.)

Once an organization has identified the possible benefits of cloud computing for its business, it will begin formulating its cloud strategy,

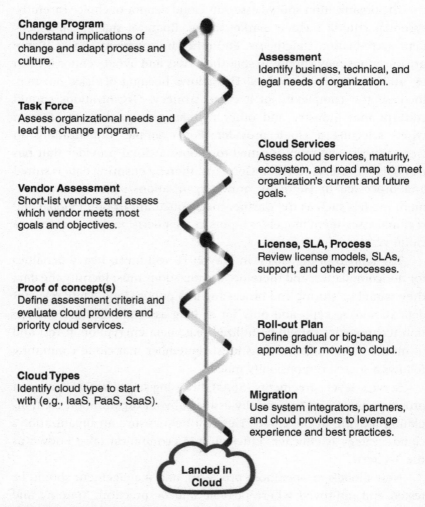

Change Program
Understand implications of change and adapt process and culture.

Assessment
Identify business, technical, and legal needs of organization.

Task Force
Assess organizational needs and lead the change program.

Cloud Services
Assess cloud services, maturity, ecosystem, and road map to meet organization's current and future goals.

Vendor Assessment
Short-list vendors and assess which vendor meets most goals and objectives.

License, SLA, Process
Review license models, SLAs, support, and other processes.

Proof of concept(s)
Define assessment criteria and evaluate cloud providers and priority cloud services.

Roll-out Plan
Define gradual or big-bang approach for moving to cloud.

Cloud Types
Identify cloud type to start with (e.g., IaaS, PaaS, SaaS).

Migration
Use system integrators, partners, and cloud providers to leverage experience and best practices.

Landed in Cloud

Figure 57 Considerations for Cloud Migration Examples

assess the cloud vendor of choice, and then assess applications it wishes to migrate to or use in the cloud (e.g., applying the R-model). Organizations should begin with applications that are low in risk and low in complexity, and that provide high business value. The banking, retail, manufacturing, education, and health care sectors see a significant presence of cloud in their industries (Economist Intelligence Unit 2016, 3–14). In the manufacturing industry, 54 percent or organizations see cloud computing as a way of supporting their goals of better supply chain management (Economist Intelligence Unit 2016, 6).

4. IDENTIFY CLOUD TYPE, CLOUD SERVICE, CLOUD VENDOR

The first two steps in the "five steps to the cloud" framework should help an organization with identifying the cloud type (i.e., private cloud, public cloud, or hybrid cloud). Step 3 (applying the 5Rs framework) should help determine the types of applications to migrate and what cloud services to consume (i.e., infrastructure as a service [IaaS], platform as a service [PaaS], or software as a service [SaaS]). Many organizations begin their journey to the cloud with IaaS, and then assess applications and other workloads and start to adopt PaaS and SaaS offerings from the cloud provider. Organizations may also utilize different services from different cloud vendors. This allows an organization to select the best possible service offering (e.g., data services, Internet of Things [IoT] services, analytics, etc.) at the most affordable price, and in the suitable location (e.g., the country where the cloud data center resides that stores and processes data). Some organizations have seen excellent returns on certain application types when migrating them to cloud services.

Such self-assessment could help organizations further identify application candidates for transitioning to the cloud, and this process is typically iterative and evolving. Organizations should begin with easy, less complicated, and less risky applications. The process would involve creating an assessment and filtering process and criteria list (e.g., business focus, technical focus, software licensing focus, risk

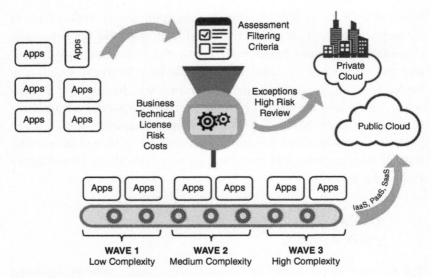

Figure 58 Cloud Migration Factory Approach

focus, and financial focus). As organizations transition more applications through the cloud, they can revisit assumptions and challenge earlier hypotheses and assumptions. This type of a structured and continuously improving process will assist with organizational goals of increasing cloud adoption. (See Figure 58.)

Some example application types providing good economic returns are listed in Table 6. Organizations should begin (e.g., wave 1) with applications that are assessed as having low complexity (e.g., no redesign necessary, no complex architecture, low data sensitivity, low risk), and then transition to more complex applications with waves 2 and 3. Moving in such waves allows organizations to test their processes, assessment criteria, assumptions, and performance of low-risk applications before moving on to the more complicated undertaking. After a few successful migrations with successful end-user testing and business-classified success of the migration, the process can be standardized and more applications can then be pushed through this process in a factorized manner. Some applications may be sensitive, and hence classified for private cloud, but such software applications could also be reassessed at a later time. Some external factors (e.g., time period to close a data center, software license

Table 6 Respondents' Views on Which Cloud Services Gave the Best Economic Return

Cloud Service Type	% of Respondents
Email/calendar/diary	7
Content management	3
Customer relationship management (CRM)	14
Accounting/back office	3
Personnel/HCM or talent management	6
Application platform as a service	4
Database management	9
Business intelligence/analytics	6
Application development and/or online testing	1
Security	9
System and network management	6
Storage online, including backup and/or disaster recovery	9
Infrastructure/compute power	7
Document sharing and management	13
Not applicable	3

Source: European Commission (2014), 42–44.

renewal period, etc.) may dictate a different or parallel process, but if possible organizations should adopt a phased approach for moving to the cloud.

Organizations will have different criteria when selecting the cloud vendor(s), and the decision will be influenced by factors such as location (of organization and vendor), cloud services available, costs, maturity, support levels (e.g., service-level agreements), and market share (i.e., stability, reputation, knowledge, experience). Other internal factors that could influence a decision for selecting a cloud vendor include the industry the organization operates in, legal requirements (global, local), the degree of risk averseness, attitude, and the organization's cloud strategy.

Some of the common factors for selecting a cloud vendor are the following:

- Location of the cloud provider
- Types of cloud services available (e.g., data, analytics, IoT, storage)

- Service levels, uptime, disaster recovery service-level agreements
- Knowledge, experience, and know-how of the vendor
- Ecosystem of the vendor (e.g., software partners, a marketplace for applications)
- Implementation partners' availability
- Independent accreditations (e.g., security)
- Market share and reputation, stability, and future availability of vendor

Table 7 highlights some common reasons that influenced the selection of a cloud vendor for different organizations (surveyed respondents were based in Europe).

While the priorities and weighting of such influencing factors vary across organizations and regions, there are some key factors that are most likely to drive organizational decisions for selecting a cloud vendor. The most common main influencing factors are highlighted in Table 8 (surveyed respondents were based in Europe, though such influencing factors and importance are likely to be similar across other regions). Price-to-value ratio and the price were noted as the most deciding factors by the respondents in the EU survey.

Table 7 Preferred Choice of Cloud Services Provider

Type of Provider	% of Respondents
Pure cloud providers headquartered outside of the European Union	16
Pure cloud providers headquartered in the European Union	15
IT service providers headquartered outside of the European Union	7
IT service providers headquartered in the European Union	11
Software providers headquartered outside of the European Union	10
Software providers headquartered in the European Union	16
Telecom service providers headquartered outside of the European Union	9
European telecom providers	9
Not applicable	7

Source: European Commission (2014), 42–44.

Table 8 Main Choice Factor for Cloud Service Provider

Factor	% of Respondents
The geographic location of the equipment providing the service	26
The location of the supplier's headquarters	29
Availability of local implementation partners	31
Price	50
Ratio quality/price of the services provided	60
The supplier's reputation	47
The service-level agreement (SLA or uptime guarantee)	38
Other/not applicable	3

Source: European Commission (2014), 42–44.

Table 9 Market Comparison of Top 25 to 100 Vendors by Origin

Origin	Number of Providers	Total Share of Top 25 to 100 Vendors' Revenue	Share per Player
EU	23	34.1%	1.48%
United States	49	60.7%	1.24%
Other	3	4.1%	1.38%

Source: European Commission (2014), p. 67.

The United States has the lion's share of the cloud market compared to Europe and other regions, reaching approximately 60 percent of the total revenue of the top 25 to 100 vendors, as shown in Table 9. The European Union (EU) is the second largest market with roughly half the number of cloud providers and revenue share from the total revenue of the top 25 to 100 vendors compared to the United States.

In terms of market share and market standing in global and European markets, a handful of vendors are listed as the top vendors in multiple independent assessments. A sample of such assessments is shown in Figures 59 and 60. Leaders in all regions are AWS, Google, Microsoft, and Salesforce (in alphabetical order).

Table 10 highlights the top 25 cloud vendors in the European market. Cloud vendors include global and local providers.

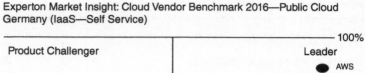

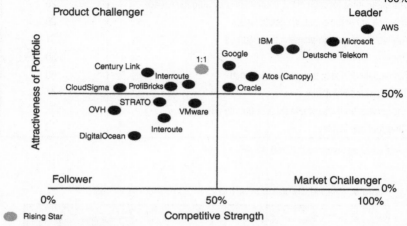

Figure 59 Cloud Vendor Benchmark 2016—Germany
Source: Henkes (2016, 9).

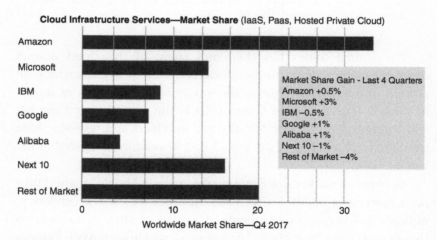

Figure 60 The Race for Public Cloud Leadership
Source: Synergy Research Group (2018).

Table 10 Estimated EU Market Shares of Top 25 Public Cloud Service Providers

Rank in Western Europe	Vendor Name	Headquarters Location	EU Market Share in 2013	Growth 2012–2013 in EU
1	Salesforce.com	United States	6.9%	183%
2	Amazon (AWS)	United States	6.0%	212%
3	Microsoft	United States	2.8%	383%
4	Google	United States	2.4%	178%
5	Oracle	United States	2.0%	153%
6	IBM	United States	2.0%	254%
7	Adobe	United States	1.8%	164%
8	SAP	Germany	1.7%	576%
9	Symantec	United States	1.6%	96%
10	Opentext (GSX)	United States	1.4%	105%
11	Cisco	United States	1.3%	18%
12	Visma	Norway	1.2%	172%
13	HP	United States	1.2%	96%
14	ServiceNow	United States	1.0%	238%
15	Citrix	United States	0.8%	122%
16	T-Systems	Germany	0.8%	328%
17	SmartFocus	France/UK	0.8%	119%
18	Concur	United States	0.8%	137%
19	Unit4	Netherlands	0.7%	203%
20	Cegid	France	0.6%	193%
21	IntraLinks	United States	0.6%	131%
22	ADP	United States	0.6%	220%
23	Zoho	United States	0.6%	204%
24	Zucchetti	Italy	0.5%	147%
25	Wolters Kluwer	Netherlands	0.5%	0156%

Source: European Commission (2014), 65–66.

5. MIGRATION FACTORY

The fifth and final phase in the "five steps to the cloud" process is assembling a migration factory for transitioning to the cloud (see Figure 61). This stage ties together the strategy, approaches, and decisions from the previous four steps as inputs. The size and

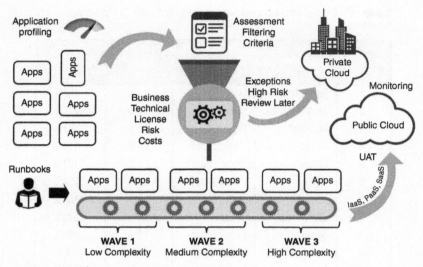

Figure 61 Cloud Migration Factory Methodology

specialized (i.e., cloud) skills of the IT department executing the migration often depend on the size of the organization undertaking the journey to the cloud. The organization can choose to run the migration factory on its own, or it can leverage implementation partners. Such partners can be consulting divisions of cloud vendors or consulting firms that specialize in such cloud advisory and delivery services. Planning and preparation are key to success, and organizations should begin the journey with small steps.

This generally involves dividing the applications to be migrated into waves depending on complexity and risk, and beginning with the low-hanging fruit (e.g., easy to migrate, low risk, business value). Organizations should define assessment criteria relevant to its business and internal governance rules, as well as incorporate best practices and experiences from implementation partners (if a joint approach is selected). Application profiling is an essential step in this process. Such profiling involves monitoring the applications to be migrated in terms of performance (e.g., key performance metrics such as average and peak CPU, memory, and disk throughputs) and user access. Application profiling should be conducted for at least 30 days to capture a reliable baseline.

These baselines can then be used as inputs for deciding the target performance sizes of the applications (e.g., size of virtual machines, size and scale of databases, web applications, etc.). Migration teams typically create "run books" to follow a standardized migration methodology and have various checks and milestones to validate and approve the migration as successful and completed. User acceptance tests (UATs) are an important stage in such a migration and should be included in the final migration validation steps.

Case Study: Netflix

Netflix is a global video streaming service that operates in the cloud. Back in 2008 the company had experienced an IT failure event, and it realized that it had to move away from its own data centers and traditional software architectures. Architects at Netflix decided a horizontally scalable and distributed system in the cloud with no single point of failure would be the best design. AWS was the cloud provider chosen by Netflix, having the scale and services required, and by 2016 all customer-facing services and data center applications had been migrated to the cloud. The number of customers for Netflix increased by more than eight times compared to in 2008, and this required a lot of computing and storage resources.

Elastic cloud resources enabled Netflix to keep pace with growing demands and add thousands of virtual servers and petabytes of storage within minutes. The global reach of AWS cloud allowed Netflix to provide its services worldwide without having to worry about infrastructure and back-end systems. Netflix leveraged services and features such as storage, computing, distributed databases, Big Data, and analytics (e.g., personalized recommendations for users).

The primary reasons Netflix decided to move to the cloud were increase capacities of compute (CPU+RAM) and storage, elastic use of resources, high availability, and agility. Cost reductions were positive side effects of moving to the cloud, compared to operating its own data centers. Although a "lift and shift" migration would have been easier and quicker, Netflix decided to redesign its applications and services and make them genuinely cloud-native. This approach required more time, costs, and effort, but was the most suitable option for Netflix to optimize benefits of the cloud.

Source: Izrailevsky, Vlaovic, and Meshenberg (2016).

CHAPTER 4

Amazon Web Services and Microsoft Azure

At the time of writing, there are two public cloud vendors that have the highest market share and are comfortably ahead of other vendors regarding market share, cloud service offerings, geographic availability, implementation ecosystem, cloud marketplace (e.g., store of applications), and cloud maturity. The two top public cloud vendors in this context are Amazon Web Services (AWS) and Microsoft (Azure). This chapter aims to provide an overview of these two public clouds and their cloud services portfolios. The focus of the first section of this chapter will be on AWS, the current global market leader, while the second section will focus on Microsoft Azure (Microsoft's cloud). An IDC assessment ranks AWS and Microsoft as the top two leaders, among others like Fujitsu, Google, IBM, and Rackspace (Mohan, DuBois, and Berggren 2017, 1).

1. AWS (AMAZON WEB SERVICES)

Amazon Web Services (AWS) began offering information technology (IT) services to the public in 2006. AWS is a separate business unit from the Amazon online retail business. The AWS public cloud operates in 18 geographic regions (190 countries) across the world and provides 49 Availability Zones (AZs) or data center groupings. There are many cloud services that AWS provides, and the list of such services continues to grow. This section aims to provide a high-level overview of crucial cloud services within the current AWS portfolio (Amazon Web Services 2017). Figure 62 provides a quick summary of the category areas.

Compute

There are several subcategories within this AWS compute classification:

- Amazon Elastic Compute Cloud (EC2)
- Amazon Elastic Compute Container Service (ECS)
- Amazon Elastic Compute Container Registry (ECR)
- Amazon Lightsail
- Amazon Elastic Beanstalk
- Amazon Lambda

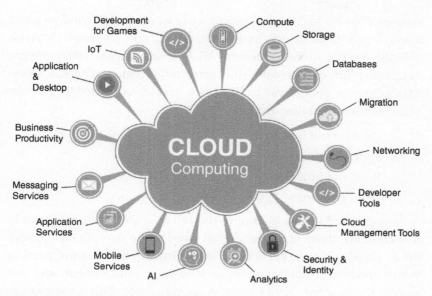

Figure 62 AWS Cloud Portfolio Categories

Amazon Elastic Compute Cloud (EC2)

This cloud service essentially provides customers with compute capacity in the cloud that comes in the form of a virtual machine (VM). It is a secure way of provisioning, accessing and using a virtual server. These virtual machines can be resized (e.g., increasing or decreasing the number of virtual central processing units [CPUs], the amount of random-access memory [RAM], or the amount and type of storage). The provisioning of such virtual machines is a self-service task via a web portal or a command line interface (special command line interface with ready-made command-lets [cmdlets] to help automate tasks for developers or administrators). The provisioning time is in minutes and can be with scale (e.g., tens, hundreds, or even thousands of servers). Amazon has designed its cloud services with web service application programming interfaces (APIs) to make automation and integration with other services more manageable, so tasks such as provisioning, decommissioning, and increasing the capacity of a virtual machine can all be done programmatically, scheduled, and automated. There are many choices of operating systems (OS) for such virtual machines (e.g., Microsoft Windows, and many Linux flavors such as Redhat, SUSE, and Ubuntu). Amazon provides a service-level agreement (SLA) commitment of 99.5 percent availability for each region (the geographic region where a cloud data center is operational). There are several cost models that an organization can choose from:

- On-demand instances
- Spot instances
- Reserved instances
- Dedicated hosts

On-demand instances (a term used to refer to virtual machines in this context) allow organizations to pay for the computing capacity on an hourly or even per second basis. Organizations do not need to worry about up-front payments or long-term commitment, and just pay for the time the cloud resources are consumed. This is the essence of the pay-as-you-go (PAYG) business model, and can be compared to the analogy of using a mobile phone—either pay via a contract with monthly costs and commitment or pay for how much is used on a running basis.

Spot instances allow organizations to take advantage of spare capacity that Amazon may have at certain times. The prices (e.g., unit costs) are heavily discounted for up to 90 percent for short time periods. The drawback of this option is that Amazon may shut down the virtual machines (VMs) at very short notice as demand for their cloud capacity increases and Amazon wishes to ensure adequate performance for premium-paying organizations or users. The applications deployed within such spot-instance VMs must be able to handle short-notice shutdowns gracefully and be able to resume or restart computing tasks at a later stage.

Reserved instances provide a discount of up to 75 percent compared to on-demand instance prices. Organizations typically select this cost model for applications (and consequently VMs) that require a steady state and a certain amount of minimum operating capacity (e.g., performance baseline with a certain amount of virtual CPUs and RAM to operate sufficiently). Amazon requires that organizations that are selecting this model commit to a one or three-year period.

Region: US East (Ohio)

	vCPU	ECU	Memory (GiB)	Instance Storage (GB)	Linux/UNIX Usage
General Purpose—Current Generation					
t2.nano	1	Variable	0.5	EBS Only	$0.0058 per Hour
t2.micro	1	Variable	1	EBS Only	$0.0116 per Hour
t2.small	1	Variable	2	EBS Only	$0.023 per Hour
t2.medium	2	Variable	4	EBS Only	$0.0464 per Hour
t2.large	2	Variable	8	EBS Only	$0.0928 per Hour
t2.xlarge	4	Variable	16	EBS Only	$0.1856 per Hour
t2.2xlarge	8	Variable	32	EBS Only	$0.3712 per Hour
m4.large	2	6.5	8	EBS Only	$0.1 per Hour
m4.xlarge	4	13	16	EBS Only	$0.2 per Hour
m4.2xlarge	8	26	32	EBS Only	$0.4 per Hour
m4.4xlarge	16	53.5	64	EBS Only	$0.8 per Hour

Source: https://aws.amazon.com/ec2/pricing/on-demand/.

	vCPU	ECU	Memory (GiB)	Instance Storage (GB)	Linux/UNIX Usage
Compute Optimized—Current Generation					
c4.large	2	8	3.75	EBS Only	$0.1 per Hour
c4.xlarge	4	16	7.5	EBS Only	$0.199 per Hour
c4.2xlarge	8	31	15	EBS Only	$0.398 per Hour
c4.4xlarge	16	62	30	EBS Only	$0.796 per Hour
c4.8xlarge	36	132	60	EBS Only	$1.591 per Hour
Memory Optimized—Current Generation					
x1.16xlarge	64	174.5	976	1 x 1920 SSD	$6.669 per Hour
x1.32xlarge	128	349	1952	2 x 1920 SSD	$13.338 per Hour
r3.large	2	6.5	15	1 x 32 SSD	$0.166 per Hour
r3.xlarge	4	13	30.5	1 x 80 SSD	$0.333 per Hour
r3.2xlarge	8	26	61	1 x 160 SSD	$0.665 per Hour
r3.4xlarge	16	52	122	1 x 320 SSD	$1.33 per Hour
r3.8xlarge	32	104	244	2 x 320 SSD	$2.66 per Hour
r4.large	2	7	15.25	EBS Only	$0.133 per Hour
r4.xlarge	4	13.5	30.5	EBS Only	$0.266 per Hour
r4.2xlarge	8	27	61	EBS Only	$0.532 per Hour
r4.4xlarge	16	53	122	EBS Only	$1.064 per Hour
r4.8xlarge	32	99	244	EBS Only	$2.128 per Hour
r4.16xlarge	64	195	488	EBS Only	$4.256 per Hour

Source: https://aws.amazon.com/ec2/.

Figure 63   AWS EC2 On-Demand Pricing Examples

Dedicated hosts allow organizations to select a physical EC2 server for their specialized use. No other organizations' workloads will be placed on such hosts. This option will enable organizations to gain high performance and a higher degree of separation with a public cloud, and can help with server-bound software licenses. Amazon will enable organizations to purchase capacity of such dedicated hosts on an on-demand basis (hourly billing) or via reservations (with up to 70 percent discounted prices compared to the on-demand option). Figure 63 provides example prices of the various Amazon cost models for Elastic Compute Cloud (EC2).

An "r4.16xlarge" instance type under on-demand pricing would cost $4.256 per hour versus $3.5394 per hour using spot instance.

Linux/UNIX Usage		Windows Usage
r4.4xlarge	$0.1489 per Hour	$0.8849 per Hour
r4.8xlarge	$0.2977 per Hour	$1.7697 per Hour
r4.16xlarge	$0.5954 per Hour	$3.5394 per Hour

Source: https://aws.amazon.com/ec2/spot/pricing/

Amazon Elastic Compute Container Service (ECS)

This cloud service offering focuses on containers (see Chapter 2 for more details), providing a scalable and "performant" container management service supporting Docker containers. Organizations can use Amazon ECS to run applications on managed clusters of Amazon EC2 instances. Containers increase application development agility, increase flexibility in designs and architecture blueprints, and can also increase the density of hosting (e.g., maximizing the use of virtual servers by running multiple containerized applications on the same virtual machine).

Amazon Elastic Compute Container Registry (ECR)

A container registry is like a library system for centralizing and managing container images. This cloud service offering integrates with Amazon's Elastic Compute Container Service (ECS) and increases the ease of use for organizations using containers and having a collaborative and standardized work flow.

Name	API Name	Memory	vCPUs	Instance Storage	Network Performance	Linux On Demand cost	Linux Reserved cost	Windows On Demand cost	Windows Reserved cost
M1 General Purpose Small	m1.small	1.7 GiB	1 vCPUs	160 GiB HDD • 900MB swap	Low	$0.044000 hourly	$0.028000 hourly	$0.075000 hourly	$0.057000 hourly
M1 General Purpose Medium	m1.medium	3.75 GiB	1 vCPUs	410 GiB HDD	Moderate	$0.087000 hourly	$0.058000 hourly	$0.149000 hourly	$0.115000 hourly
M1 General Purpose Large	m1.large	7.5 GiB	2 vCPUs	840 GiB (2 * 420 GiB HDD)	Moderate	$0.175000 hourly	$0.112000 hourly	$0.299000 hourly	$0.232000 hourly
M1 General Purpose Extra Large	m1.xlarge	15.0 GiB	4 vCPUs	1680 GiB (4 * 420 GiB HDD)	High	$0.350000 hourly	$0.224000 hourly	$0.598000 hourly	$0.465000 hourly
C1 High-CPU Medium	c1.medium	1.7 GiB	2 vCPUs	350 GiB HDD • 900MB swap	Moderate	$0.130000 hourly	$0.091000 hourly	$0.210000 hourly	$0.179000 hourly
C1 High-CPU Extra Large	c1.xlarge	7.0 GiB	8 vCPUs	1680 GiB (4 * 420 GiB HDD)	High	$0.520000 hourly	$0.364000 hourly	$0.840000 hourly	$0.719000 hourly
Cluster Compute Eight Extra Large	cc2.8xlarge	60.5 GiB	32 vCPUs	3360 GiB (4 * 840 GiB HDD)	10 Gigabit	$2.000000 hourly	$1.050000 hourly	$2.570000 hourly	unavailable
Cluster GPU Quadruple Extra Large	cg1.4xlarge	22.5 GiB	16 vCPUs	EBS only	10 Gigabit	$2.100000 hourly	unavailable	$2.600000 hourly	unavailable
M2 High Memory Extra Large	m2.xlarge	17.1 GiB	2 vCPUs	420 GiB HDD	Moderate	$0.245000 hourly	$0.111000 hourly	$0.345000 hourly	$0.249000 hourly
M2 High Memory Double Extra Large	m2.2xlarge	34.2 GiB	4 vCPUs	850 GiB HDD	Moderate	$0.490000 hourly	$0.222000 hourly	$0.690000 hourly	$0.496000 hourly
M2 High Memory Quadruple Extra Large	m2.4xlarge	68.4 GiB	8 vCPUs	1680 GiB (2 * 840 GiB HDD)	High	$0.980000 hourly	$0.444000 hourly	$1.380000 hourly	$0.991000 hourly
High Storage Eight Extra Large	hs1.8xlarge	117.0 GiB	16 vCPUs	48000 GiB (24 * 2000 GiB HDD)	10 Gigabit	$4.600000 hourly	$2.574000 hourly	$4.931000 hourly	$2.961000 hourly
T1 Micro	t1.micro	0.613 GiB	1 vCPUs	EBS only	Very Low	$0.020000 hourly	$0.014000 hourly	$0.020000 hourly	$0.015000 hourly
T2 Nano	t2.nano	0.5 GiB	1 vCPUs for a 1h 12m burst	EBS only	Low	$0.005800 hourly	$0.004000 hourly	$0.008100 hourly	$0.006000 hourly
T2 Micro	t2.micro	1.0 GiB	1 vCPUs for a 2h 24m burst	EBS only	Low to Moderate	$0.011600 hourly	$0.007000 hourly	$0.016200 hourly	$0.012000 hourly
T2 Small	t2.small	2.0 GiB	1 vCPUs for a 4h 49m burst	EBS only	Low to Moderate	$0.023000 hourly	$0.014000 hourly	$0.032000 hourly	$0.024000 hourly
T2 Medium	t2.medium	4.0 GiB	2 vCPUs for a 4h 49m burst	EBS only	Low to Moderate	$0.046000 hourly	$0.029000 hourly	$0.064400 hourly	$0.047000 hourly
T2 Large	t2.large	8.0 GiB	2 vCPUs for a 7h 12m burst	EBS only	Low to Moderate	$0.092000 hourly	$0.058000 hourly	$0.120000 hourly	$0.086000 hourly
T2 Extra Large	t2.xlarge	16.0 GiB	4 vCPUs for a 5h 24m burst	EBS only	Moderate	$0.185200 hourly	$0.115000 hourly	$0.226500 hourly	$0.156000 hourly
T2 Double Extra Large	t2.2xlarge	32.0 GiB	8 vCPUs for a 4h 3m burst	EBS only	Moderate	$0.371200 hourly	$0.230000 hourly	$0.413200 hourly	$0.292000 hourly
M5 General Purpose Large	m5.large	8.0 GiB	2 vCPUs	EBS only	High	$0.096000 hourly	$0.061000 hourly	$0.188000 hourly	$0.153000 hourly
M5 General Purpose Extra Large	m5.xlarge	16.0 GiB	4 vCPUs	EBS only	High	$0.192000 hourly	$0.123000 hourly	$0.376000 hourly	$0.307000 hourly
M5 General Purpose Double Extra Large	m5.2xlarge	32.0 GiB	8 vCPUs	EBS only	High	$0.384000 hourly	$0.245000 hourly	$0.752000 hourly	$0.613000 hourly
M5 General Purpose Quadruple Extra Large	m5.4xlarge	64.0 GiB	16 vCPUs	EBS only	High	$0.768000 hourly	$0.491000 hourly	$1.504000 hourly	$1.227000 hourly
M5 General Purpose 12xlarge	m5.12xlarge	192.0 GiB	48 vCPUs	EBS only	High	$2.304000 hourly	$1.472000 hourly	$4.512000 hourly	$3.680000 hourly
M5 General Purpose 24xlarge	m5.24xlarge	384.0 GiB	96 vCPUs	EBS only	High	$4.608000 hourly	$2.944000 hourly	$9.024000 hourly	$7.360000 hourly
M4 General Purpose Large	m4.large	8.0 GiB	2 vCPUs	EBS only	Moderate	$0.100000 hourly	$0.062000 hourly	$0.192000 hourly	$0.154000 hourly
M4 General Purpose Extra Large	m4.xlarge	16.0 GiB	4 vCPUs	EBS only	High	$0.200000 hourly	$0.126000 hourly	$0.384000 hourly	$0.308000 hourly
M4 General Purpose Double Extra Large	m4.2xlarge	32.0 GiB	8 vCPUs	EBS only	High	$0.400000 hourly	$0.240000 hourly	$0.768000 hourly	$0.616000 hourly
M4 General Purpose Quadruple Extra Large	m4.4xlarge	64.0 GiB	16 vCPUs	EBS only	High	$0.800000 hourly	$0.490000 hourly	$1.536000 hourly	$1.232000 hourly
M4 General Purpose Deca Extra Large	m4.10xlarge	160.0 GiB	40 vCPUs	EBS only	10 Gigabit	$2.000000 hourly	$1.239000 hourly	$3.840000 hourly	$3.079000 hourly

Source: https://aws.amazon.com/ec2/pricing/on-demand/.

Amazon Lightsail

This cloud service offering is aimed at helping organizations have a quick start within the Amazon public cloud. Organizations can focus on their applications while the cloud provider (Amazon) focuses on the infrastructure such as virtual machine, solid state disk (SSD) storage, domain name system (DNS) management, and static Internet Protocol (IP) address.

Amazon Batch is a similar service that aims to automate work flows for the organization. With this service, developers, data scientists, and others can submit hundreds of thousands of batch computing jobs on AWS public cloud. The AWS Batch cloud service dynamically provisions the required computing resources (e.g., virtual CPUs, virtual RAM). Batch planning, scheduling, and execution are managed by the AWS Batch cloud service.

Amazon Elastic Beanstalk

This cloud service makes it possible for organizations to deploy web applications and code while the back-end tasks are handled by the cloud service and Amazon. The infrastructure is created, provisioned, managed, and scaled automatically. This includes advanced features such as load balancing and application health monitoring. Organizations can still control the resources to assist with financial cost control.

Amazon Lambda

This cloud service makes it easy for organizations to run code in the cloud without having to worry about the infrastructure. AWS handles the provisioning and management of servers in the back end. This minimizes the operational and administrative overhead for organizations, which can then focus more on development and business-value-oriented tasks. Organizations pay for compute time only.

AWS operates in 18 geographic regions across the world, with multiple Availability Zones (data center groupings). Some cloud services may not be available in all areas, or there is a phased roll-out of services to different regions (see Figure 64).

Region & Number of Availability Zones

U.S. East
N. Virginia (6), Ohio (3)

U.S. West
N. California (3), Oregon (3)

Asia-Pacific
Mumbai (2), Seoul (2), Singapore (2), Sydney (3), Tokyo (3)

Canada
Central (2)

China
Beijing (2), Ningxia (2)

Europe
Frankfurt (3), Ireland (3), London (2), Paris (3)

South America
São Paulo (3)

AWS GovCloud (US-West) (2)

New Region (coming soon)

Bahrain

Hong Kong SAR, China

Sweden

AWS GovCloud (U.S. East)

Figure 64 AWS Global Regions for Public Cloud
Source: https://aws.amazon.com/about-aws/global-infrastructure/.

Storage

There are several key offerings within this classification:

- Amazon Simple Storage Service (S3)
- Amazon Elastic Block Store (EBS)
- Amazon Elastic File System (EFS)
- Amazon Glacier
- Amazon Storage Gateway

Amazon Simple Storage Service (S3)

This storage cloud service provides an object-based storage type through a simple web service interface (also industry standard REST APIs and SDKs) that is globally accessible (via internet connection). Organizations can use Amazon S3 for storing application data, utilize it as a data lake, or leverage it for backup and recovery. Amazon S3 has a service-level agreement (SLA) of 99.999999999 percent durability and 99.99 percent availability over a year. The cloud storage service supports more than a trillion objects that can be stored worldwide. Amazon also provides different cost models for organizations that use the storage frequently or less frequently. Data uploads to Amazon S3 are via secure socket layer (SSL) transmission, and Amazon S3 offers encryption for data at rest (within S3 storage bucket), and provides user access and security management through AWS Identity and Access Management (IAM). Organizations have control over where this cloud service will be leveraged, allowing control over latency or helping organizations adhere to regulatory requirements for data that is sensitive.

Amazon Elastic Block Store (EBS)

This storage type provides consistent block storage volumes for Amazon EC2 instances (virtual machines). These storage volumes are available after a reboot of a virtual machine and are automatically replicated within an Availability Zone (AZ) to provide high availability to organizations. An Availability Zone is a generally a cluster of three data centers within one region. Data and virtual machines can be replicated to such data center clusters to provide high availability and help protect from disasters. The method of replication can be asynchronous or synchronous (e.g., writing data from one application to two locations at the same time to safeguard data). Scaling of EBS volumes can be done within minutes, and organizations pay for only what they provision (disk volume is provisioned and available to the organization even if not actually written to). Organizations can choose between traditional hard disk drives (HDDs) or solid state disks (SSDs) for their Amazon EBS volumes. HDDs are cheaper and can be of larger sizes, whereas SSDs are well suited for applications or processes requiring high throughput (i.e., fast read and write). Each Amazon EBS volume is designed to provide 99.99 percent availability, and data is encrypted at rest or in motion between Amazon EC2 instances and Amazon EBS volumes.

Amazon Elastic File System (EFS)

The Amazon Elastic File System (EFS) cloud service provides scalable file storage for Amazon EC2 instances. As the name suggests, the Amazon EFS cloud service offers elastic storage capacity that grows and shrinks as the organization's needs change. If the Amazon EFS is mounted to an Amazon Elastic Compute Cloud (EC2) instance, then the access and interoperability are seamless for applications and other tools. It is also possible for multiple EC2 instances to access an Amazon EFS file system at the same time. Organizations could leverage the Amazon EFS as a centralized data source for workloads and applications across multiple EC2 instances. When utilizing a virtual private network (VPN) connection (a more secure and dedicated virtual network tunnel connection between a source and a target) between on-premises and Amazon public cloud, organizations can use Amazon EFS and a VPN to migrate or back up data from their on-premises location to the Amazon cloud. Amazon EFS aims to be highly available and provide the necessary performance for a broad set of applications and workload types.

Amazon Glacier

The Amazon Glacier cloud service is a low-cost and secure storage option for archiving data and storing data backups for the long term. This type of storage service is aimed at long-term storage and infrequently accessed data. Amazon provides cost models for varying speeds of data retrieval, which can require minutes or several hours.

Amazon Storage Gateway

This Amazon cloud service provides a hybrid storage option between on-premises and the Amazon cloud. Amazon offers a multiprotocol storage appliance (an appliance is typically a preconfigured, out-of-the-box device tailored for the purpose) with efficient network connectivity to the Amazon cloud storage services. Organizations can leverage such a gateway to migrate data to the cloud, or for bursting data into the cloud if there is a local storage shortage.

Databases

There are several databases and database services that Amazon offers in its public cloud. These include the following:

- Amazon Aurora
- Amazon Relational Database Service (RDS) supporting the following databases:
  - Amazon Aurora
  - PostgreSQL
  - MySQL
  - MariaDB
  - Oracle
  - Microsoft SQL Server
- Amazon DynamoDB
- Amazon Elasticache

Amazon Aurora

This Amazon cloud service is a managed service—a platform as a service (PaaS) offering. The Amazon Aurora database is a database engine that is compatible with MySQL (e.g., version 5.6) and PostgreSQL database engines (e.g., version 9.6). This makes it easy for organizations to migrate to this database as no software code changes should be necessary, and applications should be cross compatible. Amazon states that this database provides up to five times better performance than the MySQL database, or twice the throughput of a PostgreSQL database, and provides security, availability, and reliability equivalent to a database at the commercial enterprise level, all at a fraction of the cost. Amazon Aurora database can support up to 500,000 reads per second and 100,000 writes per second. Using read replicas (multiple copies of a database to allow greater parallel read performance), this scale can be increased further, with latency as low as 10 ms.

Amazon Aurora provides high security by leveraging virtual private networks (VPNs), secure transmission via secure socket layer (SSL), and data encryption (e.g., data at rest, backups, snapshots, and replicas within the same cluster). The virtual machine instance types for Amazon Aurora database can be small (e.g., 2 vCPUs, 4 GB RAM) to large (e.g., 32 vCPU, 244 GB RAM). The underlying storage for the database automatically grows as needed, and storage can range from 10 GB to 64 TB. Organizations can also deploy up to 15 low-latency read replicas across three Amazon Availability Zones for improved read performance. The Amazon Aurora cloud service is designed for 99.99 percent availability, and the failover of an instance is typically within 30 seconds. The underlying storage for the database is designed for fault tolerance. There are six copies of an organization's data that are replicated across three Amazon Availability Zones, and continued backups to Amazon S3 occur.

Amazon Relational Database Service (RDS)

The Amazon RDS cloud service makes it easier and less time-consuming for organizations to set up, operate, or scale a relational database in the Amazon public cloud. The cloud vendor (i.e., Amazon) is responsible for managing the time-consuming and mundane database administrative tasks (e.g., patching, upgrading), allowing an organization's database administrators (DBAs) to focus more on business value and organization-specific tasks. The Amazon RDS cloud service supports six database engines:

1. Amazon Aurora
2. MariaDB
3. Microsoft SQL Server
4. MySQL
5. Oracle
6. PostgreSQL

Amazon DynamoDB

The Amazon DynamoDB database is a fully managed (PaaS) NoSQL database cloud service. A NoSQL database can support SQL-like queries and typically supports the following types of data storage:

- Columnar store
- Document store
- Key-value store
- Graph database
- Multimodel

Amazon DynamoDB supports document store and key-value store database types. NoSQL database types have evolved to solve different challenges of the Big Data, connected devices, and advanced analytics era. A columnar store allows data retrieval by columns, which provides much faster read and analytical tasks than a traditional row-by-row read and analysis. A document store allows increased flexibility and agility as no fixed database schema (data model) is required. Instead, data can be stored in documents such as JavaScript Object Notation (JSON) and data designers do not have to worry about defining a data model or schema. Data can be inserted into a list, and there are no constraints to consider at insertion time (e.g., data types, data length, the order of data to be entered). This method is also referred to as a schema-on-read approach, as data can be inserted in any way or form, and applications later define how they will read and extract information. The relational databases use a schema-on-write approach, where a data model is predefined, and constraints must be met at insertion time. Both types have pros and cons, and it depends on the use case for when to use a relational database versus a nonrelational database (i.e., NoSQL). Some applications and analytics require fast read performance and can benefit from modern NoSQL database types. Relational database systems are typically used for online transactional processing (OLTP) in financial transactions for example, or in online analytical processing (OLAP) use cases where advanced analytics are required (e.g., multidimensional data aggregation and complex analytics).

A key-value store is a simple database type that stores data in the association with a key. Each key is associated with only one value.

The key can be a filename, a uniform resource identifier (URI), or a hash. The value can be of any data type, such as an image or a document. Storage of values is in binary large object (BLOB) format, which means there is no need for a database schema. Key-value stores are useful for quick and simple storage and analysis.

Amazon Elasticache

The Amazon Elasticache cloud service provides an in-memory cache in the public Amazon cloud for organizations. The use of memory versus solid state disks (SSDs) or hard disk drives (HDDs) offers far better performance (read and write throughput). Amazon supports two open-source in-memory caching engines: Redis and Memcached. The Amazon Elasticache cloud service with Redis is a fully managed service from Amazon. Depending on the size of data an organization frequently requires, the service can scale from one single node to 15 nodes in a cluster with up to 3.55 TB of in-memory data. As this Amazon cloud service supports the two most common in-memory caching engines, it is easier for organizations to migrate to this service, as there should be no need to modify software code, applications, or tools that are used with Redis or Memcached. Such fast performance is beneficial for a web application, mobile apps, gaming, or the Internet of Things (IoT).

Migration

To make it easy for an organization to transition to the public cloud, Amazon (Amazon Web Services [AWS]) provides several services and products:

- AWS Application Discovery
- AWS Database Migration Service
- AWS Server Migration Service (SMS)
- AWS Snowball
- AWS Snowball Edge
- AWS Snowball Mobile

AWS Application Discovery

This Amazon service is aimed at helping system integrators identify an organization's applications that are running on-premises. This discovery includes monitoring and recommending performance profiles based on baselines (e.g., tracking for 30 days and then having average and peak utilization data for key metrics such as CPU, RAM, network, and storage throughput). Identifying and mapping application dependencies is a crucial stage in the application discovery service. This ensures all required applications are migrated together to continue to provide the overall application service. The data that is collected via this discovery service is encrypted and stored in an AWS Discovery Service database. System integrators or organizations can export the data to CSV or XML that can then be used as inputs in visualization tools for easier planning and management of the migration.

AWS Database Migration Service

The Amazon migration service helps organizations migrate their on-premises databases to the Amazon public cloud. Most commercial and open-source databases are supported, and this service also allows organizations to migrate from one vendor to the same vendor in the cloud (e.g., Oracle to Oracle), or switch database vendors (e.g., Oracle to Microsoft SQL Server). This service can also be used to migrate data from sources such as Amazon Aurora, PostgreSQL, MySQL, MariaDB, Oracle, SAP ASE, and Microsoft SQL Server to Amazon Redshift (a data warehouse).

AWS Server Migration Service (SMS)

This Amazon service provides an agentless service (meaning no software agent is installed on servers that are being considered for migration to the cloud), enabling organizations to migrate their on-premises servers to the Amazon public cloud. The Amazon SMS makes it easier for organizations to automate and schedule server migrations. Such tools are useful in a "migration factory" approach.

AWS Snowball

The AWS Snowball is an Amazon data transport solution in the form of a secure appliance (an out-of-the-box hardware appliance with particular security, e.g., tamper-proof, with encryption) that can scale to petabyte storage size. The organization can leverage this service if it has large volumes of data and is concerned about the transfer times or costs via network (e.g., internet) interfaces.

AWS Snowball Edge

AWS Snowball Edge is a specialized hardware appliance from Amazon aimed at helping organizations transfer up to 100 TB of data into and out of the Amazon public cloud. Organizations can also use the device as temporary storage for large data sets. This device can be utilized by organizations in situations where there is no access to the cloud, or when organizations require their data to be processed on-premises.

AWS Snowmobile

The AWS Snowmobile is a 45-foot-long shipping container that is pulled by a semitrailer truck. The container is ruggedized, encrypted (e.g., with 256-bit encryption and keys managed through Amazon Key Management Service), and secured with dedicated security personnel, GPS tracking, alarm monitoring, and 24/7 video surveillance, and it is even possible to have a security vehicle escort the container while it is in transit. An organization's data is transported via such a device to Amazon cloud (AWS), where the data is imported into Amazon S3 storage or Amazon Glacier storage.

Networking

Amazon has several cloud offerings in the networking category. These can complement or replace systems and methods currently used by organizations wishing to transition to the cloud. The networking portfolio of Amazon can be divided into the following categories:

- Amazon Virtual Private Cloud (Amazon VPC)
- Amazon CloudFront

- Amazon Route 53
- Amazon Direct Connect
- Amazon Elastic Load Balancing (ELB)

Amazon Virtual Private Cloud (VPC)

An Amazon VPC enables an organization to logically isolate resources of the public cloud, which can communicate via a virtual network that is specific to the organization. Organizations have full control over defining an Internet Protocol (IP—unique address for computers) address range, configuring subnets (a logical subdivision of an IP network), as well as full control over the configuration of route tables (tables that define the way network traffic will flow) and network gateways (devices or software that let two networks communicate with each other). Amazon VPC supports IPv4 and IPv6 standards. Organizations can also create a hardware virtual private network (VPN) connection (a virtual, secured network tunnel) between its environment and the Amazon VPC, allowing the Amazon cloud to be used as an extension to the on-premises resources.

Amazon CloudFront

This Amazon cloud service provides a global content delivery network (CDN) to organizations that need to deliver content such as websites, video content, and the like to global consumers of such resources. Amazon defines "edge locations" that are distributed throughout the world and located in AWS regional data centers. End-user requests for content are serviced via these edge locations that are closest to the requesting source (e.g., a European user is serviced by a European location, or users in the United States are serviced by areas in the United States). Such a delivery process ensures adequate performance for end users and consumers of content (e.g., websites for online retailers, or video streaming services for on-demand services). Amazon provides a PAYG cost model for organizations using this cloud service, so costs are based on how much content is delivered through Amazon CloudFront.

Amazon Route 53

The Amazon Route 53 cloud service is a domain name system (DNS) web service. A DNS can be used to translate human-readable address names such as www.acme.com to a unique numeric IP address (e.g., 192.168.0.1). Computers use the numeric IP address for communication, and this Amazon service supports IPv4 and IPv6. The Amazon Route 53 cloud service connects user or application requests to infrastructure (e.g., EC2 instances—Virtual Machines, S3 storage, etc.) running in the AWS cloud. Organizations can use this Amazon service to configure latency-based routing, geography-based DNS routing, or weighted round robin, connecting to a single AWS region or multiple AWS regions across the world. Through this Amazon service, organizations can also purchase and manage domain names (e.g., acme.com).

Amazon Direct Connect

Organizations can create a dedicated network connection from their premises to the Amazon cloud via AWS Direct Connect. Such a link may provide lower costs and consistent and higher bandwidth throughput to organizations. Industry-standard virtual LANs (vLANs) are supported by this Amazon cloud service. Organizations can use the same connection to access different resources in the Amazon cloud such as Amazon EC2 instances or Amazon S3 objects.

Amazon Elastic Load Balancing (ELB)

The Amazon Elastic Load Balancing cloud service is used to distribute application requests across multiple Amazon EC2 instances automatically. There are two types of load balancers available through this service. The Classic Load Balancer is the first type, and routes traffic based on application or network-level provided information. The second type of load balancer is the Application Load Balancer, and this advanced type routes traffic based on application-specific information contained within the request. The classic load balancer type is suited for simple load balancing of traffic across multiple Amazon EC2 instances. Organizations should select the Application Load Balancer when microservices and container architectures are in use.

Developer Tools

Amazon provides several tools for helping organizations develop applications for the cloud in a more accessible, faster, and more collaborative way. Organizations using the Amazon cloud can leverage the following tools for development:

- Amazon CodeCommit
- Amazon CodeBuild
- Amazon CodeDeploy
- Amazon CodePipeline
- Amazon X-Ray

Amazon CodeCommit

This is a managed cloud service enabling organizations to store source code of their application development in private Git repositories. Amazon operates the back-end resources required to scale with increased needs of the organizations utilizing this service.

Amazon CodeBuild

With this Amazon-managed cloud service, organizations can compile source code, run tests, and produce software packages. Organizations do not have to worry about building, configuring, or managing servers — it is a managed cloud service.

Amazon CodeDeploy

This cloud service makes it easier for organizations to deploy software code to virtual machines running on-premises or in the Amazon cloud (e.g., on EC2 instances).

Amazon CodePipeline

Amazon CodePipeline is a cloud service from Amazon that aims to help organizations quickly perform infrastructure updates. This service enables an organization to build, test, and deploy software code to its infrastructure whenever there is a software code change.

Amazon X-Ray

This cloud service helps developers to debug or analyze applications that are deployed in preproduction or production environments. The X-Ray service helps a developer gain a detailed view of how requests and information flow through an application and can be used for simple architectures (e.g., client-server) or for more advanced designs that utilize microservices.

Cloud Management Tools

To help organizations use resources in the cloud effectively and economically, Amazon provides several tools assisting with management, monitoring, orchestration, and governance. Such tools can be categorized as follows:

- Amazon CloudWatch
- Amazon EC2 Systems Manager
- Amazon CloudFormation
- Amazon CloudTrail
- Amazon Config
- Amazon OpsWorks
- Amazon Service Catalogue
- Amazon Trusted Advisor
- Amazon Personal Health Dashboard
- Amazon Managed Services

Amazon CloudWatch

The Amazon CloudWatch cloud service helps organizations monitor cloud resources and applications in the Amazon cloud. Organizations can utilize this cloud service for recording and observe key metrics (hence the name "watch"), capture and review log files, define alarms (triggered notifications or actions based on thresholds of parameters (e.g., percentage of CPU usage rising above 80 percent). This cloud service helps organizations collect and highlight usage data of resources and log files, providing a holistic view of cloud resource utilization, application health, and performance.

Amazon EC2 Systems Manager

Organizations can use the Amazon EC2 Systems Manager cloud service to automate the collection of software inventory (useful for governance, compliance, and auditing), for applying software patches to operating systems, or for creating virtual machine images (templates for EC2 instances). The Amazon EC2 Systems Manager can be used for on-premises or Amazon cloud environments (virtual infrastructure, i.e., virtual machines — EC2 instances).

Amazon CloudFormation

Amazon CloudFormation provides an easy way for developers or administrators to create and operate cloud resources in a standardized manner. Templates are used to increase standardization and reduce errors and effort. Organizations can leverage sample templates provided by Amazon, or they can create their own templates. This cloud tool can be complemented by the Amazon CloudFormation Designer, which visualizes templates as diagrams, and administrators can edit these via a drag-and-drop interface.

Amazon CloudTrail

The Amazon CloudTrail cloud service can be used to record API calls for an organization's Amazon cloud subscription. Such information is stored in log files, which can be parsed later and used as an audit trail or for troubleshooting. API calls made via user interfaces (e.g., Amazon Management Console), common line tools, or Amazon Software Development Kit (SDK) can all be recorded. The type of information that can be recorded includes:

- The identity of person or service making the API request
- The time stamp of when the API call was made
- IP address origin from where the API call was made
- Parameters included in the API request
- Response values returned by the Amazon cloud service (Amazon Web Service [AWS])

Amazon Config

Organizations can use the managed Amazon Config cloud service to record configuration history, document inventory of cloud resources, and enable notifications for when configuration changes are made. This cloud service can therefore assist with security and governance rules of an organization. It is possible to view information regarding existing resources in the Amazon cloud, as well as details from deleted resources in the Amazon cloud. Organizations can use this service to check compliance of rules against its resources in the Amazon cloud. The service can be useful in auditing, security analysis, troubleshooting, and change-tracking situations.

Amazon OpsWorks

The Amazon OpsWorks cloud service is used for configuration management of servers via Chef (a platform for IT infrastructure automation). Chef Recipes are the templates or instructions to automate tasks in a repeatable and standardized manner. With Amazon OpsWorks (using Chef) organizations can automate the configuration and deployment of servers on-premises or as EC2 instances (virtual machines) in the Amazon cloud. More information regarding Chef can be found at this URL: www.chef.io.

Amazon Service Catalogue

Organizations can use the Amazon Service Catalogue service for creating and managing a catalog of IT services that are internally approved for use in the Amazon cloud. Users and departments within an organization can select IT services (such as virtual machines, platform as a service offering, or software as a service offering) from such catalogs with the internal assurance that they will be compliant with governance, compliance, and security requirements of their organization.

Amazon Trusted Advisor

The Amazon Trusted Advisor tool aims to help organizations be cost-effective in the Amazon cloud, increase possible performance, and ensure that best practices and security principles are applied. This tool provides real-time suggestions for organizations to improve their usage of the Amazon cloud according to best practices.

Amazon Personal Health Dashboard

Operational resources (e.g., administrators, center of excellence operations) within an organization can use the Amazon Personal Health Dashboard to quickly view information relevant to its cloud resources. Events or issues that are occurring on Amazon resources that may affect an organization are displayed in a personalized view (e.g., depicting only an organization's Amazon resources). IT staff can then use such information proactively to plan accordingly or inform organizational users of the Amazon cloud of any potential issues, performance bottlenecks, or outages.

Amazon Managed Services

Organizations can use Amazon Managed Services as an IT process outsourcing concept specific to cloud infrastructure. Organizations can focus on business value and their applications, and let Amazon automate everyday IT tasks such as change requests, monitoring, backups, security, or configuration and patching.

Security and Identity

To help organizations with security and identity management challenges, Amazon provides several cloud services, such as the following:

- Amazon Cloud Directory
- Amazon Identity and Access Management (IAM)
- Amazon Inspector
- Amazon Certificate Manager
- Amazon CloudHSM
- Amazon Directory Service
- Amazon Key Management Service (KMS)

- Amazon Organizations
- Amazon Shield
- Amazon Web Application Firewall (WAF)

Amazon Cloud Directory

Organizations can leverage this cloud service to create logical directory listings of various information types, such as organizational charts, device listings, or content catalogs. One difference of this type of directory service compared to directories based on Active Directory Lightweight Directory Services or Lightweight Directory Access Protocol (LDAP) is that the Amazon Cloud Directory can use multiple directories across multiple dimensions. This provides additional flexibility for organizations wishing to use the information in different ways; for example, an organizational chart could be navigated via different hierarchies in a management reporting structure, or for reporting by location, or for financial cost center purposes. This cloud service is a managed service and can scale to hundreds of millions of objects. Amazon is responsible for the infrastructure, and an organization defines a schema, creates a directory, and then starts populating the index with its information and objects (e.g., server lists, people listings, etc.).

Amazon Identity and Access Management (IAM)

Amazon IAM enables organizations to control access to Amazon cloud services and cloud resources that the organization uses and pays for. It is possible to create users and groups with Amazon IAM. Organizations can create granular security controls for allowing or denying access to resources in the Amazon cloud. It is possible to define the use of access keys, passwords, and even multifactor authentication with the help of devices or software applications on devices (e.g., smartphones). An Amazon cloud service that is utilized by an organization can assume the IAM role assigned to it by an organization and adhere to the security principles defined. It is also possible to allow federated users (users and groups within an organization) access to the organization's resources within the Amazon cloud through Amazon IAM.

Amazon Inspector

The Amazon Inspector is a cloud service for assessing applications deployed in the Amazon cloud for vulnerabilities and deviations from best practices. The results of the inspection are highlighted in detailed listings sorted by the highest risk of departure from best practices. Best practices rule sets are regularly updated by Amazon security teams to ensure optimum protection for organizations.

Amazon Certificate Manager

Organizations can use this Amazon cloud service to manage and deploy security certificates (i.e., for secure sockets layer [SSL] and transport layer security [TLS]) that are to be leveraged by Amazon services that the organization utilizes. These SSL and TLS certificates are used to verify secure network communication via the internet. The Amazon Certificate Manager Service makes it easier for organizations to request, deploy, and renew certificates.

Amazon CloudHSM

Some industries have more stringent regulatory and security requirements than others based on the data being held or processed. A dedicated hardware security module (HSM) can be used to generate, store, and manage cryptographic keys that are used for data encryption. The Amazon CloudHSM instances are isolated from other tenants (other customers in the cloud) and are provisioned within an Amazon Virtual Private Cloud (VPC) of an organization's Amazon resources, thus providing further security and isolation.

Amazon Directory Service

This cloud service is also known as the Amazon Microsoft Active Directory (AD) as it specializes in directory services for Microsoft AD. Organizations do not need to replicate or synchronize their on-premises AD data to the cloud. Through this service an organization can join Amazon EC2 instances or Amazon Microsoft SQL Server instances to its domain, and allow single sign-on, making it easier for organizational users, departments, or applications to communicate across resource environments (on-premises and the Amazon cloud).

Amazon Key Management Service (KMS)

The Amazon Key Management Service (KMS) is a managed cloud service and is used to control encryption keys that are used to encrypt an organization's data. Hardware security modules are used to protect the encryption keys that organizations use. The Amazon CloudTrail cloud service can be used to record and log the use of encryption keys. This helps organizations with meeting regulatory requirements.

Amazon Organizations

Amazon Organizations are logical groupings used to manage multiple subscriptions that an organization may have. Such subscriptions can then be centrally managed, and billing can become more straightforward.

Amazon Shield

This Amazon cloud service provides protection services against distributed denial of service (DDoS) attacks on web applications that an organization has active in the Amazon cloud. Amazon offers two options for organizations—standard and advanced. The standard edition is free of charge for Amazon cloud customers. Organizations wishing to have further protection for their applications that are running on Amazon Elastic Load Balancers or Amazon CloudFront can subscribe to the advanced edition of Amazon Shield. The advanced version provides near real-time information on attacks, integrates with Amazon Web Application Firewall (WAF), and gives organizations access to the Amazon DDoS Response Team.

Amazon Web Application Firewall (WAF)

Organizations can use the Amazon WAF cloud service to protect their web applications from common exploits via the web. Amazon WAF gives organizations control over what traffic they wish to allow or block via rule sets. Such rule sets can be activated within minutes, enabling organizations to respond quickly to security threats. Amazon also provides an application programming interface (API) to automate the creation, deployment, and updating of rule sets.

Analytics

Amazon provides several cloud services to assist organizations with their analytical needs and challenges. These services can be categorized as follows:

- Amazon Athena
- Amazon Elastic Map Reduce (EMR)
- Amazon CloudSearch
- Amazon Elasticsearch Service
- Amazon Kinesis
- Amazon Redshift
- Amazon QuickSight
- Amazon Data Pipeline
- Amazon Glue

Amazon Athena

Amazon Athena makes it easy for organizations to analyze data that is stored in Amazon S3 via standard Structured Query Language (SQL). Data scientists or users who need to perform analytics merely make a connection to Amazon S3 via a data schema (defines the data structure, dimensions, data types, and formats) and can then query data via SQL. This cloud service is also known as a serverless service as organizations do not have to worry about any infrastructure to manage. Amazon scales and maintains the required infrastructure, and organizations pay for only the queries they execute. Data can remain in Amazon S3, and there is no need for any extract, transform, load (ETL) process or tools.

Amazon Elastic Map Reduce (EMR)

Amazon Elastic Map Reduce (EMR) is a managed service of a Hadoop (horizontally scalable framework for Big Data and some analytics scenarios) environment via elastically scaling Amazon EC2 instances. Organizations can use this service with other frameworks such as Apache Spark or Amazon data stores like Amazon S3 or Amazon

DynamoDB. Organizations can use this cloud service in a variety of use cases where Big Data is present, such as log analysis, machine learning, science, or medicine.

Amazon CloudSearch

Organizations can leverage the managed Amazon CloudSearch service to add a scalable search solution for a website or application. The service supports 34 languages and provides key features like auto-completion of search terms or geospatial search capabilities.

Amazon Elasticsearch Service

This managed cloud service provides scalable search capabilities for analyzing log files, full-text search, and more. The service can integrate with Amazon Kinesis Firehose, Amazon Lambda, or Amazon CloudWatch. Organizations can thus gain insights quickly with less effort and let data remain at its original location.

Amazon Kinesis

Organizations can use the Amazon Kinesis cloud service for streaming data into the Amazon cloud. It is especially useful in scenarios where fast data ingestion and rapid analysis must occur. Connected devices (e.g., IoT, industrial sensors, wearables, etc.) and mobile devices produce vast volumes of data at fast rates, and this cloud service makes it easier and more affordable for organizations to utilize the Amazon Kinesis framework. At the time of writing Amazon (AWS) provides three cloud services in this area:

- Amazon Kinesis Firehose
- Amazon Kinesis Analytics
- Amazon Kinesis Streams

Amazon Kinesis Firehose enables fast ingestion of data from hundreds of thousands of data sources into the Amazon cloud and Amazon Kinesis Analytics, Amazon S3, Amazon Redshift, or the Amazon Elasticsearch service. Amazon manages the service, so organizations do not have to worry about the underlying infrastructure or any administration. The service scales with the data needs of an organization and can provide batch functionality for processing data, compression for economical storage, and encryption for secure storage.

Amazon Kinesis Analytics lets organizations process streaming data in near real time through standard SQL. The services automatically scale with the volume and throughput of data required.

Amazon Kinesis Streams enables organizations to build custom applications for processing or analyzing streaming data. The cloud service can automatically scale to capture, process, and store terabytes of data per hour via hundreds of thousands of data sources. Scenarios in which this service could be useful include clickstream analysis (e.g., from websites), financial transactions, social media, or location tracking (e.g., wearables). Data can be further shared with Amazon S3, Amazon Redshift, Amazon EMR, or Amazon Lambda.

Amazon Redshift

Amazon Redshift is a managed data warehouse that can scale to petabyte size and serve data to business intelligence tools. This Amazon data warehouse uses columnar stores (data stored and accessible in virtually organized vertical columns) and data compression to enhance significantly the performance required for analyzing and reporting on large volumes of data sets. This cloud service is designed for massive parallel processing (MPP) data warehousing, providing high performance for analytics, business intelligence, and reporting. Locally attached storage is used to maximize throughput, and Amazon allows organizations to choose between hard disk drives (HDDs) and solid state disks (SSDs).

Amazon QuickSight

Organizations can utilize this Amazon cloud service to create business intelligence visualizations and reports. It is possible to generate visualizations and business intelligence dashboards that can be viewed via a web browser or a mobile device (e.g., tablet or smartphone).

Amazon Data Pipeline

This cloud service helps organizations transfer data from on-premises sources to the Amazon cloud, or move data between resources within the Amazon cloud. Data transfer can be scheduled, and data flows are visually represented. Data can be transformed or processed, and tasks can be triggered by the data pipeline flow. End targets can be Amazon S3, Amazon Redshift, Amazon DynamoDB, or Amazon EMR.

Amazon Glue

Organizations can utilize this managed cloud service to extract, transform, and load (ETL) data from one data location to another. This cloud service aims to simplify and automate data discovery (e.g., identifying the data, the data types, and formats), data conversion, and job scheduling (i.e., an ETL job). Amazon Glue supports Amazon S3, Amazon RDS, Amazon Redshift, and any data source compliant with Java Database Connectivity (JDBC). Organizations can continue using tools they are comfortable and experienced with (e.g., Python or Spark). There is no infrastructure for organizations to manage, and organizations pay for only the resources used to process ETL jobs.

Artificial Intelligence (AI)

Amazon offers several cloud services to help organizations with artificial intelligence (AI) for voice or image recognition, text-to-voice functionality, and machine learning (ML). The Amazon AI services can be categorized as follows:

- Amazon Machine Learning (ML)
- Amazon Lex
- Amazon Polly
- Amazon Rekognition

Amazon Machine Learning (ML)

Organizations can quickly begin using machine learning technologies via the Amazon ML cloud service. This cloud service has a visual interface and work flow guiding a user through the creation of ML models that leverage complex ML algorithms and technologies. Machine learning algorithms are used by organizations to discover patterns in vast amounts of data in an automated and scientific manner. Machine learning is often used for prescriptive analytics.

Amazon Lex

With the Amazon Lex cloud service, organizations can build an interface for conversational communication (i.e., voice and text) into their applications. Amazon Lex uses deep learning for automating speech recognition (ASR) and converting human speech into text, including natural language understanding (NLU), which recognizes the intent within the text. Such services help organizations deploy smart chatbots for websites or mobile applications. Cloud services such as Amazon Lex make it easy and affordable for organizations to offer advanced interactivity for their consumers.

Amazon Polly

The Amazon Polly cloud service transforms text into human-like speech. Organizations can thus use such services to create speech-enabled products or services. Amazon Polly also uses deep learning to simulate up to 47 human voices supporting 24 human languages. Audio results can be streamed in near real time as responses to interactive dialogue sessions with end users, or they can be stored in common audio formats such as MP3.

Amazon Rekognition

Organizations can utilize the Amazon Rekognition cloud service for including analysis of images in their applications. With this type of artificial intelligence service, it is possible to identify faces or objects in images. It is also possible to search for images within images or sets of images. This technology is based on Amazon's research and experience in the Amazon Prime Photos cloud-based service (customers can store photos in the cloud) where billions of images are analyzed daily. Organizations using this cloud service simply pay for the pictures analyzed and the metadata (information about images) stored.

Mobile Services

Many organizations are developing and providing mobile applications to their customers, as consumers are becoming more tech-savvy and connected, wanting products, services, or information on demand when it suits them. Amazon provides a range of cloud services to help organizations with such challenges:

- Amazon Mobile Hub
- Amazon Cognito
- Amazon Pinpoint
- Amazon Device Farm
- Amazon Mobile SDK
- Amazon Mobile Analytics

Amazon Mobile Hub

This cloud service assists organizations with the development of mobile applications. The service provides a console for developers, who can integrate back-end features into a mobile application. Developers select the features they require for the mobile application, and the Amazon Mobile Hub adds the necessary components in the back end. There are many Amazon cloud services that are supported by the Amazon Mobile Hub, such as:

- NoSQL database
- Application analytics
- Cloud logic
- Application content delivery
- Conversation bots
- User data storage
- User sign-in
- Push notifications

Amazon Cognito

The Amazon Cognito cloud service makes it easier for developers to add user sign-up (registering for a mobile or web application service) or sign-in features to their mobile and web applications. Amazon Cognito also supports authentication via trusted identity providers such as Facebook, Twitter, or an organization's identity system. Developers can configure Amazon Cognito to store user data locally on user devices, thereby enabling the use of the mobile or web application even if off-line (not connected to the internet). Functionalities such as user authentication, user management, or information synchronization across devices are handled by the Amazon Cognito cloud service, allowing developers to focus on features that set their organization's application apart from others.

Amazon Pinpoint

Organizations can leverage the Amazon Pinpoint cloud service to execute personalized campaigns (user specific or targeted messages or promotions) within mobile applications (mobile apps). This cloud service helps organizations understand mobile application user behavior, identify the users to target, understand what message to send and when to send it, and then also track the results of the personalized campaigns. Using a data-driven approach (e.g., collecting and analyzing user behavior and application usage patterns to drive actions), organizations can gain higher response rates than with a generic mass push campaign. Amazon charges for only the number of users an organization targets with its campaigns and for the events that an organization collects.

Amazon Device Farm

This cloud service specializes in application testing. Organizations can test their applications across multiple platforms such as Android, iOS, or web. Application testers can review logs, performance-related data, screenshots, or video to assess the quality of their application before releasing it for general availability (GA).

Amazon Mobile SDK

Organizations can use the Amazon Mobile SDK to increase the ease of development of mobile applications. The integration with various Amazon cloud services such as Amazon Lambda, Amazon S3, Amazon DynamoDB, Amazon Machine Learning, or Amazon Mobile Analytics makes it possible to quickly develop advanced mobile applications for use on Android, iOS, or FireOS (Amazon devices with the tailored operating system).

Amazon Mobile Analytics

The Amazon Mobile Analytics cloud service helps organizations measure usage of their mobile applications, as well as measure the revenue resulting from the use of those mobile applications. Key metrics such as new or returning user, data regarding the retention of application users, or in-app behaviors are tracked and recorded. Organizations can view such data via the Amazon Mobile Analytics console, or export such data to Amazon S3 or Amazon Redshift for more specialized analysis and reporting.

Application Services

To help organizations with their development of applications or services for their customers, Amazon provides several specialized cloud services:

- Amazon Step Functions
- Amazon API Gateway
- Amazon Elastic Transcoder
- Amazon Simple Workflow (SWF)

Amazon Step Functions

This cloud service helps organization design distributed applications and microservices via a visual work flow interface. Components of an application are visualized as steps within the Amazon console user interface. Diagnosis of application bugs (software defects) becomes easier as each step can be traced sequentially, and log files are recorded for each step in the application work flow. The underlying infrastructure is managed and scales via the Amazon Step Functions cloud service, allowing developers to concentrate on application development rather than having to spend time on configuring and managing required infrastructure.

Amazon API Gateway

Organizations can leverage this managed cloud service to make it easier for its developers to create, update, deploy, and monitor application programming interfaces (APIs). An API Gateway is used as an interface (or connector) between front-end applications and back-end systems. Using a gateway increases standardization, security, and ease of use, as multiple applications communicate via such a gateway instead of requiring individual connections from each application or cloud service. The Amazon API Gateway handles authorization (e.g., verifying credentials and privileges for an application-based request to back-end services such as a database), access controls, monitoring, and more, making the life of a developer much more manageable. This cloud service can process hundreds of thousands of concurrent API calls.

Amazon Elastic Transcoder

Transcoding is the process of converting a video from one format to another. This could use different video and audio codecs to convert video from one format to another (e.g., an MPEG2 video with Dolby Digital audio into an H.265 video with AAC audio). Such transcoding provides content in different formats for use on various devices (e.g., television, tablets, and smartphones), as well as for streaming scenarios (e.g., on-demand video-streaming services). Transcoding processes are very CPU intensive, and a higher number of CPUs and graphics processing units (GPUs), more memory, and fast storage can all increase the speed of transcoding. Amazon Elastic Transcoder is a cloud-based media transcoder providing scalability and cost-effectiveness for organizations to transcode media content.

Amazon Simple Workflow (SWF)

This cloud service can help organizations track the state of application processing. If the tasks of an application are failing, and developers need to recover or retry such jobs, then the Amazon SWF service may be able to help.

Messaging Services

The Amazon cloud (AWS) provides several cloud services to help organizations with messaging, and these can be classified as follows:

- Amazon Simple Queue Service (SQS)
- Amazon Simple Notification Service (SNS)
- Amazon Simple Email Service (SES)

Amazon Simple Queue Service (SQS)

Amazon SQS is a managed cloud service providing message queuing functionality. Organizations can use Amazon SQS to transmit large volumes of data, and the service guarantees "at-least-once processing" and first-in, first-out (FIFO) processing. Applications must be able to adapt to such technologies (e.g., handle a message that is delivered once or multiple times).

Amazon Simple Notification Service (SNS)

This is a managed cloud service for pushing messages to single recipients or many recipients. Such messages can be used in mobile applications, in email, or with other notification services. Amazon SNS supports sending notifications to Apple, Google, Fire OS, and some niche devices like Windows or in geographic areas such as China.

Amazon Simple Email Service (SES)

Organizations can leverage this cloud-based email service to send emails, marketing messages, and other content to their customer bases. Amazon SES can also be used to receive content and consequently store information in Amazon S3 or to trigger other processes.

Business Productivity

To help organizations with their goals of increasing office productivity, Amazon offers the following cloud services:

- Amazon WorkDocs
- Amazon WorkMail
- Amazon Chime

Amazon WorkDocs

This managed cloud service provides a secure enterprise-level storage and file-sharing option for organizations. Files are centrally stored through this service, avoiding multiple versions being proliferated via email (a standard way of sharing and reviewing documents). Business users can upload files to a central storage repository, update versions centrally, and rest assured that the service provides the security required. As it is a cloud service, users can use any device—for example, Microsoft Windows-based PCs, macOS (Apple's operating system for desktop devices), tablets, or smartphones.

Amazon WorkMail

Amazon WorkMail is a managed cloud-based email service providing a business email and calendar service for organizations using desktop or mobile email clients, including probably the most common business mail application, Microsoft Outlook. With this cloud service, business users can access their work emails via a web browser interface, iOS (e.g., iPad, iPhone devices), or Android-based email applications.

Amazon Chime

Organizations requiring a secure, enterprise-grade cloud service for online conferencing, including video, audio, chatting, and content sharing, can use this Amazon Chime cloud service.

Application and Desktop Streaming

Amazon provides several cloud services for streaming applications or desktops from a cloud environment to end-user devices:

- Amazon Workspaces
- Amazon AppStream 2.0

Amazon Workspaces

This is a cloud-based desktop service that allows business users to access their virtual desktop hosted in the public Amazon cloud from any supported device (e.g., Microsoft Windows and Apple macOS computers, Google Chromebooks, iPad or Android tablets, Chrome and Firefox web browsers) via the internet. Organizations can select hourly or monthly billing options. The public cloud service offering may be cheaper than on-premises virtual desktop infrastructure (VDI) solutions.

Amazon AppStream 2.0

The Amazon AppStream 2.0–managed cloud service provides application streaming functionality to organizations. It is possible to securely stream desktop applications running in the public Amazon cloud to devices supporting a web browser (should be HTML 5 compatible). If the devices have an internet connection, enterprise users can connect to the cloud service and stream their required applications to any location. Centrally managed applications provide standardization, a consistent user experience, and security assurance as no data is stored on end-user devices.

Internet of Things (IoT)

"The Internet of Things (IoT) builds out from today's internet by creating a pervasive and self-organizing network of connected, identifiable and addressable physical objects enabling application development in and across key vertical sectors through the use of embedded chips (integrated circuits or microprocessors), sensors, actuators and low-cost miniaturisation" (Schindler et al. 2012, 8). The Cisco GCI estimates that by the year 2021 people, machines, and things will generate 850 ZB of data (Cisco Global Cloud Index 2016–2021, 23). A city of one million is estimated to create 200 million GB of data per day (Cisco Global Cloud Index 2015–2020, 14). As shown in Figure 65, the economic potential of the industrial internet in the United States is forecasted at $32.3 trillion (Evans and Annunziata, 2012, 13).

The Internet of Things (IoT) can provide enormous earning potential for an organization and help with improving its operations throughout the value chain. IoT can also help organizations become more data-driven with a smart and digital value chain, increasing the speed of informed or autonomous decisions.

Cloud computing facilities are well suited for helping organizations collect, process, and store Big Data. Organizations can also utilize cloud-based computations to instruct IoT devices to take coordinated and distributed action (European Commission:, 2013, 11). There are some concerns about using IoT (e.g., security and the sensitivity of

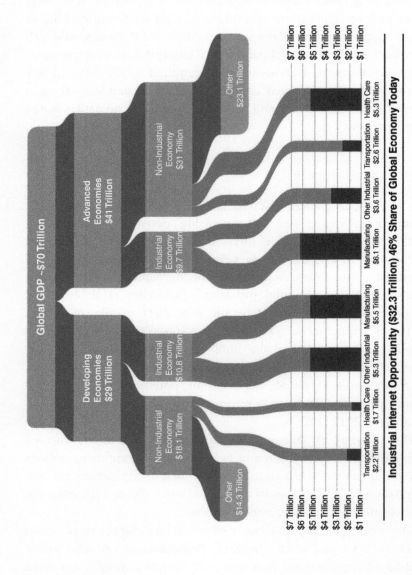

Figure 65 Industrial Internet Economic Potential

Source: Evans and Annunziata (2012, 13); original sources: World Bank (2011) and General Electric.

data), and adoption of IoT by an organization will depend on the industry it operates in (e.g., regulations) and on the organization's risk averseness.

As the demand for IoT services is increasing, public cloud vendors such as Amazon offer the following cloud services to help organizations with their IoT strategies and goals:

- Amazon IoT Platform
- Amazon Greengrass
- Amazon IoT Button

Amazon IoT Platform

Amazon IoT is a managed cloud service enabling an organization to connect its devices to the Amazon cloud, and to cloud-based applications or other Amazon cloud services that an organization utilizes. This cloud service can support billions of devices and trillions of messages from such devices. It is also possible to interlink this cloud service with other Amazon cloud services such as Amazon Lambda, Amazon Kinesis, Amazon S3, Amazon Machine Learning, or Amazon DynamoDB. Organizations can therefore create IoT-enabled applications quickly and efficiently, ingesting, processing, analyzing, and storing data from connected devices.

Amazon Greengrass

This Amazon software makes it possible to execute messaging or data caching locally on a connected device, and communicate with other such devices even if the IoT devices are not connected to the internet. Data upload to the Amazon cloud can occur intermittently; that is, batches of data can be uploaded on an hourly or daily basis. This may help save money for organizations or assist in situations where a live connection to the internet is not always possible or feasible. For example, an airplane may collect vast amounts of data via IoT devices on board, and this data may then be uploaded to the cloud in batch mode when the aircraft has docked at an airport where internet connectivity is faster and cheaper.

Amazon IoT Button

The Amazon IoT Button is a unique hardware device in the shape of a button that is based on the Amazon Dash button (the retail business of Amazon). It is a Wi-Fi-enabled device, and developers can program the logic of a button press to perform a number of actions, such as ordering something (as in the case of the Amazon Dash button), calling a contact number, switching on/off a home appliance such as a Wi-Fi-enabled lightbulb, and so forth.

Development for Games

The final cloud service category in the current Amazon cloud portfolio is for games development. The games market provides high revenue potential for organizations, and Amazon delivers two cloud services to help game developers:

- Amazon GameLift
- Amazon Lumberyard

Amazon GameLift

This managed cloud service makes it easier for organizations to deploy and elastically scale virtual servers for multiplayer games. Organizations are charged for the computing resources and bandwidth consumed by the game players, and organizations do not have to worry about monthly or annual contractual obligations.

Amazon Lumberyard

Amazon provides this cross-platform 3D game engine for free, allowing developers to focus on creating game play and amassing communities of users, rather than having to spend time and effort on infrastructure or the game engine.

■ ■ ■

In summary, Amazon Web Services (AWS) cloud is multinational public cloud provider that is recognized as the market leader in the public cloud computing space. It has an extensive portfolio of cloud services helping organizations adopt the cloud through either

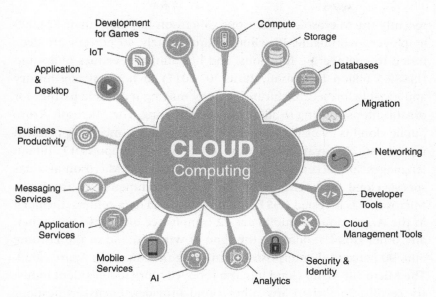

Figure 66 AWS Cloud Service Portfolio

infrastructure as a service (IaaS), platform as a service (PaaS), or even software as a service (SaaS). (See Figure 66.) Organizations have varying degrees of cloud adoption maturity and goals, and the mixed model of cloud services (IaaS, PaaS, SaaS) provides choices and opportunities for organizations across industries and the globe. The PaaS and SaaS market is rapidly growing, and competition from other vendors (e.g., Microsoft, Google) is increasing. This competitiveness provides further choices for organizations regarding decreasing costs. Paas and SaaS will probably offer more differentiating features for cloud vendors than IaaS, as they provide more growth and innovation opportunities for cloud providers and consumers alike.

2. MICROSOFT AZURE

Microsoft (MSFT) was founded in 1975, and the company is probably most famously known for its operating system called Windows. Other popular products include Microsoft Office, Microsoft Dynamics, Microsoft SQL Server, Microsoft Xbox game console, and more recently the Microsoft Azure cloud. Microsoft has more than 124,000 employees worldwide, of whom approximately 40 percent are dedicated to engineering functions, and has annual revenues of around US$89.5 billion (Microsoft, June 30, 2017). It has a strong history and a stable foreseeable future, thereby making it a viable partner for organizations wishing to adopt cloud computing. The Microsoft Azure public cloud is available in 42 geographic regions (including planned regions not yet available) across 140 countries, supports 17 human languages, and accepts 24 currencies for payment. Microsoft also has special cloud data centers for the U.S. Government and Germany. Microsoft has invested US$15 billion into cloud data centers. Included in the Azure cloud portfolio are 62 compliance offerings—more than any other cloud vendor (at the time of writing), and of the Fortune 500, 90 percent of enterprises are utilizing the Microsoft Azure cloud. The Microsoft Azure cloud has also received more independent industry certifications than any other cloud provider. Such certifications include (not a complete listing):

- ISO/IEC (e.g., ISO 27001, ISO 27017, ISO 27018, ISO 20000-1:2011, ISO 22301:12012)
- Cloud Security Alliance (CSA)/Cloud Controls Matrix (CCM)
- International Traffic in Arms Regulations (ITAR)
- Criminal Justice Information Services (CJIS)
- Health Insurance Portability and Accountability Act (HIPPA), Internal Revenue Service (IRS) 1075, Federal Risk and Authorization Management Program (FedRAMP)
- Service Organization Control (SOC) 1 and SOC 2
- Australian InfoSec Registered Assessors Program (IRAP) and Singapore Multi-Tier Cloud Security (MTCS)
- UK G-Cloud (government-approved cloud for government use)

This section aims to provide a high-level overview of key cloud services within the current Microsoft Azure portfolio. Microsoft categorizes these cloud services as follows (see Figure 67):

- Compute
- Networking
- Storage

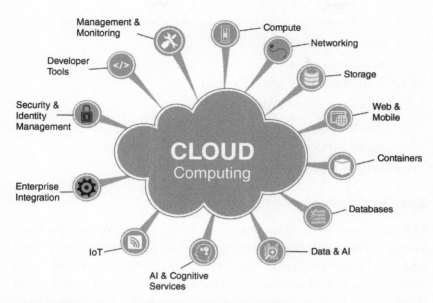

Figure 67 Microsoft Azure Cloud Portfolio Categories

- Web + Mobile
- Containers
- Databases
- Data + Analytics
- Artificial Intelligence and Cognitive Services
- Internet of Things (IoT)
- Enterprise Integration
- Security + Identity
- Developer Tools
- Monitoring + Management

Compute

Microsoft Azure provides the following cloud services in the compute category:

- Azure Virtual Machines (VMs)
- Azure Virtual Machine Scale Sets

- Azure Reserved Virtual Machine Instances
- Azure App Service
- Azure Functions
- Azure Container Service (AKS)
- Azure Container Instances
- Azure Batch
- Azure Service Fabric
- Azure Cloud Services

Azure Virtual Machines

This cloud service enables organizations to deploy virtual machines (VMs) in the cloud. Organizations can select VM images (preinstalled and can be preconfigured) from the public Azure marketplace (an online repository of software by Microsoft or third-party independent software vendors), or from an organization-specific set of images. Such virtual machines support Microsoft Windows and Linux operating systems (OSs). The OS within a virtual machine is commonly referred to as the guest OS. It is important to note that Microsoft has adopted an open source and choice philosophy within recent years. This provides organizations with more choices of platforms, technologies, development communities, and innovation potential. The Microsoft Azure cloud portfolio reflects this openness, as many services are based on open-source software.

Microsoft Azure cloud provides a service-level agreement (SLA) of 99.95 percent for one virtual machine instance for VMs that have two or more instances within one availability set (a logical grouping of VMs to aid management, high availability, and maintenance options). For single-instance virtual machines with premium storage (guest OS and data), there is a 99.9 percent uptime SLA. Microsoft Azure also provides flexible business models for organizations, allowing them to choose between pay-as-you-go (PAYG) or reserved (e.g., one-year, three-year) cost models. Microsoft Azure has different categories of virtual machines, and the specifications possible within a virtual machine family are aimed at specific use cases. The Microsoft Azure Virtual Machines categories are as follows:

- General-purpose
- Compute-optimized
- Memory-optimized
- Storage-optimized
- GPU-optimized use cases
- High-performance compute (HPC)–optimized

To review the latest sizes and prices of resources of Azure, visit the following URLs:

General-purpose virtual machines URL:
https://docs.microsoft.com/en-us/azure/virtual-machines/windows/sizes-general

Compute-optimized virtual machines URL:
https://docs.microsoft.com/en-us/azure/virtual-machines/windows/sizes-compute

Memory-optimized virtual machines URL:
https://docs.microsoft.com/en-gb/azure/virtual-machines/windows/sizes-memory

Storage-optimized virtual machines URL:
https://docs.microsoft.com/en-gb/azure/virtual-machines/windows/sizes-storage

GPU-optimized virtual machines URL:
https://docs.microsoft.com/en-us/azure/virtual-machines/windows/sizes-gpu

High-performance compute (HPC)–optimized URL:
https://docs.microsoft.com/en-us/azure/virtual-machines/windows/sizes-hpc

Azure Virtual Machine Scale Sets

Organizations can create scalable application architectures by deploying and managing identical virtual machines as a logical set. These Microsoft Azure VM Scale Sets leverage the Azure Resource Manager platform (a way of standardizing resource deployments within the Azure cloud). They integrate with Azure load balancing and autoscaling. Organizations can deploy Windows VMs, Linux VMs, and custom VM images. It is possible to deploy hundreds of identical VMs within minutes. Azure Autoscale provides the elastic resources (e.g., expanding from one VM to four) required for serving workload demands dynamically. Workloads can be distributed across VMs in an Azure VM Scale Set through mechanisms such as Microsoft Azure Load Balancer or Azure Application Gateway. These VMs can house containers, clusters of microservices, or stateless web front ends.

Azure Reserved Virtual Machine Instances

Organizations can save up to 72 percent with reserved instances (RIs) compared to the standard pay-as-you-go (PAYG) model, and cost savings can be increased to 82 percent if Azure Hybrid benefit is utilized (combining on-premises resources and public cloud resources). Such VMs are purchased for one-year or three-year terms, and although payment is made at the beginning of the contract term, organizations can exchange or cancel at any time. Organizations may find such a cost model easier to budget and forecast than a PAYG cost model. Another benefit to organizations using Azure RIs is that such resources receive prioritized compute capacity.

Azure App Service

This managed cloud service (i.e., platform as a service [PaaS]) helps organizations create enterprise-class web applications or mobile applications, regardless of platform or end device. Such applications can then be deployed and scaled on the Azure cloud infrastructure. Both Windows and Linux are supported, as well as many of the popular programming languages such as dot Net (.Net), Java, Ruby, Node.js, PHP, and Python. Developers can use Microsoft Visual Studio as their integrated development environment (IDE) and benefit from easy integration with Microsoft Azure cloud, including continuous integration and continuous deployment (CI/CD), making updates to applications easier. The service also makes it easier to integrate with Docker Hub (for container technologies) and GitHub (software code repository technology). This service can integrate with other Azure services such as Azure Active Directory to provide single sign-on (SSO) and authentication capabilities. Developers can spend more time on their applications rather than on managing infrastructure and building components for everyday tasks (e.g., sign-on, authentication).

Azure Functions

Developers can utilize Azure Functions for building HTTP end points that are accessible by connected devices (e.g., IoT) or mobile devices. Azure Functions provide event-driven computing, for example executing code at regular intervals (using Cron job syntax) or parsing a new text file that appears in Azure Blob storage. Azure Functions can run API calls and integrate with other services, allowing organizations to build sophisticated work flows. Many popular programming or scripting languages are supported, such as JavaScript, C#, F#, PHP, Bash, Batch, or PowerShell. This type of cloud service is referred to as serverless, as an organization does not have to manage any servers or infrastructure. Such back-end resources are automatically deployed, configured, scaled, and maintained by the cloud vendor and service.

Azure Container Service (AKS)

Organizations can leverage this cloud service to orchestrate, deploy, and scale container-based applications that use Docker Swarm and Apache Mesos. These are favorite open-source tools for container technologies, and organizations already using such platforms can move to Azure cloud with minimal effort. The AKS cloud service utilizes Kubernetes, an open-source system for automating deployment, management, and scaling of containerized applications. Organizations can use the managed Kubernetes platform or deploy unmanaged Kubernetes, Docker, or DC/OS (distributed OS—Mesosphere). Organizations are charged for consumed resources, and there is no per-cluster charge.

Azure Container Instances

With this cloud service, organizations can focus on their applications housed within a container and active in the cloud. There is no need to learn or to acquire skills in orchestrations tools for containers. The cost model of this service allows for a per-second billing, providing very granular cost control for organizations. Container images (template-driven to increase standardization and ease of use) can be obtained from Docker Hub or Azure Container Registry. Microsoft provides guidance for organizations for selecting the suitable technologies for container usage. Visit this URL for more information: https://azure .microsoft.com/en-us/services/container-instances/.

Azure Batch

The Azure Batch cloud service makes it easier for organizations to run high-performance computing (HPC) and parallel workloads in the Azure cloud. This cloud service can be used to execute tasks from a queue, parallelize workloads, and enable applications to offload compute jobs to be processed in the Azure cloud. Organizations can choose to run batch jobs on Windows or on Linux with the tools they need and are charged on consumption of cloud resources. Scaling can be to thousands of virtual machines, and infrastructure is managed by this service, meaning organizations can focus on their applications instead.

Azure Service Fabric

This is a cloud service for microservice architectures that help cloud-enable applications. Developers do not have to worry about infrastructure and can spend more time on developing enterprise-level applications. Organizations can choose their programming languages to use, and this service supports Windows or Linux in Azure cloud or on-premises and even other clouds. The cloud service can scale up to thousands of virtual machines to handle the workloads. Microsoft itself leverages this service for business solutions such as Skype for Business.

Azure Cloud Services

Azure Cloud Services helps organizations create, deploy, and manage cloud-enabled applications. Developers do not have to worry about managing infrastructure as that is handled by this cloud service. Popular programming languages such as dot Net (.Net), Java, Node.js, Ruby, PHP, and Python are supported. The underlying resources can autoscale to suit application requirements. Customers using this service include Dell, Aviva, and AccuWeather.

Networking

Microsoft Azure provides the following cloud services in the networking category:

- Azure Virtual Network
- Azure Load Balancer
- Azure Application Gateway
- Azure VPN Gateway
- Azure DNS (Domain Name System)
- Azure Content Delivery Network
- Azure Traffic Manager
- Azure ExpressRoute
- Azure DDoS Protection
- Azure Network Watcher

Azure Virtual Network

Organizations can use this cloud service to create private logical virtual networks in the Azure cloud and have full control over the IP addresses, Domain Name Systems (DNS) servers, and security rules required by the organization. It is possible to connect on-premises networks to the Azure cloud via a virtual private network (VPN) tunnel, or by using a dedicated and secure connection through the Microsoft Azure ExpressRoute service. Virtual Networks provide isolation and security for the organization to run its applications in the cloud. Microsoft has invested vast amounts of money into building a dedicated network for all of its geographic regions. All traffic between Azure resources therefore remains on this dedicated network, including intergeographic traffic. Organizations can also leverage third-party networking via the Azure Marketplace (e.g., Palo Alto, Barracuda, or F5).

Azure Load Balancer

This cloud service is for distributing traffic among healthy (e.g., up and running VMs) servers or services to ensure adequate performance of applications. The cloud service includes health checks (e.g., of virtual machine instances configured to be reachable by the Load Balancer) and IPv6.

Azure Application Gateway

The Azure Application Gateway is a managed cloud service. It provides HTTP load balancing or cookie-based sessions (a cookie is stored on application devices to help with session or preference management) for web applications. The web applications can be for private or public use. Secure sockets layer (SSL) is offloaded to the Azure Application Gateway, and a web application firewall can help organizations protect their web applications from web vulnerabilities. Microsoft provides a 99.95 percent service-level agreement.

Azure VPN Gateway

An Azure VPN Gateway helps organizations create a secure virtual network tunnel connection between virtual networks in the Microsoft Azure cloud, or between on-premises networks and the Azure cloud. Industry-standard site-to-site IPSec VPNs are supported with a service-level agreement of 99.9 percent uptime.

Azure DNS (Domain Name System)

This cloud services lets organizations host their DNS in the Azure cloud benefiting from global reach, redundancy, and fast responses. Azure DNS utilizes Anycast networking to automatically route DNS queries to the nearest name servers for rapid responses. DNS record updates typically require only a few seconds to be updated on DNS servers and reflected in new address queries.

Azure Content Delivery Network

Organizations can use the Azure Content Delivery Network (CDN) to host static content across the Azure cloud regions and serve front-end applications locally. Such a globally distributed CDN provides low-latency responses to client applications and end users and offers high availability of content. Use cases for content include serving web pages, media streaming, and software updates for connected devices. The cloud service provides granular controls to help organizations control their content. Near real-time analytics help organizations gain an insight into what content is requested the most and where.

Azure Traffic Manager

This cloud service enables organizations to route network traffic across Azure services within one Azure data center or multiple Azure data centers across the globe. Customers that leverage this service include Heineken and AccuWeather. There are four traffic routing methods available through the Azure Traffic Manager:

1. Failover
2. Performance
3. Geography
4. Weighted round-robin

Azure ExpressRoute

Azure ExpressRoute is used by organizations to create private and dedicated network connections between their on-premises data center and the Azure data center. Traffic via ExpressRoute is via dedicated networks and does not use the Internet.

For cost examples, visit the URL (https://azure.microsoft.com/en-us/pricing/details/expressroute).

Notes:
Outbound data transfer is charged at $0.025/GB for Zone 1, $0.05/GB for Zone 2, and $0.15/GB for Zone 3.

Organizations can connect to other regions within the same geographic region even after the initial ExpressRoute connection is made. No additional costs or add-ons are required. For example, if an organization connects an ExpressRoute to an Azure region in Europe, it can send or receive data to/from any Azure region in Europe without any additional costs.

- Up to 10,000 routes for private and public peering
- Global connectivity to Azure regions
- More than 10 VNet links per ExpressRoute circuit (depends on the bandwidth)

Global connectivity to other Azure regions is not available if an organization creates an ExpressRoute circuit in Azure Government, Azure Germany, or Azure China on account of the isolation and sovereignty requirements of those regions.

Azure DDoS Protection

Microsoft applies its insights and experience in security to this service to help protect organizations from distributed denial of service network attacks. The service protects against layer 3/4 attacks.

Azure Network Watcher

Organizations can leverage this Azure cloud service to monitor and diagnose network health and issues. The cloud service includes tools to visualize and diagnose network information, allowing network administrators to capture network packets of a virtual machine and to visualize network topology.

Storage

To help organizations with storage challenges and strategies, Microsoft Azure provides the following cloud services in the storage category:

- Azure Storage
- Azure Blob Storage
- Azure Archive Storage
- Azure Queue Storage
- Azure File Storage
- Azure Disk Storage

- Azure Data Lake Store
- Azure StorSimple
- Azure Backup
- Azure Site Recovery

Azure Storage

This cloud storage service provides nonrelational data storage. Organizations are charged for only what they consume, and with cloud storage, it is unlikely that an organization's demand will be higher than the scalable supply. The following four storage services fall under this category.

Azure Blob Storage

This cloud service provides object storage based on Representational State Transfer (REST) web protocol for organizations to store unstructured data. Organizations can save any raw data type such as images, documents, or media files. It is possible to save hundreds of billions of objects, and organizations can choose from hot, cold, or archive tiers. Hot storage is for fast and frequently incoming or accessed data types. Cold storage is generally for slow-moving or infrequently accessed data, and archive storage is for long-term cold storage. Prices start from $0.002 per GB per month.

Three Blob types can be selected to provide the best performance for organizational use cases:

- Block Blob
- Page Blob
- Append Blob

Azure Archive Storage

This cloud service is aimed at archival needs of organizations, which vary depending on the industry they operate in; for example, financial, medical, or employee data must be archived for several years to comply with regulatory requirements. This storage tier has the lowest prices compared to the other Azure storage services. Data at rest is automatically encrypted with AES 256-bit encryption.

Azure Queue Storage

Organizations can use this cloud service for affordable and straight-forward message queuing. Industry-standard REST APIs provide easy and global access to the data. Asynchronous message queuing is used for communication between application components. Messages are buffered in case some elements of an organization's application architecture go down, and resume once these become available again.

Azure File Storage

This cloud service is a managed file sharing cloud service providing access via industry-standard Server Message Block (SMB) protocol. Azure File shares can be mounted on multiple operating systems, such as Windows, Linux, and macOS. Data at rest and in transit is secured via SMB 3.0 and HTTPS.

Azure Disk Storage

Organizations can use this cloud service for persistent disk storage assigned to virtual machines. Solid state disks (SSDs) provide fast throughput (I/O) for demanding applications, and standard hard disk drives (HDDs) are for general use cases or for offering accept-able performance at affordable costs. Maximum disk throughput per virtual machine can be up to 80,000 IOPS and 2,000 MB per second. The Azure disks provide 99.999 percent availability, and an organization's data on these disks is replicated three times, providing high durability in case of hardware failure. Data at rest is encrypted by default. Business solutions such as Microsoft Dynamics AX, Microsoft Dynamics CRM, or Microsoft SharePoint farms are certified to run on premium Azure disk storage.

Azure Data Lake Store

This cloud service supports an organization's Big Data strategy by allowing it to store data of any type, at any size, and at any speed (the 3-Vs of Big Data). Azure provides enterprise-level security for storing, sharing, and collaborating with such data. Data can be ingested from connected devices (e.g., IoT), or from other sources, handling hot (fast-moving) or cold (slowly moving) data equally well. Azure Data Lake can be used alongside other cloud services such as Azure HDInsight (HDFS—Hadoop framework) and other Big Data platforms such as Hortonworks, Cloudera, or MapR. The Azure Data Lake scales with the demands of an organization and can handle fast or slow streams of data from many sources. Data types can be structured, semistructured, or unstructured, and a single file can be greater than one petabyte (1 petabyte = 1,000 terabytes). The cloud service is designed to support trillions of files an organization may need to store in a data lake. Data in motion is encrypted via secure socket layer (SSL), and data at rest is encrypted via Azure Key Vault (an Azure cloud service for managing encryption keys) or a self-managed hardware security module (HSM). If an organization leverages the Azure Active Directory, then it can utilize security features such as:

- Single sign-on (SSO)
- Multifactor authentication
- POSIX-based access control lists (ACLs) providing granular role security controls

Microsoft Azure Data Lake Store offers a 99.9 percent service-level agreement (SLA) and 24/7 support for organizations. Some Azure cloud services may not be available in all regions, as services are rolled out depending on Microsoft criteria (e.g., customer demand for service in geographic areas, data center capabilities, etc.). The Azure Data Lake service is not available in the Western European region, for example (as of December 2017). For cost examples, visit the URL https://azure.microsoft.com/en-us/pricing/details/data-lake-store. To review the Azure cloud services available in different geographic regions (e.g., United States, Europe) visit the URL https://azure .microsoft.com/en-us/regions/services/.

Azure StorSimple

This cloud service aims to help organizations with storage, archiving, and disaster recovery challenges. The Azure StorSimple uses a hybrid approach by placing physical storage arrays in data centers and virtual arrays in smaller environments—for example, remote offices using storage technologies such as network attached storage (NAS). Azure StorSimple can be used to automatically archive inactive data to the cloud, and help organizations with backup and disaster recovery challenges and needs. Software policies are used for data archiving and retrieval instead of traditional forms such as tape backups and tape rotation schedules.

Azure Backup

Azure Backup can help organizations protect business-critical data stored on corporate laptops, and it can also help protect business-critical applications (e.g., Microsoft SharePoint, Microsoft SQL Server, Microsoft Exchange), or Hyper-V virtual machines (Microsoft hypervisor virtualization technology) through integration with Microsoft System Center Data Protection Manager (DPM). Azure Backup can be used with Windows, Linux, VMware (virtualization technology), and Microsoft Hyper-V. Information regarding backups performed can be visualized via Microsoft Power BI (a business intelligence reporting tool).

Azure Site Recovery

This cloud service, which offers disaster recovery as a service (DRaaS), helps organizations protect business-critical applications by replicating private clouds to off-site locations (i.e., Azure public cloud). Azure Site Recovery can be used to replicate physical servers, VMware-based virtual machines, and Microsoft Hyper-V virtual machines. The service integrates with Microsoft System Center and Microsoft SQL Server AlwaysOn technologies. Disaster recovery can be orchestrated through Windows PowerShell scripts and Microsoft Azure Automation runbooks. Communication with the Microsoft Azure cloud is encrypted, safeguarding an organization's sensitive data. Azure Site Recovery remotely monitors protected instances (e.g., servers). If an organization chooses to replicate data between two sites it manages itself, then the data remains on the organization's network. If an organization decides to replicate data to the Microsoft Azure cloud (Azure then being its secondary disaster recovery site in this example), then the data transfer and data at rest are encrypted.

Web and Mobile

To help organizations to create modern applications for the web and mobile devices, Microsoft Azure provides the following cloud services:

- Azure App Service
  - Azure Web Apps
  - Azure Mobile Apps
  - Azure Logic Apps
  - Azure API Apps
- Azure Content Delivery Network (CDN)
- Azure Media Services
  - Azure Live and On-Demand Streaming
  - Azure Media Player
  - Azure Content Protection
  - Azure Media Analytics
- Azure Search
- Azure API Management
- Azure Notification Hubs

Azure App Service

This cloud service can enable organizations to develop web and mobile applications that can leverage the cloud. Supported programming languages include dot Net (.Net), Java, Node.js, Python, PHP, and Ruby. Both Microsoft Windows and Linux operating system platforms are supported, providing flexibility for developers and organizations.

Organizations can leverage Azure Web Apps to create enterprise-level web applications. Common deployment frameworks such as Git, Microsoft Team Foundation Server, and GitHub are supported. Developers can leverage WordPress, Umbraco, or Drupal technologies also.

Azure Mobile Apps can be used to build mobile applications that run on mobile operating system platforms such as iOS, Android, and Windows phone. Such applications can support back-end processing via programming languages such as C# or Node.js. Organizations can leverage support for frameworks such as Xamarin or PhoneGap to develop advanced mobile apps for enterprise use. Customers that utilize this type of cloud service include NBC News and Paramount (https://azure/microsoft.com/en-us/services/app-service/mobile).

The Azure Logic Apps service helps organizations build application logic via a visual work flow interface. Microsoft Azure cloud provides ready-to-use connectors for accessing systems such as Microsoft Office 365, Salesforce (SFDC), and Google services. Support for electronic data interchange (EDI) means organizations can more easily exchange data via standards such as EDOFACT, X12, AS2, aiding business operations.

Azure API Apps helps organizations to create APIs for cloud deployment quickly. Supported API written languages include dot Net (.Net), Java, Python, PHP, and Node.js.

Azure Content Delivery Network (CDN)

Organizations can use the Azure Content Delivery Network (CDN) to host static content across the Azure cloud regions and serve front-end applications locally. Such a globally distributed CDN provides low-latency responses to client applications and end users and offers high availability of content. Use cases for content include serving web pages, media streaming, and software updates for connected devices. The cloud service provides granular controls to help organizations control the content. Near real-time analytics help organizations gain an insight into what content is requested the most and where.

Azure Media Services

This cloud service enables organizations to ingest media, encode or format media, protect media content, and support streaming of content (both on-demand and live streaming). Streaming capabilities integrate with Azure Content Delivery Network functionalities. Customers leveraging this service include Microsoft Xbox or NBC Sports (https://azure.microsoft.com/en-us/services/media-services).

Organizations can leverage this cloud service to deliver live and on-demand streaming of media content with just-in-time AES encryption and digital rights management (DRM). Integration with the Azure Content Delivery Network (CDN) provides global availability. As new media encoding formats are created, the cloud service will incorporate them, making it easier for organizations to focus on content and not worry about media formats and re-encoding.

The Azure Media Player automatically selects the most suitable media format for the end-user device to which content is being streamed. Modern media-rich technologies such as HTML 5, Apple HTTP Live Stream (HLS), or legacy platforms like Microsoft Silverlight are supported.

Azure Content Protection helps protect an organization's media content from the time it is uploaded to the Azure cloud to playback time. Content can be secured via Advanced Encryption Standard (AES), including real-time media delivery. Security keys provide easy and secure management of encryption, and should an organization's content ever become compromised it merely has to change its encryption key instead of worrying about having to re-encrypt its entire media content repository.

Azure Media Analytics can help organizations analyze content (e.g., for police and security-related media content), extract audio to text, utilize facial recognition (e.g., for face emotion use cases), and even redact content to protect identities. Since it is a cloud service, new features are added constantly, such as a content moderation feature (in preview status at the time of writing) to help organizations prevent the proliferation of content of racial, violent, or child pornographic nature, for example.

Azure Search

Azure Search is a managed cloud service enabling organizations to add advanced search capabilities to their web or mobile applications. By utilizing this cloud service, organizations can take advantage of Microsoft's knowledge and experience of natural language processing. Such knowledge has been used in Microsoft products such as Bing and Office for more than a decade. Billing for this service occurs on an hourly or monthly basis, and documents hosted can range from thousands to millions.

Azure API Management

The Azure API Management service helps organizations to securely and efficiently publish and manage APIs to in-house developers or external partners. Using API Gateways helps with standardization, maintenance, or changes as developers focus on a universal gateway instead of multiple individual connectors between software components. Management capabilities support REST API, PowerShell, and Git.

Azure Notification Hubs

This cloud service provides push notification services that can scale to suit organizational needs, and supports sending millions of messages. Organizations can use this service to send push notifications to applications across popular platforms such as iOS, Android, Kindle, and Microsoft Windows. Supported push notification services include Apple Push Notification (APN), Google Cloud Messaging (GCM), Windows Push Notification Service (WNS), and Microsoft Push Notification Service (MPNS). Back-end systems that integrate with Azure Notification Hubs (i.e., generating content of the message) can use dot Net (.Net), Java, Node.js, or PHP, and the back-end systems can be cloud or on-premises.

Containers

Microsoft Azure provides several cloud services that aim to help organizations leverage technologies such as containers (a technology to increase the density of hosted applications—squeezing maximum use out of computing resources—to provide sandbox environments, and to make development and updates of applications easier) or microservices. Microsoft Azure provides the following container-related cloud services:

- Azure App Service
- Azure Batch
- Azure Container Registry
- Azure Container Instances
- Azure Service Fabric
- Azure Container Service (AKS)

Azure App Service

This managed cloud service helps organizations create enterprise-class web applications or mobile applications, regardless of platform or end device. Such applications can then be deployed and scaled on the Azure cloud infrastructure. Both Windows and Linux are supported, as well as many of the popular programming languages such as dot Net (.Net), Java, Ruby, Node.js, PHP, and Python. Developers can use Microsoft Visual Studio as their integrated development environment (IDE) and benefit from easy integration with Microsoft Azure cloud, including continuous integration and continuous deployment (CI/CD), making updates to applications easier. The service also makes it easier to integrate with Docker Hub (for container technologies) and GitHub (software code repository technology). This service can integrate with other Azure services such as Azure Active Directory to provide single sign-on (SSO) and authentication capabilities. Developers can spend more time on their applications rather than on managing infrastructure and building components for everyday tasks (e.g., sign-on, authentication).

Azure Batch

This type of cloud service makes it easier for organizations to execute parallel processing jobs and high-performance computing (HPC) workload types. Organizations can scale batch computing jobs from tens to thousands of virtual machines. HPC and large batch job workloads are typical in engineering or scientific industries, and organizations operating in such sectors can leverage the Microsoft Azure cloud for scalable and affordable compute resources. Cost models available include pay-as-you-go (PAYG) low priority, PAYG normal priority, and one-year or three-year reserved instances (providing 40 to 60 percent discounted prices).

Azure Container Registry

Organizations can utilize the Azure Container Registry service for centrally storing and managing container images, supporting Docker

Swarm, Kubernetes, Azure Batch, Azure Service Fabric, or Mesophere DC/OS. The Azure Container Registry is compatible with open-source Docker Registry v2, making it easier for organizations to switch to the cloud, reusing skills, tools, and scripts that they may already be using.

Azure Container Instances

With this cloud service, organizations can focus on their applications housed within a container and active in the cloud. There is no need to learn or to acquire skills in orchestrations tools for containers. The cost model of this service allows for per-second billing, providing very granular cost control for organizations. Container images (template-driven to increase standardization and ease of use) can be obtained from Docker Hub or Azure Container Registry. Microsoft provides guidance for organizations for selecting the suitable technologies for container usage.

Azure Service Fabric

This is a cloud service for microservice architectures that help cloud-enable applications. Developers do not have to worry about infrastructure and can spend more time on developing enterprise-level applications. Organizations can choose their programming languages to use, and this service supports Windows or Linux in Azure cloud or on-premises and even other clouds. The cloud service can scale up to thousands of virtual machines to handle the workloads. Microsoft itself leverages this service for business solutions such as Skype for Business.

Azure Container Service (AKS)

Organizations can leverage this cloud service to orchestrate, deploy, and scale container-based applications that use Docker Swarm and Apache Mesos. These are popular open-source tools for container technologies, and organizations already using such platforms can move to Azure cloud with minimal effort. The AKS cloud service utilizes Kubernetes, an open-source system for automating deployment, management, and scaling of containerized applications. Organizations can use the managed Kubernetes platform or deploy unmanaged Kubernetes, Docker, or DC/OS (distributed OS—Mesosphere). Organizations are charged for consumed resources, and there is no per-cluster charge.

Databases

Microsoft has a strong background in database technologies through Microsoft SQL Server and related technologies. Big Data, analytics, online analytical processing (OLAP), online transactional processing (OLTP), and the increased speed of storing, processing, and analyzing (gaining business insights) are common challenges to organizations worldwide, and the Azure cloud platform provides several services and technologies to help with such problems:

- Azure SQL Database (cloud-based version of Microsoft SQL Server)
- Azure Database for MySQL
- Azure Database for PostgreSQL
- Azure SQL Data Warehouse
- Azure SQL Stretch Database
- Azure Cosmos DB
- Azure Redis Cache
- Azure Database Migration Service

Azure SQL Database

The Azure SQL Database service is the cloud-based version of the popular Microsoft SQL Server relational database server and has evolved to take advantage of the cloud and related services. This cloud database has been modernized to provide additional features (beyond merely being a relational database) such as in-memory OLTP, handling JSON, spatial, or XML data, and it is a fully managed cloud service currently operating in 38 Azure data centers (at the time of writing) around the world. Microsoft development is generally first on the Azure cloud-based SQL database version, and then features are later included in the on-premises version (Microsoft SQL Server), so organizations requiring the most up-to-date features should probably consider the Azure SQL Database version. The SQL Database utilizes intelligence to assess usage patterns and consequentially tunes the database automatically to ensure adequate performance. This can proactively prevent issues and saves administrator time, especially for organizations having thousands of databases.

Application developers can use DevOps and tools such as Microsoft Visual Studio and SQL Management Studio, and develop applications with popular programming languages such as dot Net (.Net), Java, PHP, and Ruby. The cloud service provides a 99.99 percent service-level agreement (SLA) and can help with disaster recovery objectives—for example, a recovery point objective (RPO) of around five seconds if the active geo-replication feature is enabled. This ensures there is minimal loss of business-critical information (e.g., disaster minus five seconds from the earlier example) in the event of an emergency (e.g., hardware or power failures, or other disasters affecting an entire data center). In-memory technologies of Azure SQL Database can identify heavily accessed database tables (e.g., during peak business times like Christmas holidays) and move them into memory for substantially faster response times. Microsoft notes up to 30 times speedier response times when such heavily used data tables are automatically transferred into memory, and a staggering 100 times faster analytics to help with use cases like financial fraud detection where every millisecond counts. Organizations can benefit from these in-memory features without changing the service tier they use, providing consistency and cost control.

Clustered columnar store (physical storage of an entire SQL table) index technologies are included with the Azure SQL Database. Such indexes are used to store and query large fact data tables, and can provide up to 10 times better query performance and up to 10 times better data compression compared to traditional row-based storage. Columns store values of the same data dimension (e.g., zip code, postal address code) in one column. The same data type makes compression efficient, and queries are also significantly improved, as the in-memory footprint is smaller and all like data is in one columnar store. Reading selected columns (i.e., during a query) provides superior performance compared to a row-by-row reading of record sets. Azure SQL Database also supports nonclustered indexes, which are secondary indexes based on row store tables. Row stores represent data logically organized in the traditional row and column matrix of a relational database table.

Organizations can choose among four Azure SQL Database service tiers for their performance needs and budget:

- Basic
- Standard
- Premium
- Premium RS

It is possible to change between service tiers at any time, and administrators can do this manually or programmatically to ensure required performance to meet business needs. For more information, visit the URL https://docs.microsoft.com/en-gb/azure/sql-database/sql-database-service-tiers-dtu.

To help organizations dynamically adapt to unpredictable workloads and reduce administration time and effort, the Azure SQL Database cloud service provides a feature called "elastic pools." With this performance design concept, an organization pays for a pool of resources instead of individual databases, whereby the pool allocates resources to the demanding databases (e.g., DB 1) when needed and reallocates them to other databases (e.g., DB 2) when no longer required for DB 1. Organizations can mix and match single databases with elastic pools, benefiting from maximum flexibility, performance gains, ease of use, and cost efficiencies. To help organizations understand possible resource requirements and decide on service tiers and whether to use single databases or elastic pools, Microsoft uses performance metrics called data transaction units (DTUs) and elastic data transaction units (eDTUs) (for elastic pools, as the name implies), respectively. A DTU is a blend of CPU, memory, and read-write rates. A DTU calculator and related tools are available for estimating the DTUs required (http://dtucalculator.azurewebsites.net).

Data such as transactional data, an online store product database, or a customer orders database are critical to the business of an organization. Failures of such data platforms can have a devastating financial effect on an organization. To help with disaster recovery planning, the Azure SQL Database service includes the following availability features:

- Automatic backups (e.g., full, differential—delta from last backup, transactional log backups)
- Point-in-time restore
- Active geo-replication
- Failover groups

Organizations can restore an Azure SQL database to a recovery point in time as long as it is within the automatic backup retention period.

Active geo-replication is a feature that allows an organization to configure up to four read-only secondary databases in the same geographic region or another region. For example, an organization with an online web store operating worldwide may choose to have a primary database in the United States while configuring secondary read-only databases in Europe and the Asia-Pacific region for performance, latency, availability, and user experience reasons.

Failover groups help protect databases against failure where, if the primary group fails, applications automatically failover to the secondary group. Such groups can also be used in load balancing situations.

To help safeguard sensitive and confidential data, the Azure SQL Database provides four key security features:

1. Transparent data encryption (TDE)
2. Always encrypted—encryption of data in motion
3. Dynamic data masking
4. Row-level security (RLS)

Transparent data encryption provides real-time encryption/decryption of databases, database backups, and database transaction log files of data at rest. Always encrypted encrypts and decrypts data in motion (e.g., between database and application). Dynamic data masking leaves underlying data intact but masks out critical pieces of information (e.g., the majority of credit card number sequence, such as xxxx-xxxx-xxxx-9437). Row-level security helps organizations protect data at a granular level; for example, John Doe has access to human resource data but not salary data, which may be stored as a row in the database table.

Azure Database for MySQL

This is a managed cloud service for the popular MySQL relational database. The community version of MySQL is used, and the service provides a global availability of 99.99 percent service-level agreement (SLA). Developers can utilize their preferred frameworks such as WordPress or Drupal, and this cloud service also integrates with Azure Web Apps. Organizations can benefit from the elasticity of the database for times of unexpected demand (e.g., during a sales promotion or after a marketing event), and use a MySQL database to store product data and customer sales order data. For more information, visit the URL https://azure.microsoft.com/en-us/pricing/details/mysql.

Azure Database for PostgreSQL

Organizations can leverage this managed cloud service based on another popular relational database called PostgreSQL. Tasks such as patches, updates, and maintenance are handled by the cloud service provider (Microsoft). This database cloud service utilizes the community edition of PostgreSQL. Developers can continue to use programming languages and frameworks of their choice, such as Java, Node.js, Python, PHP, C++, or C#. The managed cloud service scales compute and storage independently to match the needs of an organization.

Azure SQL Data Warehouse

Azure SQL Data Warehouse is a specialized cloud service that provides an enterprise-level elastic data warehouse that scales with an organization's needs in the cloud or on-premises (organization's data center). The data warehouse is built on massive parallel processing (MPP) architecture design and is built on the powerful SQL engine of Microsoft SQL Server. This warehouse dynamically scales up or down to meet data and reporting requirements. The Azure SQL data warehouse integrates with other Azure services such as Azure Data Factory, Azure HDInsight (Hadoop framework for Big Data), Azure Machine Learning, or Microsoft Power BI (business intelligence visualization and reporting).

Azure SQL Stretch Database

This service enables organizations to dynamically stretch both slow and fast moving transactional data (i.e., cold and hot data, respectively) from on-premises MS SQL Server databases (e.g., SQL Server 2016) to Microsoft Azure. Organizations can thus benefit from the elastic storage capabilities of the cloud when local storage is exhausted. Both cold and hot data can be accessed as if they were local data, and no changes to existing applications are required to work with this Microsoft SQL Server Stretch Database. Organizations can further benefit from security features such as always encrypted (encrypting data at rest and in motion) and row-level security. Organizations have full control over what data remains on-premises and what can be stretched to the Azure cloud via software policies. The service automates the stretching of data once policies are defined. Stretched data is automatically backed up in the Azure cloud.

Azure Cosmos DB

Azure Cosmos DB is a managed cloud-based NoSQL database that specializes in storing unrelational data (e.g., data without a schema, without a predefined structure), and is a true cloud-native database with global availability. It was purposely developed by Microsoft to be a globally distributed and multimodel (types of nonrelational data models) NoSQL database. The design of this NoSQL database provides horizontal scaling for transactional throughput and storage, and scales elastically (expands when more resources are needed, and shrinks when fewer resources are required). The Azure Cosmos DB service guarantees a less than 10 millisecond latency worldwide (less than 10 milliseconds on read and less than 15 milliseconds on indexed write latency) and a 99.999 percent high-availability service-level agreement. Data is stored on solid state disks. This database service is well suited for scenarios such as globally distributed product database instances in e-commerce and retail, for example. Microsoft itself leverages these technologies in its Windows Store and Xbox Live gaming services. Customers utilizing this service include Domino's Pizza, Toyota, and Asos (source: https://azure.microsoft .com/en-us/services/cosmos-db/?v=17.45b). Supported APIs include SQL, MongoDB, Gremlin, JavaScript, and Azure Table Storage. Data at rest and in motion is automatically encrypted, including backups.

Compliance certification includes the following:

- Payment Card Industry (PCI)
- Health Insurance Portability and Accountability Act (HIPAA)
- ISO 27001, ISO 27018, EU Model Clauses (EUMC)
- Federal Risk and Authorization Management Program (FedRAMP), IRS 1075, UK Official (IL2)
- Health Information Trust Alliance (HITRUST)

The Azure Cosmos DB NoSQL database supports the following types of data models (referred to as multimodel support):

- Key-value
- Graph
- Column family
- Document

The key-value data model is a simple database type that stores data in association with a key. Each key is associated with only one value, and the key used is a hash function. Hashing is often used to help ensure an even distribution of keys across the data storage. This way of storing keys is exceptionally well suited for parallel partitioning of data, as the hashing function provides randomness that provides more even distribution of data shards across data nodes (e.g., multiple server nodes). This parallelization increases read and write speeds. Storage of values is in binary large object (BLOB) format, which means there is no need for a database schema. Key-value stores are useful for quick and simple storage and lookups based on the keys. Values are written following atomic operation principles (a way of ensuring data consistency), so could take some time if "values" are substantial. The values in a key-value store could be simple numerical values, text, image files, or other. An example

Table 11   Key-Value Data
Store Example

Key	Value
C173DX	John Doe
CustID12345	Jane Doe
00001	Michael Doe

could be C173DX (hash key) and John Doe (key value), as shown in Table 11. Keys do not have to be hashed (e.g., randomized) and can be sequential (e.g., product IDs or customer IDs).

A graph data model makes it easier to query interconnected data with data nodes that may have many relationships (referred to as edges), and can also store directional data of edges. Edges are also used to describe the relationships between data nodes. Such relationships can help provide more holistic information about a potential customer, returning results such as tastes, activities, cities traveled to, other friends with similar tastes or hobbies, and so on. Such interconnection details could be useful in retail scenarios (e.g., recommending products or services that may be relevant to the prospect consumer). Another use case could be in crime scenarios (e.g., linking suspects, events, locations, etc.). Visualization of graph data with nodes and edges is more helpful to the human eye than tabular representation. For information visit the URL https://docs.microsoft.com/en-us/sql/relational-databases/graphs/sql-graph-sample.

The column family data store type groups relevant data into logical rows and columns and data does not have to be normalized. There can be multiple column families, and rows within such a column family do not have to contain data for each column, which can help with storage efficiencies. The concept of this data model type provides flexibility of schema design. The keys used to uniquely identify values are usually sequentially specified rather than hashed (randomized). For example, one column within a column family could be a CustomerID with a sequence such as C0001, C0002, C0003, and so forth. This CustomerID column could then be used to link multiple column families such as Names, Address, State, and so on. Figure 68 showcases a simple example of column families.

CustomerID	Column Family 1: Name
C001	First Name: John Last Name: Doe
C002	First Name: Jane Last Name: Doe
C003	First Name: Harry Last Name: Doe

CustomerID	Column Family 2: Address
C001	1, Acme Street, 27513
C002	2, Acme Street, 27513
C003	3, Acme Street, 27513

CustomerID	Column Family 3: State-Country
C001	State: North Carolina Country: U.S.
C002	State: North Carolina Country: U.S.
C003	State: North Carolina Country: U.S.

Figure 68   Column Family Data Model Example

A document data model type is conceptually similar to a key-value data store model, except that it can store multiple data fields and values (referred to as documents). JavaScript Object Notation (JSON) is a popular document store format, and it provides excellent flexibility, as data schemas can change within documents or from one document to another. JSON is supported by many database engines or reporting engines, making it easy to store, query, and report on data. Product databases or shipment orders are typical examples of document stores, as fields (schema) can be changed or added easily without complex data schema design and application (writing, querying) rewriting. Documents can store single or multiple data observations or records as showcased in Table 12.

Azure Cosmos DB provides a choice of five consistency levels for the organization to choose from to ensure its data consistency and latency needs are met. These five levels are:

1. Strong

2. Bounded staleness

3. Consistent-prefix

4. Session

5. Eventual

Strong consistency selection ensures ultimate data consistency but requires the most time, whereas eventual consistency provides

Table 12 Document Data Model Example

Key	Document 1	Document 2
Key	0001	0002

	```{```
	``` "CustomerID": C001,```
	``` "Orders": [```
	``` {"ProductID":P001,```
	``` "Quantity": 1,000```
	``` },```
	``` {"ProductID":P002,```
	``` "Quantity": 2,000```
	``` },```
	```]```
	``` "DateOfOrder":01/01/2017"```
	```}```
		```{```
		``` "CustomerID": C001,```
		``` "Orders":[```
		``` {"ProductID":P001,```
		``` "Quantity": 1,000```
		``` },```
		```]```
		``` "DateOfOrder":02/01/2017"```
		```}```

the lowest latency but data is only eventually consistent, so recent application/data queries of values may not immediately return the accurate data value. Organizations must select the correct type based on their applications that utilize this globally distributed database service. Financial transactions are an example where strong consistency is mandatory.

Azure Redis Cache

This managed cloud service is based on the open-source Redis cache engine and provides data caching capabilities for Azure-based cloud applications that an organization develops. This engine can be used as a database, cache, or message broker. The data model of Redis is an advanced key-value data store where values supported include hashes, strings, sorted sets, and sets. Lua scripting language is also supported, making migrations and open-source compatibility easier for organizations. There are three service tiers for this cloud service:

1. Basic
2. Standard
3. Premium

The basic option provides single node and multiple sizes, but there is no service-level agreement (SLA). This option is suitable for dev/test or noncritical workload types. With the standard option, organizations benefit from a high-availability SLA and a replicated cache over two nodes (primary and secondary failover nodes). Finally, the premium option provides organizations all the features of the standard option, as well as better performance (e.g., above 53 GB memory size), better disaster recovery, data cache persistence, and enhanced security through a Microsoft Azure Virtual Network (providing configuration options such as subnets and access control policies). The basic and standard options offer a cache size up to 53 GB in memory, whereas the premium cache can grow up to 530 GB (data sharding across multiple Azure Redis nodes).

Azure Database Migration Service

This is a process-led option for organizations themselves to migrate on-premises Microsoft SQL Server databases or Oracle databases to the Azure SQL Server database cloud service. Organizations will require a Microsoft Azure account and a direct connection (e.g., Azure ExpressRoute, or VPN) from their premises to the Azure cloud to start this process.

Data and Artificial Intelligence

To help organizations with data and Big Data challenges (e.g., data ingestion—hot and cold), data orchestration, data storage, analytics, and reporting, Microsoft and the Azure cloud platform provide the following data and artificial intelligence cloud services:

- Azure HDInsight
- Azure Stream Analytics
- Azure Bot Service
- Azure Data Lake Analytics
- Azure Data Lake Store (ADLS)
- Azure Data Factory
- Azure Power BI Embedded

- Azure Data Catalog
- Azure Log Analytics
- Azure Apache Spark for Azure Insight
- Azure Text Analytics API
- Azure Analysis Services
- Azure Custom Speech Service
- Azure Event Hubs
- Azure SQL Data Warehouse

Azure HDInsight

This is a fully managed cloud service for organizations to leverage open-source data and analytics platforms such as Hadoop, Spark, Hive, Kafka, Storm, and R (a favorite data science language and platform; Microsoft has a modified and more "performant" version of the community version of R). Organizations do not have to worry about setting up, configuring, or managing such platforms, which generally are time-consuming and complicated tasks. Azure HDInsight can be used for business needs such as data warehousing, machine learning, IoT, and many other areas. For some cost examples, visit the URL https://azure.microsoft.com/en-us/pricing/details/hdinsight. Some cloud services are not always available in all geographic regions that the Microsoft Azure cloud operates in (some services are rolled out to other regions over time, for example). For checking cloud service availability in different regions, visit the URL https://azure.microsoft.com/en-us/regions/services.

Azure Stream Analytics

This cloud service is designed for analyzing streaming data (hot data—fast-moving data) from devices such as sensors (e.g., IoT, IIoT), wearables, or other cloud services and data sources. Azure Stream Analytics is an event-processing engine helping organizations analyze streaming data in near real time, which can help with dashboard (business intelligence) reporting, with anomaly detection (e.g., data point above a reasonable range), or even with initiating other actions based on the analysis (e.g., send an alert). Organizations can develop complex event process (CEP) pipelines with an SQL-like language to implement temporal logic. Azure Stream Analytics integrates with the Azure IoT Hub and Azure Event Hubs cloud services. Integration with Azure IoT Edge makes it easier for the organization to leverage artificial intelligence off-line or on-premises and upload data to the Azure cloud when feasible. Business insights and actions can therefore occur much closer to an event. At the time of writing the service is available in 19 geographic regions that the Microsoft Azure cloud operates in. Organizations pay for only each process job (pricing units referred to as streaming units). With Azure Stream Analytics an organization could capture demand signals near real time from connected devices and take the corresponding action (e.g., increase or decrease product shipments from a distribution center to a retailer).

Azure Bot Service

The Azure Bot Service helps an organization to develop and publish intelligent bots for its applications or web interfaces. Customer interactions are with bots that respond more naturally. Some example uses are Facebook Messenger, Microsoft Skype, or Microsoft Teams. These Azure bots can leverage Azure cognitive services that can let the bot interpret information more like a human (e.g., sentiment analysis via text recognition, image, or audio recognition). The transport and logistics company UPS uses Azure, bots, and cognitive services to help provide more advanced customer service (https://customers.microsoft .com/en-us/story/ups).

Azure Data Lake Analytics

This cloud service is based on Apache YARN (standing for yet another resource negotiator), which provides a method for applications to access and process data on a Hadoop. Microsoft Azure has developed a unique language called U-SQL that lets organizations build SQL-like code with expressive features for accessing and querying data. Execution of U-SQL can scale horizontally (e.g., distributed across computer nodes) and access different data sources such as Azure SQL Databases or Azure SQL Data Warehouses. Organizations can also use other languages such as dot Net (.Net), Python, or R to perform parallel data transformations. Costing for this service is based on processing used per data job, and is based on a metric called an analytics unit (AU). This AU is a blend of CPU cores and memory. At the time of writing, one AU is equivalent to 2 CPU cores and 6 GB RAM. One AU costs $2 per hour in the central United States or €1.687 per hour in Northern Europe. As noted earlier, some cloud services are not (at least initially) available in all Azure geographic regions.

Azure Data Lake Store (ADLS)

This cloud service supports an organization's Big Data strategy by allowing it to store data of any type, at any size, and at any speed (the 3-Vs of Big Data). Azure provides enterprise-level security for storing, sharing, and collaborating with such data. Data can be ingested from connected devices (e.g., IoT), or from other sources, handling hot (fast-moving) or cold (slowly moving) data equally well. Azure Data Lake can be used alongside other cloud services such as Azure HDInsight (HDFS—Hadoop framework) and other Big Data platforms such as Hortonworks, Cloudera, or MapR. The Azure Data Lake scales with the demands of an organization and can handle streams (fast or slow) of data from many sources. Data types can be structured, semistructured, or unstructured, and a single file can be larger than one petabyte (1 petabyte = 1,000 terabytes). The cloud service is designed to support trillions of records, and an organization may need to store them in a data lake. Data in motion is encrypted via secure socket layer (SSL), and data at rest is encrypted via Azure Key Vault (an Azure cloud service for managing encryption keys) or a self-managed hardware security module (HSM). If an organization leverages the Azure Active Directory, then it can utilize security features such as:

- Single sign-on (SSO)
- Multifactor authentication
- POSIX-based access control lists (ACLs) providing granular role security controls

Microsoft Azure Data Lake Store offers a 99.9 percent service-level agreement (SLA) and 24/7 support for organizations. Specific Azure cloud services may not be available in all regions, as services are rolled out depending on Microsoft criteria (e.g., customer demand for service in geographic regions, data center capabilities, etc.). The Azure Data Lake service is not available in the Western European region, for example (as of December 2017).

Azure Data Factory

Azure Data Factory (ADF) is a managed cloud service providing a visual data work flow and data management (e.g., ETL) and orchestration interface that can also include actions (e.g., triggering other processes). Many data connectors are provided, enabling organizations to leverage data from multiple sources. Such data jobs (commonly referred to as data pipelines) can be scheduled and accept data from the cloud or on-premises. (See Figure 69.)

Azure Power BI Embedded

With this cloud service, an organization can embed visualizations into its applications without having to develop such functionality itself. Microsoft Power BI is a business intelligence (BI) application and service for visualization of data and reporting that can leverage data from many sources (e.g., SAP enterprise resource planning (ERP) systems, databases, flat files, Azure cloud services, or third-party data sources). Data can be cold (i.e., slow moving or static such as data residing in data warehouses) or hot (i.e., fast moving, such as results from streamed data). Streamed data is typically ingested and analyzed in near real time, stored in a data format or platform, and can then be consumed via a reporting and visualization interface such as Power BI. To use this Power BI Embedded service, an organization will have to be an Azure Active Directory (AAD or AD) tenant and have a paid Power BI Pro license. Power BI is a cloud service available in many Azure geographic regions.

Figure 69   Data Flow Example

Azure Data Catalog

This is a managed cloud service for cataloging data and for classifying and tagging metadata (i.e., information about the data) to data sources. Such a data catalog can help an organization understand the data it has stored in various locations, avoiding the Dark Lake phenomenon (Veritas 2016). Data is not moved, and information capturing can be manual or partially automated (partially as tagging and classification still require human knowledge and interaction). Connection details to data sources are stored with metadata, but controlled via access security. Such a cloud service and metadata cataloging could assist organizations with data governance and regulations such as the EU General Data Protection Regulation (GDPR; www.eugdpr.org).

Azure Log Analytics

Azure Log Analytics enables organizations to capture, understand, and even visualize log data such as application log files, event log files, or networking log files. Such analysis can help with troubleshooting events, failures, configuration changes, and more. Supported sources include Azure cloud and on-premises. IT dashboards can be customized to suit the needs of an organization, and be available via the web, tablets, or mobile devices. Azure Machine Learning (ML) is leveraged to power the intelligent analytics of this service. The Azure Log Analytics cloud service can integrate with other cloud services such as Azure Automation or Azure Functions to help IT staff receive data and react promptly.

Azure Apache Spark for Azure Insight

This cloud service is related and integrated with the Azure HDInsight service. Apache Spark is an open-source (Apache software foundation) framework that provides a common in-memory compute engine for processing and querying Big Data. This framework was designed for sizable parallel processing and querying, and integrates specialized packages such as Apache Spark SQL, Spark Streaming, Apache MLlib (machine learning), and Apache GraphX (graph computation). Organizations can leverage this service without having to worry about infrastructure management or configuration). Such analytics and querying can be used on cold and hot data (i.e., batch processing or real-time streaming). In this framework model, data is persisted in memory, providing fast query performance. As it is an open-source model, there is integration and support for IntelliJ IDEA (a Java integrated development environment), Scala, Java, Jupyter notebooks, and Python. This service also integrates with Microsoft R Server, a modified community version of R that provides parallelization, terabyte data size machine learning, and much higher performance gains compared to the unmodified community edition of R (https://azure .microsoft.com/en-gb/services/hdinsight/r-server). The Azure cloud service also supports integration with standard business intelligence reporting tools such as Microsoft Power BI, QlikView, SAP Business Objects Lumira, or Tableau.

Azure Text Analytics API

This service is part of the Azure Cognitive services portfolio and can be leveraged for sentiment analysis. An organization could use such data to gain an insight into product perception for example, and could then alter promotions, prices, marketing, and more to help safeguard demand for its products. Consumers are increasingly connected via social media platforms, and inertia via such followings can affect consumption of products. It is therefore becoming more important than ever to analyze such data, which can assist with an organization's goal of becoming more data-driven. Sentiments from the end consumers in the supply chain are important signals an organization should not ignore. Even if such data is not used initially, or if it is not found to be influencing enough (e.g., on-demand forecasts), it could still be included in data capture pipelines (digital supply chain) and analyzed when the time is right. Having historical data over more extended time periods available in the future will generally improve analytical results. Organizations can leverage such technologies as text and sentiment analytics from the Microsoft Azure Text Analytics cloud service for language detection, for extracting key phrases, and for sentiment analysis. To try an example, visit the URL https://azure.microsoft.com/en-us/ services/cognitive-services/text-analytics.

Azure Analysis Services

Azure Analysis Services is a platform as a service (PaaS) offering from Microsoft Azure cloud, and organizations can quickly deploy such an environment via the Azure web portal or Azure Resource Manager (ARM) and PowerShell (a dominant scripting language of Microsoft most commonly used for administrative and automation tasks). With Azure Analysis Services an organization can build a semantic business-focused data model (a logical design of the data using business-friendly labels, calculated metrics, and more). Conceptually it can be considered close to data virtualization, as data remains at the original locations while allowing business users and reports to include different data sources, formats, and mix and match data for the analytics required. These Analysis Services are built from the Microsoft SQL Server Analysis Services (SSAS) supporting Tabular Object Model (TOM) and Tabular Model Scripting Language (TMSL). Microsoft Visual Studio (including SQL Server Data Tools for Visual Studio) makes it easier to deploy Microsoft SQL Server 2016 Tabular Models to the Azure cloud.

There are two compatibility modes, namely 1400 and 1200. Compatibility 1400 is currently the latest version and represents features compatible with Microsoft SQL Server 2017 Analysis Services. There are three service tiers an organization can choose from:

1. Developer
2. Basic
3. Standard

It is possible to upgrade computational resources within a tier or upgrade to a higher tier, but downgrades from an upper tier to a lower tier are currently not permitted. Costing is based on a metric called a query processing unit (QPU) representing relative computational and data processing performance, and depends on the underlying virtual server instance selected. A general rule of thumb is that one virtual core equates to 25 QPUs. In the United States, a B1 basic tier selection would provide 40 QPUs with 10 GB of memory at a price of $0.43 per hour, or €0.363 per hour in the Western Europe Azure geographic region. As noted earlier, some Azure cloud service is not available in all regions.

For more information visit the URL https://azure.microsoft.com/en-gb/pricing/details/analysis-services/. Organizations can perform data exploration with common tools of their choice, including Microsoft Excel, Microsoft Power BI, or Tableau.

Azure Custom Speech Service

The Azure Custom Speech cloud service is part of the Azure Cognitive services portfolio and can be leveraged by organizations to help solve speech recognition challenges such as speaking styles, or background noise in the audio.

Azure Event Hubs

Microsoft Azure Event Hubs is also a cloud-based data ingestion service that focuses on hot data. It enables organizations to stream in data and log millions of events per second in near real time. A key use case is that of telemetry data (e.g., IoT devices). It is a cloud-managed service, meaning an organization does not have to worry about development, deployment, maintenance, and the like. Azure Event Hubs can be integrated with other cloud services, such as Azure Stream Analytics. The Azure Event Hub service focuses on the near real-time analysis of the hot data being streamed into the cloud, and it can help with rapidly automated decision-making processes (e.g., anomaly detection). Services like this could be used to help with industry 4.0 solutions, digitalizing a supply chain more, receiving near real-time location data of network nodes in a supply chain, or ingesting demand signals from connected devices such as soda streaming machines or point of sale (POS) scanners at retailers. For more information visit the URL https://azure.microsoft.com/en-us/pricing/details/event-hubs.

Azure SQL Data Warehouse

Azure SQL Data Warehouse is a specialized cloud service that provides an enterprise-level elastic data warehouse that scales with an organization's needs in the cloud or on-premises (organization's data center). The data warehouse is built on massive parallel processing (MPP) architecture design and is built on the powerful SQL engine of Microsoft SQL Server. This warehouse dynamically scales up or down to meet data and reporting requirements. The Azure SQL data warehouse integrates with other Azure services such as Azure Data Factory, Azure HDInsight (Hadoop framework for Big Data), Azure Machine Learning, or Microsoft Power BI (business intelligence visualization and reporting).

Artificial Intelligence and Cognitive Services

The world is creating digital assets at an exponential rate, highlighted in the Cisco Global Cloud Index where it is estimated that 850 ZBs of data (from people or machines) would be generated by the year 2021 (Cisco Global Cloud Index 2016–2021, 23). Utilizing, understanding, and identifying such vast amounts of data and formats present a challenge. As Microsoft has different business areas and services in various industries, such as office productivity, computer gaming, audiovisual communication, and a search engine, it can leverage such technologies, research, and experience in its Azure Machine Learning and Azure Cognitive Services. There are far too many functional and technology areas in this category of the Azure portfolio to go into details of each one of them, so this section aims to highlight the different types available.

In general, this category of services focuses on machine learning (ML), artificial intelligence (AI), speech, audio and visual intelligence, search engine technologies (leveraging the research and experience of Microsoft Bing—a search engine similar to the popular search engine called Google), and a new and exciting area called Genomics. Microsoft invests a lot of resources (i.e., monies, people, time) into research for improving human life via services such as Microsoft Genomics. A lot of software (i.e., code, programs) is shared back with the research community as open-source software, and prices of leveraged cloud services are comparatively low.

The Azure AI and Cognitive Services include the following:

- Azure Machine Learning Services
- Azure Machine Learning Studio
- Azure Bot Service

- Azure Cognitive Services
  - Computer Vision API
  - Face API
  - Content Moderator
  - Emotion API
  - Custom Vision Service
  - Video Indexer
  - Translator Speech API
  - Speaker Recognition API
  - Bing Speech API
  - Custom Speech Service
  - Language Understanding (LUIS)
  - Text Analytics API
  - Bing Spell Check API
  - Translator Text API
  - Web Language Model API
  - Linguistic Analysis API
  - Recommendations API
  - Academic Knowledge API
  - Knowledge Exploration Service
  - QnA Maker API
  - Entity Linking Intelligence Service API
  - Custom Decision Service
  - Bing Autosuggest API
  - Bing Image Search API
  - Bing News Search API
  - Bing Video Search API
  - Bing Web Search API
  - Bing Custom Search API
  - Bing Entity Search API
- Azure Batch Artificial Intelligence (AI)
- Microsoft Genomics

Image recognition could help identify objects such as cars and number plates, and such technologies are already in use in many carparks. It could also be possible to use such technologies in smart factories and manufacturing scenarios. Face recognition is commonly used in crime fighting scenarios, could be used in missing person situations, or could merely be used to speed up and automate recognition and tagging (metadata tagging—adding information about images), which can then later be used for classification and searching. For more information, visit the URL https://azure.microsoft.com/en-us/services/cognitive-services/face.

Similar technologies are used in photographic cameras, for example (usually referred to as face recognition or smile detection features). Devices are using such technologies to add additional security for verification of a person (e.g., Microsoft Window laptops with the "Hello" feature or the iPhone X). Speech recognition is increasingly being used in telephone banking, search engines (e.g., Siri, Google), or home automation products, and could also be leveraged in other devices or work flows such as manufacturing, or in the use of speech to direct a business intelligence reporting tool to create a specific report (e.g., "Show me next month's sales forecasts").

Point of sale (POS) scanners are becoming more intelligent by identifying products visually instead of by QR or bar codes, making the customer experience more comfortable. Quality assurance could be enhanced by visually verifying possible defects of parts in a supply chain or manufacturing process.

Recommendations API services could be used by online retailers to help shape demand by understanding the historical purchase history of a consumer and linking products of possible interest into a personalized recommendation. This could be a near real-time promotion and marketing or price promotion to help drive sales. An organization could become more demand and data driven using historical data, understanding influencing factors (e.g., price sensitivity, events, weather) through demand-driven forecasting, AI and ML, and taking appropriate actions (e.g., making tailored recommendations or a promotion). Organizations could interrelate inventory data—for example, viewing inventory levels and trying to reduce stock by understanding causal factors with the help of demand-driven forecasting and digitalization of the supply chain and data availability (e.g., Big Data, historical data, data of various variables).

Internet of Things (IoT)

The Internet of Things (IoT) and Industrial Internet of Things (IIoT) are global phenomena that will continue to grow exponentially, generating hot (fast-moving) and vast amounts of data that organizations need to capture, analyze, and act upon. Many industries could benefit from these types of technologies, from connectivity, and from near real-time data. Connected medical devices could help improve patient care with data insights and aid telemedicine or telehealth. Of doctors surveyed, 85 percent reported that connected wearables are assisting patients to engage more with their health (Safavi and Ratliff 2015). Retail industries, for example, could receive data in near real time or much shorter time windows to sense demand signals and amend demand-driven forecasts if required.

Supply could be matched better to demand in a demand-driven supply chain using a pull design of a digitalized or digitally aware and data-aware supply chain and supply network. Data could be combined to provide a holistic overview, and organizations could leverage analytics (including Big Data, AI, ML, etc.) for demand forecasting, inventory optimization and replenishment, and collaboration (i.e., internal and with external supply chain network nodes and partners) to form more data-driven decisions and improve resource planning. GE refers to such IoT data integration with insights and actions within its smart manufacturing process as an "Industrial Internet Data Loop"—see Figure 70 (Evans and Annunziata 2012, 10). GE research estimates that 46 percent of the global economy or US$32.3 trillion of global output could benefit from IoT and IIoT (Evans and Annunziata 2012, 14).

To help organizations with such challenges, the Microsoft Azure cloud platform provides the following services:

- Azure IoT Hub
- Azure IoT Edge
- Azure Stream Analytics
- Azure Machine Learning Studio

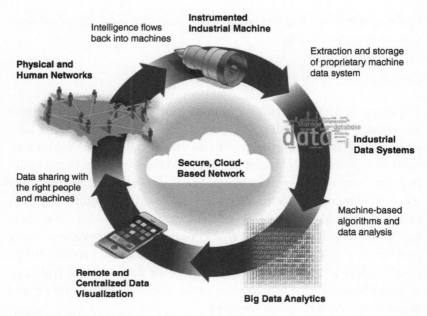

Figure 70   Industrial Internet Data Loop
Source: Evans and Annunziata (2012, 10).

- Azure Time Series Insights
- Azure Cosmos DB
- Azure Event Grid
- Azure Logic Apps
- Azure Notification Hubs
- Azure Event Hubs
- Azure Location-Based Services

Azure IoT Hub

This cloud service makes it easier for organizations to connect, control, and monitor IoT devices emitting telemetry data continually or intermittently. Bidirectional communication is also possible with connected devices and the Azure cloud. Organizations like ThyssenKrupp and Rockwell Automation are leveraging this cloud service (https://azure.microsoft.com/en-us/services/iot-hub).

Azure IoT Edge

This is similar to the Azure IoT Hub in that it aims to capture telemetry data and enable data upload and device management in the cloud. The key additional feature or unique selling point (USP) is that it allows intelligence and analytics at the "edge of the cloud"—at the connected devices level instead of having to wait until data arrives in the cloud to be processed and analyzed. This provides faster actions and is ideal for areas where connectivity is intermittent (off-line by design or due to weak connection areas). Smart factories can benefit from such technologies; for example, machine health could be monitored and predicted (i.e., predictive maintenance) faster and on-premises. Connected devices in a digital supply chain network could upload data in batches to the cloud instead of in constant streams. Sometimes continuous streaming of telemetry data is not possible due to the volume and cost involved (e.g., airplanes), or there could be situations where such data should be analyzed on-premises for speed, data protection (i.e., not allowed in a public cloud), or safety reasons.

Azure Stream Analytics

This cloud service is designed for analyzing streaming data (hot data—fast-moving data) from devices such as sensors (e.g., IoT, IIoT), wearables, or other cloud services and data sources. Azure Stream Analytics is an event processing engine helping organizations analyze streaming data in near real time, which can help with dashboard (business intelligence) reporting, with anomaly detection (e.g., data point above a normal range), or even with initiating other actions based on the analysis (e.g., send an alert). Organizations can develop complex event process (CEP) pipelines with an SQL-like language to implement temporal logic. Azure Stream Analytics integrates with the Azure IoT Hub and Azure Event Hubs cloud services. Integration with Azure IoT Edge makes it easier for the organization to leverage artificial intelligence off-line or on-premises and upload data to the Azure cloud when feasible. At the time of writing, the service is available in 19 geographic regions that the Microsoft Azure cloud operates in. With Azure Stream Analytics an organization could capture demand signals near real time from connected devices and take the corresponding action (e.g., increase or decrease product shipments from a distribution center to a retailer).

Azure Machine Learning Studio

Azure Machine Learning (ML) Studio is a web browser–based user interface (studio) providing a visual and drag-and-drop user experience for data scientists of all levels. Popular packages of data science platforms such as R and Python are included, making it easy to leverage this cloud-based scalable and "performant" platform. The Azure ML Studio can be leveraged to solve all types of data challenges and thereby benefit organizations across many different industries. For more information, visit the URL https://azure.microsoft.com/en-us/services/machine-learning-studio.

Azure Time Series Insights

This is a managed cloud service delivering storage, analytics, and visualization of time series data. It is designed explicitly for IoT time-series data (millions or billions of events) and stores up to 400 days of historical data.

Azure Cosmos DB

Azure Cosmos DB is a managed cloud-based NoSQL database that specializes in storing unrelational data (e.g., data without a schema, without a predefined structure). This type of database works well with time-series data (Dunning and Friedmann, 2014) and the interplay with IoT data (fast moving and globally distributed). Data and compute can scale with Cosmos DB, providing very low latency and high availability across many Azure regions. Refer to the Azure databases section of this chapter for more details of the Cosmos DB.

Azure Event Grid

Organizations can leverage this cloud service to develop event-driven applications, serverless applications (organizations do not have to manage or set up back-end infrastructure for serverless cloud services), and triggering logic based on events from various sources. This way applications can listen instead of polling other services and can trigger actions and functions based on events.

Azure Logic Apps

The Azure Logic Apps service helps organizations build application logic via a visual work flow interface. Microsoft Azure cloud provides ready-to-use connectors for accessing systems such as Microsoft Office 365, Salesforce (SFDC), Google services, and more. Support for electronic data interchange (EDI) means organizations can more easily exchange data via standards such as EDIFACT, X12, and AS2, aiding business operations.

Azure Notification Hubs

This cloud service provides push notification services that can scale to suit organizational needs, and supports sending millions of messages. Organizations can use this service to send push notifications to applications across popular platforms such as iOS, Android, Kindle, and Microsoft Windows. Supported push notification services include Apple Push Notification (APN), Google Cloud Messaging (GCM), Windows Push Notification Service (WNS), and Microsoft Push Notification Service (MPNS). Back-end systems that integrate with Azure Notification Hubs (i.e., generating content of the message) can use dot Net (.Net), Java, Node.js, or PHP, and the back-end systems can be cloud or on-premises.

Azure Event Hubs

Microsoft Azure Event Hubs is also a cloud-based data ingestion service that focuses on hot data. It enables organizations to stream in data and log millions of events per second in near real time. A key use case is that of telemetry data (e.g., IoT devices). It is a cloud-managed service, meaning an organization does not have to worry about development, deployment, maintenance, and the like. Azure Event Hubs can be integrated with other cloud services, such as Azure Stream Analytics. Services like this could be used to help with industry 4.0 solutions, for digitalizing a supply chain more, for receiving near real-time location data of network nodes in a supply chain, or for ingesting demand signals from connected devices such as soda streaming machines or point of sale (POS) scanners at retailers.

Azure Location-Based Services

This is a service providing location APIs for geospatial data mapping. Organizations can use such APIs to develop a location-aware application on the Azure platform—for example, integrating maps or searching based on the current locale of the consumer.

Enterprise Integration

There are several components and related cloud services that can help organizations integrate enterprise-level applications and work flows (application and data work flows). The cloud services in this category include:

- Azure Logic Apps
- Azure Service Bus
- Azure API Management
- Azure StorSimple
- Azure SQL Server Stretch Database
- Azure Data Catalog
- Azure Data Factory
- Azure Event Grid

Azure Logic Apps

The Azure Logic Apps service helps organizations build application logic via a visual work flow interface. Microsoft Azure cloud provides ready-to-use connectors for accessing systems such as Microsoft Office 365, Salesforce (SFDC), Google services, and more.

Azure Service Bus

This type of cloud-managed service bus, also referred to as messaging as a service (MaaS), enables message exchange between applications.

It is the intermediary messaging infrastructure providing greater scalability and performance by decoupling messaging from applications, and allowing application architecture design to use one service bus component — the Azure Service Bus. Organizations can leverage this cloud service for first-in, first-out (FIFO), brokered client-server messaging and publish/subscribe to usage scenarios.

Azure API Management

The Azure API Management service helps organizations to securely and efficiently publish and manage APIs to in-house developers or external partners. Using API Gateways helps with standardization, maintenance, or changes as developers focus on a universal gateway instead of multiple individual connectors between software components. Management capabilities support REST API, PowerShell, and Git.

Azure StorSimple

Azure StorSimple can be used to automatically archive inactive data to the cloud, and help organizations with backup and disaster recovery challenges and needs. Software policies are used for data archiving and retrieval instead of traditional forms such as tape backups and tape rotation schedules.

Azure SQL Server Stretch Database

This service enables organizations to dynamically stretch both slow and fast moving transactional data (i.e., cold and hot data, respectively) from on-premises MS SQL Server databases (e.g., SQL Server 2016) to Microsoft Azure. Refer to the Azure databases section earlier in this chapter for more details.

Azure Data Catalog

This is a managed cloud service for cataloging data and for classifying and tagging metadata (i.e., information about the data) to data sources. Refer to the Azure data and AI sections earlier in this chapter for more details.

Azure Data Factory

Azure Data Factory (ADF) is a managed cloud service providing a visual data work flow and data management (e.g., ETL) and orchestration interface that can also include actions (e.g., triggering other processes). Many data connectors are provided, enabling organizations to leverage data from multiple sources. Such data jobs (commonly referred to as data pipelines) can be scheduled and accept data from the cloud or on-premises.

Azure Event Grid

This cloud service can be used to develop event-driven applications, serverless applications (organizations do not have to manage or set up back-end infrastructure for serverless cloud services), and triggering logic based on events from various sources. This way applications can listen instead of polling other services and can trigger actions and functions based on events.

Security and Identity Management

Security and identity and access management are vital to all organizations across industries and the world. To help with security and identity management challenges that are amplified by diverse systems and large and distributed global user bases, the Microsoft Azure cloud makes the following services available to organizations:

- Azure Security Center
- Azure Key Vault
- Azure Active Directory (often referred to as Azure AD or AAD)
- Azure Active Directory B2C
- Azure Active Directory Domain Services
- Azure Multi-Factor Authentication

Azure Security Center

Azure Security Center provides a unified security concept across on-premises and cloud workloads. Security policies and access control can be applied to applications on-premises and in the Azure cloud, and the service includes the automated discovery of cloud resources (e.g., new virtual servers deployed by an organization). Anomaly detection and machine learning are leveraged to identify cyber attacks.

Azure Key Vault

With this cloud service, organizations can securely store keys for hardware security modules (HSMs). Cryptographic keys and passwords can be stored in the Azure Key Vault that has been certified with FIPS 140-2 level 2 and Common Criteria EAL4+ security standards. Microsoft itself (the cloud provider in this case) cannot see or use an organization's security keys stored in Azure Key Vault. Azure Key Vault makes it possible to centralize key management in the public cloud.

Azure Active Directory

Azure Active Directory (often referred to as Azure AD or AAD) is an extensive identity and access control management solution that extends far beyond the traditional Microsoft Windows environment. The service supports multiple sources of identities and supports many devices and single sign-on. An organization can use one identity and access management solution for cloud and on-premises use cases. There are three editions from which organizations can choose:

1. Free
2. Basic
3. Premium

The cloud service supports multifactor authentication (i.e., requiring two devices for authentication or verifying an identity to increase security) with software as a service (SaaS) and integrates with Salesforce (SFDC), Microsoft Office 365, Box, Citrix, MyDay, and other services (Microsoft or third party). The service includes security monitoring and alerting, and leverages machine learning to detect anomalies in access (e.g., location or times). Organizations can also integrate on-premises Microsoft Active Directory with Azure Active Directory, providing a hybrid and synchronized solution for enterprises. Supported protocols and access methods include the following:

- Security Assertion Markup Language 2.0 (SAML 2.0)
- WS-Federation

- OpenID
- O-Auth 2.0

Azure Active Directory B2C

This cloud service is designed to enable organizations to add authentication mechanisms to their consumer-facing applications (business to consumer). Open standards, social accounts (e.g., Facebook, Google+, LinkedIn) and emails are supported, as are platforms such as iOS and Android. Supported protocols include OpenID Connect, SAML, and OAuth 2.0. Since this is a cloud service, organizations can scale resources to support hundreds of millions of end customers of applications.

Azure Active Directory Domain Services

With this service, an organization should find it easier to migrate on-premises applications (from an identity management point of view) to the cloud as it can leverage managed domain services and underlying technologies of Windows Server Active Directory. Computer resources typically managed by on-premises domain controllers can be managed by Azure Active Directory Domain Services - providing a domain controller as a service.

Azure Multi-Factor Authentication

Multifactor authentication is a process of using at least two forms of authentication or identity verification to increase security. This could be used for authentication to enterprise resources such as computers, applications, or mobile devices. Industries such as banking commonly use such mechanisms to verify remote users for online banking log-ins. For example, the first authentication step could be knowing user ID and password to log into an online banking portal. The second authentication step could then be through a smartphone with an application that generates single random-use authentication codes or receives a one-time passcode (OTP) via an SMS message sent by the banking institution. Such an example is also referred to as a two-pass authentication process (two steps involved), whereas the use of two different authentication formats (e.g., user ID and password combination, and another code received on a separate device) typically defines a multi-factor mechanism.

This solution can be deployed on-premises or in the Azure cloud, and supports other technologies such as VPN, Radius, and LDAP. Azure Machine Learning (ML) is leveraged to detect unusual behaviors (e.g., location, times, or multiple attempts). Organizations can use a Software Development Kit (SDK) to add such strong security for authentication in their applications, safeguarding access to applications, resources, and information.

Developer Tools

The Azure cloud platform provides several cloud-based applications to help organizations with the development of applications, collaboration, work flow, and life cycle management of software applications. The following services are available:

- Microsoft Visual Studio Team Services
- Microsoft Visual Studio App Center
- Azure DevTest Labs
- Azure Application Insights
- Azure API Management
- Azure HockeyApp

Microsoft Visual Studio Team Services

This service is charged separately from Microsoft Azure services and is aimed at collaborative application development, including centrally hosting and managing software code. Organizations can develop in the software language of their choice. Visual Studio is an integrated development environment (IDE), and organizations can also utilize favorite tools such as Eclipse and others.

Microsoft Visual Studio App Center

This development environment makes it easier for organizations to develop applications for iOS, Android, macOS, and Windows. Being located in the cloud, it can help monitor worldwide usage of an application.

Azure DevTest Labs

Organizations can use this service to create standardized (i.e., template-driven) environments for Windows and Linux in which to test their software applications. Organizations can define quotas and policies for their development staff and automate the shutting down of such environments to help save costs.

Azure Application Insights

This service can be used to identify possible problems with an organization's web applications. Application monitoring can help detect possible performance or scalability issues, and the service integrates with DevOps, Microsoft Visual Studio Teams Services, and GitHub tools and work flows. Visually engaging and interactive dashboards help organizations more easily detect trends, events, and possible issues. Machine learning is leveraged to identify outliers in the data (data about the applications being monitored). Monitoring of applications is possible regardless of the software development language used (e.g., Java, Python, Node.js, .Net).

Azure API Management

The Azure API Management service helps organizations to securely and efficiently publish and manage APIs to in-house developers or external partners. Using API Gateways helps with standardization, maintenance, or changes as developers focus on a common gateway instead of multiple individual connectors between software components. Management capabilities support REST API, PowerShell, and Git.

Azure HockeyApp

The Azure HockeyApp helps organizations beta test applications by making it easier to distribute beta versions and collect log files (e.g., application crash or performance data). Applications could be developed in Android, iOS, macOS, Windows, and Xamarin.

Management and Monitoring

The final category of the Azure cloud platform (at the time of writing) provides several services to help organizations with understanding the use of the cloud (e.g., costs, usage, health of IT services); improving automation; helping with governance, compliance, and security; or just making the use of the cloud easier. The following services are available:

- Azure Advisor
- Microsoft Azure Portal
- Azure Mobile app
- Azure Resource Manager
- Azure Application Insights
- Azure Log Analytics
- Azure Automation
- Azure Backup
- Azure Site Recovery
- Azure Scheduler
- Azure Traffic Manager
- Azure Monitor
- Azure Security & Compliance
- Azure Protection and Recovery
- Azure Automation and Control
- Azure Insight and Analytics
- Azure Network Watcher
- Azure Cloud Shell
- Azure Service Health
- Azure Cost Management
- Azure Policy
- Azure Managed Applications
- Azure Migrate

There are too many functional areas in this category of the Azure portfolio to go into details of each one of them, so this section aims to highlight the different types available and showcase some examples instead. In general terms, these services aim to help an organization monitor costs, assist with chargeback goals (e.g., to various departments or projects), highlight performance and resource health, automate tasks, and provide possible improvements (e.g., Azure Advisor). Improvement suggestions within the Azure Portal (e.g., improve high availability or increase service tier of a service or virtual server) make it easier for organizations to use the cloud effectively, efficiently, and economically. The Azure portal is a simple dashboard interface. Administrators or cloud users can create customized dashboards to suit their needs and work flows. Icons on the left of the dashboard (vertical strip of icons) provide quick links to cloud resources. The top right noticeboard pane offers notifications, search, or quick controls. A dashboard can have several widgets "pinned" to it, such as "Quickstart Tutorials," "Service Health," or the status of virtual servers (i.e., Test VM is stopped in this current example).

EXAMPLE: DEMAND FORECASTING WITH AZURE CLOUD

EXAMPLE

URL: https://gallery.azure.ai/Solution/Demand-Forecasting-for-Shipping-and-Distribution-2

Microsoft provides business solution examples that are bundled into templates to make it easier to deploy them to the Azure cloud and try them. Such templates offer automation and are very easy and quick to implement. There is a simple web-wizard interface for providing some initial information, and the actual deployment and configuration of cloud resources (e.g., virtual servers, databases, web services) and components required for such solution templates are entirely automated. Azure Functions are leveraged for automating tasks such as setting up an Azure SQL database or setting up Azure Blob Storage. The example used in this case relates to demand forecasting and showcases how different cloud services and components can work together to solve business challenges. The information provided in this example is for illustration purposes and uses simple sample data to highlight possibilities. The URL provided earlier includes more details for deploying and following this example. It should generally take about 30 to 60 minutes to complete such a test example (includes reading, possible customizations, automated deployment, and waiting some time for simulated data to populate the data model), and estimated daily costs are about $5. To avoid unnecessary costs, such deployments should be deleted once no longer required. This example solution leverages several cloud services of Azure such as:

- Azure Data Factory
- Azure SQL Server
- Azure Blob Storage
- Azure Machine Learning (ML)
- Microsoft Power BI

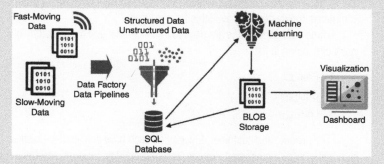

Figure 71 Microsoft Demand Forecasting Example

Azure Data Factory is leveraged to orchestrate the data flow between components and cloud services. The Machine Learning service executes R forecasting code. Azure Blob Storage is used to store temporary forecast results before such data is loaded into the Azure SQL database used in this example. Azure SQL Server is leveraged to store historical data (e.g., orders) and forecast parameters. Both of these database tables are referred to as input tables. Forecast parameters in this example define the statistical forecast models used (e.g., exponential smoothing, ARIMA), the historical period for inclusion in the forecast (e.g., representative sample period), the forecast horizon (future forecast period, e.g., next month), and forecasting techniques used (e.g., bottom-up). Time series are grouped by dimensions and hierarchies used to produce forecasts for demand planning, such as demand planning at a product category level, a location, or a retailer level.

The Azure SQL Database is also used to store two output tables for permanently storing forecast results (e.g., forecasts of products over future time horizon, and grouped forecasts for different dimensions such as product, customer, and location), as well as forecast history metadata such as the forecast models used and forecast accuracy metrics (e.g., mean absolute percentage error [MAPE], mean absolute scaled error [MASE]). Finally, to visually represent such data, Microsoft Power BI (a visualization and business intelligence reporting solution—web, desktop, mobile) is leveraged in this deployment example, and visualizations are already prebuilt (although requiring some wait time of approximately 20 to 30 minutes to allow data to be simulated, forecasted, and available for reporting).

Three data dimensions are used in this example, and the hierarchy of each dimension is flat:

1. Product
2. Customer
3. Location

The product and customer dimensions each have two values: plastics and metal, and Contoso and Protoso, respectively. The location dimension has three values of China, India, and the United States.

Overall, this sample deployment provides an excellent example of what is possible in the era of cloud computing, advanced analytics, Big Data, IoT, and more. Data ingested (hot and cold) and used could be from multiple sources such as on-premises, in the cloud, or telemetry data. Information and, more importantly, business insights and demand signals could be available to an organization in a more timely fashion. Organizations can store and possibly use various data (e.g., Big Data philosophy) at any time. The use of advanced analytics can help identify possible influencing factors on demand forecasts, spot trends, or produce forecasts for products that have no historical data (e.g., using surrogate data and advanced analytics for new product forecasting). Cloud computing and related technologies can especially help provide data ingestion and storage options, and provide scalable and elastic compute resources that an organization may require for demand forecasting. Such scalability can be very relevant when demand forecasts use large volumes of data and advanced analytics. Advanced analytics is used to produce demand-driven forecasts with assessment of multiple causal factors, automatically applying different statistical forecast models to different time series in a product hierarchy, or identifying surrogate products (like products) with historical data whose time-series data can be used as inputs into new product forecasts that have no past data but may have similar product traits.

■ ■ ■

In summary, selecting either AWS or Microsoft Azure as a provider of a public cloud platform is a good option. These are currently (at the time of writing) the top two global public cloud vendors. Both vendors provide extensive cloud services and are continually expanding their portfolios, adding new features to existing portfolios, integrating a marketplace into their platforms, and building partnerships with system integrators and consulting firms to help organizations select, implement, manage, and operate cloud and related solutions. The depth of a cloud service offering or partner solutions may further influence the choice of vendor in the selection process. Costs, security, and meeting local and regulatory requirements are other influencing factors for an organization choosing between local public cloud and global public cloud vendors.

CHAPTER **5**

Case Studies of Demand-Driven Forecasting in AWS

The focus of this chapter is on two real-world case studies of two organizations requiring an advanced demand-driven supply chain solution (i.e., forecasting, collaborative demand planning, and inventory optimization) that would run in the cloud. Some details are deliberately vague or excluded to protect the organizations involved. Other information such as architecture designs or performance examples are generally mentioned, but should not be seen as representative practices or results, as each organization will have different needs, budgets, and time. Nevertheless, there are several principles that can be adopted as best practices by other organizations.

CASE STUDY 1: NEWS AND MEDIA COMPANY

This first case focuses on a news and media company. The enterprise produces printed news content such as newspapers, magazines, and newspaper supplements (e.g., special small brochures or leaflets). It has many retail outlets that it ships its products to. Product surplus is expensive (i.e., production, distribution), as is having too much stock at the wrong location and not enough stock at another location (leading to lost sales). The primary business challenge for this organization was to enhance its forecasting process. There was a need for improvement in forecast accuracy across three dimensions (product, outlet, and location) and within the hierarchy of each dimension.

Forecast results needed to be available much faster than was possible with the current solution and work flow. Forecasts could take a day or more to complete with the current software solution and process. The forecast results would then feed into a demand-planning process and consequently into inventory optimization and resource planning. News cycles are becoming shorter, so an organization operating in such an industry might need to forecast multiple times a day, week, or month, depending on its forecast view and process. The shorter the time period for producing forecasts, the better, as it provides more agility and flexibility for organizations (e.g., new forecast based on new data, or new forecast based on new statistical models). Improvements in forecast accuracy were estimated to have a substantial impact on costs of production, distribution, and inventory.

The organization in the context of this case study posed three main challenges for a business solution specializing in demand forecasting. The first challenge was that the solution should be able to improve forecast accuracy across three data dimensions (product, outlet, and location) and time series that match any grouping and combination of these three dimensions. For example, a demand planner may wish to see forecasts for the products he or she is responsible for. Another demand planner may want to look at the forecasts grouped by location (e.g., territory or regional manager). The business solution should therefore be able to sort data and time series and generate forecasts accordingly with minimal human effort. An advanced business solution for demand-driven forecasting should also be able to apply multiple statistical forecast models (should have a large model repository) across different time series and across a hierarchy automatically, selecting the most suitable models with minimal human intervention.

As data is fed into a demand signal repository (DSR), the business solution should be able to identify influencing and causal factors of demand. For example, specific events, marketing promotions, historical milestones, calendar seasons, income levels in geographic regions, demographics, and more may influence or shape demand. An advanced forecasting solution should also be able to apply top-down, bottom-up, or middle-out forecasting techniques. A demand planner should also require minimal effort to be able to select the time horizon of the forecasts (e.g., daily, weekly, or monthly) in an ad hoc or automated manner.

An advanced forecasting solution should also be able to generate forecasts for new products that do not have any historical data. Advanced analytics would be applied to such scenarios, identifying surrogate products (like products or similar products) that possess traits similar to those of the new product. Classification and clustering techniques could help select possible time series, causal factors, and statistical models, and apply these to forecasts of the new products to be launched. Forecast confidence levels and performance metrics (e.g., mean absolute percentage error [MAPE], mean absolute deviation [MAD]) should be available to the forecasting personas of the organization to help with the forecasting and demand planning process.

To help with the demand planning process of the organization, statistical (system-generated) forecasts should be fed into a demand planning work flow, which could be another system or integrated workbench. Demand planners should be able to review system-generated forecasts and human forecasts side by side and override demand forecasts where required. A demand planner may have certain experience or knowledge about specific events (not available to the forecasting system and data) that could influence demand, in which case overrides would be plausible. These were just some of the key requirements of an advanced forecasting solution that the organization in this example required.

The second challenge for a forecasting and supply chain business solution was providing adequate performance for completing the tasks of the advanced forecasting (refer to examples of the first challenge). This was defined as having forecast results available within one or two hours, therefore enhancing the organization's forecasting and demand planning process. The solution should be able to handle large volumes of data (e.g., a large amount of order history data and a high number of time series), possibly with complex data models (e.g., depth of the hierarchy, or multiple causal or influencing factors — independent variables). The organization has different products for which it requires different forecasting cycles (e.g., daily, weekly, or monthly). Forecasts must be completed within the time required for each type of product and forecast cycle. The information technology (IT) architecture design should be able to support the computing and storage requirements of the solution. This could mean appropriate vertical (i.e., CPUs, memory—RAM) or horizontal scaling of servers to support the workloads. Performance sizing should allow for planned growth and unexpected workloads. Storage sizing should support a growing demand signal repository (DSR) with all relevant data, staging areas, and final record sets.

The third challenge posed by the organization in this example was that a new forecasting and supply chain optimization solution should run in the cloud. The organization's IT strategy involved moving to a public cloud. This would help save costs (e.g., data center costs), provide more agility, and assist with flexibility (e.g., provisioning infrastructure or leveraging expansion of storage when required). The organization leveraged infrastructure as a service (IaaS), platform as a service (PaaS), and software as a service (SaaS), and a new forecasting solution should comply with one of these cloud service models. AWS was the public cloud vendor chosen by the organization, and assessment criteria included:

- Recognized as a leader in global public cloud services
- Cloud being the primary business (at least of the AWS division of Amazon)
- Local and global presence
- Affordable costs
- Good engagement and strategic partnership interest with the organization

A new demand forecasting and supply chain optimization solution should therefore be able to run in the Amazon cloud (AWS). The cloud service model itself (i.e., IaaS, PaaS, and SaaS) was not as relevant as the advanced forecasting functionality, analytics, and domain expertise. Therefore, as long as these requirements were met, the organization could select IaaS. The architecture design (e.g., single-tier, multitier) should provide the performance required, and there should be two environments to support dev/test and production workloads and tasks.

The challenges of this project were divided into four phases (see Figure 72):

1. Functional and advanced analytics assessment for meeting advanced forecasting needs
2. Test and verification of whether a solution can run on the Amazon cloud (IaaS)
3. A performance test to satisfy concerns
4. Assistance with organization's business case and assessment of software vendor

The team of the software vendor engaged throughout this project was confident that the business solution for demand-driven forecasting and supply chain optimization (a suite that supports demand forecasting, collaborative demand planning, inventory

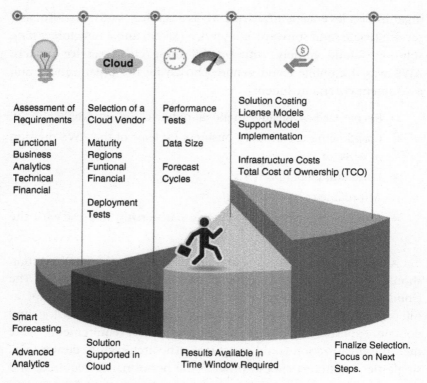

Figure 72 Example Methodology—Solution Assessment for Cloud

optimization and replenishment, and visual analytics) would meet all the success criteria required. The software vendor had over 40 years of experience in advanced analytics, and its forecasting and supply chain optimization solution suite leveraged such technologies (e.g., advanced analytics, machine learning, high-performance forecasting, in-memory analytics, operations research, etc.). The solution included a purpose-built demand signal repository, data integration (e.g., studio interface to extract, transform, and load data), and business and advanced forecaster user interfaces and work flow to provide the level of sophistication for demand-driven forecasting and supply chain optimization required by the organization. All the previously mentioned forecasting requirements (the first challenge) would be met by the current version of the business solution.

Since the software vendor had a strategic partnership with AWS, it had already tested deploying many of its software solutions into the AWS cloud. To demonstrate this to the customer, the vendor's engagement team implemented the solution several times to an AWS environment managed by the software vendor. The repeatability assured the customer organization that the solution was well tested in AWS. Well-documented installation, configuration, and testing protocols helped provide evidence to the customer organization that the software vendor was experienced and followed a scientific and structured approach.

The third phase of the methodology utilized in this case was to run performance tests to ensure forecasting results would be available within the time frames required by the organization. Different types of demand planners required different forecasts (e.g., based on product responsibility or regional responsibility). The software vendor worked with the customer organization to discover possible test scenarios that would reflect the actual business.

Four scenarios were identified for the performance test. The customer organization was sure these scenarios would be above current forecasts but wanted such tests to be executed to instill confidence in adopting a new solution. The engagement team of the software vendor mapped these scenarios to other benchmarks conducted by research and development (R&D), product management, and professional services to understand possible design options and set expectations. Such scenario mapping made it possible to select a viable architecture deployment option.

A simple two-tier deployment (client machine, server machine) was chosen to keep the tests simple, and the computing specifications accepted provided the performance required. Computational tasks were performed on the server machine that hosted logical tiers such as an analytics server, middle-tier (e.g., web tier) components, and a data tier. The client tier provided a user interface for initiating forecasts and viewing results. Virtual machines were used for deploying the software solution. The server tier was assigned 32 vCPUs, 244 GB RAM, and 3 TB of storage. The client tier was a simple 2 vCPU, 4 GB RAM desktop-style machine.

The four test scenarios represented approximately 250,000, 500,000, 750,000, and 1 million time series, respectively. The demand signal repository (DSR) was configured to use two data dimensions, namely product and location. Customer data was molded (e.g., facts such as sales data, product details, location details, and calendar events specific to promotions of the customer's marketing efforts) to fit into this solution-specific DSR, and the data integration tools required for such tasks were included in the business solution suite.

Each dimension had several hierarchy levels. Six levels of the product dimension and five levels of the location dimension were used. Test scenarios used an increasing number of values (e.g., number of products and number of locations) with test scenario 1 using the lowest selection and test scenario 4 using the highest selection of these tests.

The combination of selections drove the number of time series. One causal factor for the demand forecasts was included in all four test scenarios. Four events were included to help with the accuracy of forecasts. The inclusion of such data helped the statistical models with identifying promotional events that could drive demand or assist with outlier detection.

The time horizon was defined as 12 weeks, and the demand forecasts were defined as weekly. In summary, the following settings were used for the performance tests:

- Two-tier deployment architecture
- Server virtual machine with 32 vCPUs, 244 GB RAM, 3 TB storage
- Four test scenarios (250,000, 500,000, 750,000, 1 million time series)
- Two dimensions (product, location)
- Six product levels
- Five location levels
- One causal factor (independent variable)
- Four events
- Twelve-week time horizon
- Weekly forecasts

The actual results are not relevant and are excluded from this case study for confidentiality reasons. Performance requirements were met (e.g., forecast results available within the time window required by the customer organization). Ample evidence was provided that the solution could be deployed in AWS as virtual machines. Deployment architectures and sizing would be part of detailed discovery workshops at the beginning of implementation. The software vendor of the business solution issued a support statement for the solution in AWS providing further assurance to the customer organization. The deployment of the solution into the AWS cloud was a simple rehost scenario. The solution was not truly cloud-aware (e.g., elastic, dynamic), and the deployment architecture and licensing model would therefore not leverage full cloud benefits (e.g., pay-as-you-go [PAYG] financial model).

This was not a concern for the customer organization, as the business solution would be used daily, and virtual machines that would be used could be shut down in a controlled manner over weekends if required. Reserved instances of virtual server machines would probably be the long-term option selected to provide better value.

The business solution provided the advanced analytics that were required to produce advanced demand-driven forecasts and use such results as inputs into demand planning and inventory optimization systems and processes. The organization would focus on one business area at a time, beginning with demand forecasting. Improvements in forecast accuracy (evaluation metrics such as MAPE, bias, etc. were defined before and used as a baseline for comparison) met target objectives, and this translated to increased cost savings (e.g., production, inventory, and distribution). The impact of forecast accuracy results (i.e., financial cost savings by optimization in production, inventory replenishment) is what interests management (Mendes 2011, 46; Mentzer 1999).

The customer organization was satisfied with the global experience, industry knowledge, reference customers, global implementation, and customer support that the software vendor could provide. Stable growth of the software vendor over 40 years and a continuously improving software solution road map further satisfied the customer organization.

CASE STUDY 2: OIL AND ENERGY COMPANY

This second case focuses on an oil and energy company. Over- or underforecasting was causing financial costs that the organization wanted to reduce. Inventory costs were high with excess supply in the case of overforecasting, and express shipments were more costly in the case of underforecasting. It was also difficult for the organization to plan inventory replenishment in its distributed supply chain network. Having the business insights to place the right amount of inventory at the distribution center closest to demand would significantly increase business and financial efficiencies. Improvements in forecasting and becoming more demand-driven were seen as the first step to assist with this goal, and the second step would be to feed demand forecasts into an inventory planning system.

The organization was also assessing whether the use of a public cloud could help with cost reductions and efficiencies (e.g., reducing the data center footprint and related costs). Some stakeholders were skeptical of the cloud, while others were ready to adopt and try it. Therefore the organization would probably begin with infrastructure as a service (IaaS), especially as it wanted to maintain full control of the virtual servers and business solution deployed on such virtual machines (VMs). The organization had not yet finalized the selection of a public cloud provider. Therefore the organization was also looking at advice from the solution vendor as to whether there was a preference or experience of one cloud vendor versus another.

The methodology used for this project was similar to the one mentioned in the previous case study, and focused on four phases:

1. Functional and advanced analytics assessment for forecasting and inventory optimization
2. Advice on cloud vendor and verification of business solution functioning in the cloud
3. Benchmarks or performance test to satisfy concerns of the time window for the process
4. Finalizing cloud vendor selection and business solution

The organization in this example had similar forecasting requirements as in the previous case study. It had already experimented with different products and solutions but was not happy with the forecast accuracies produced. The organization was searching for a business solution that would apply advanced analytics to help with its supply chain optimization goals. Requirements were broken down into two streams:

1. Demand-driven forecasting
2. Inventory optimization and replenishment

Demand-Driven Forecasting

As the organization had already tried different solutions unsuccessfully, it was looking for a new solution that would provide more "smart forecasting." This was defined as having the following possibilities:

- Vast repository of statistical models at disposal
- A demand signal repository (DSR) design
- The ability for demand planners to forecast at different levels (e.g., product, location)
- Possibility to include multiple causal factors or independent variables
- Top-down, bottom-up, and middle-out forecasting techniques
- Option to customize statistical models
- Work flow to support demand planners and advanced forecasting personas
- Data integration with inventory optimization system

Inventory Optimization

The organization was looking for a solution that could handle multi-echelon optimization to support inventory planning across multiple network nodes of its supply chain. The organization wanted to see the effects of service levels on inventory costs, and use demand-driven insights to plan the location of inventory (storage and distribution). Both of these requirements would assist with the goals of reducing inventory and distribution costs (especially express delivery costs), and at the same time ensure its customers would not be short of supply. The organization had had negative experiences with internal projects trying to integrate data from different systems and processes for its demand planning and sales and operations planning (S&OP) process.

Therefore, a new solution should be able to avoid or minimize such consulting time, effort, and costs. A proof of concept (PoC) with sample data was used to showcase the "smart forecasting" capabilities, work flow, and interface options for demand planners and advanced forecasters. The customer organization was satisfied with the goals being met. The business solution suite provided a demand signal repository design that included data marts for individual workbenches of the solution.

The demand signal repository, in this case, had a data mart tailored for demand forecasting, a data mart customized for collaborative demand planning, a data mart for inventory optimization and replenishment (leveraging data inputs from the forecasting and demand planning workbenches), and finally a data mart specialized for reporting (e.g., visual analytics and visualization). (See Figure 73.) Tight data and work flow integration using a collaborative forecasting, demand planning, and inventory replenishment approach would be likely to lead to forecast accuracy improvements, increased growth in sales revenues, shorter lead and cycle times, as well as a reduction of cost of goods sold and other operating costs (Mendes 2011, 59–65;

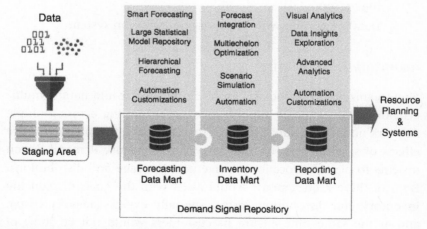

Figure 73 Supply Chain Optimization Solution Suite

Oliver Wight Americas 2005). The business solution suite included data integration tools and outside-the-box data flows to integrate data between business workbenches (i.e., data marts) of the solution suite. Such data flows could be automated based on the work flow; for example, as soon as a forecasting cycle is completed (i.e., system forecasts, and collaborative demand planning if utilized), the finalized forecasts are sent as inputs into the inventory optimization and replenishment system (workbench).

As the organization had limited experience with cloud computing, the solution vendor was requested to provide inputs into the selection process. The software vendor has a strategic partnership with AWS, and it had conducted numerous tests of its solutions on the AWS platform. Moreover, the majority of its other customers were either existing AWS customers or inquiring about AWS as their public cloud vendor. This made it plausible to recommend AWS as the public cloud vendor for the oil and energy company. AWS is a large multinational public cloud provider and already was at the top of the customer organization's list of possible cloud vendors.

In its own assessment efforts, AWS was classified as being far ahead of the competition (local and global). The customer organization wanted to maintain control over the virtual environment, including the virtual machines, users, data, and solution deployed on those virtual machines. Maintenance and patching, as well as solution-specific tasks, should be handled by the organization's IT team. This meant that infrastructure as a service (IaaS) was the suitable cloud model for the organization. Figure 74 shows an example of the deployment.

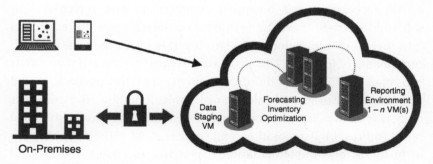

Figure 74 Case Study—Deployment Example

Forecasts and inventory planning were to be performed on a weekly basis. Ideally, the results of the system-generated forecasts should be available within the same day (within business hours). Forecasts could be scheduled or manually started, and this was typically done on Monday after new data was loaded into the demand signal repository on Sunday through a batch job. The organization was satisfied being presented with detailed benchmark results that the software vendor had conducted (e.g., R&D and product management testing performance of its solution). Previous customer references were also used to reassure the organization.

Discovery workshops would be used to identify requirements and recommend a suitable architecture. If there were to be many reporting user persona types, then there could be a need to deploy a grid of computer nodes to handle such reporting needs. This would not affect the data flow or work flow, and would merely add parallel computing nodes for visual analytics tasks. Horizontal scaling is especially important, as the visual analytics solution utilizes in-memory analytics and technologies, and vertical scaling may reach limitations at some points. Hence an architecture design with horizontal scaling for this task might provide better performance.

The business solution and license model was not cloud-aware (not leveraging elasticity and dynamic capabilities), but this did not pose a problem for the organization. The virtualization and use of IaaS provided initial benefits required to meet internal goals. Virtual machines would be shut down outside of business hours (e.g., evening, weekends), and reserved instances may be explored in the future.

To provide the business benefits required to optimize the supply chain, the customer organization would implement the demand-driven forecasting and inventory optimization and replenishment solution together. Leveraging improved forecast results as inputs into inventory simulation and planning was estimated to assist with cost-saving objectives. The estimated return on investment (ROI) was high (e.g., several hundred percent) and the payback period was forecasted to be within a year of implementation. The customer organization was looking for a business solution vendor with global reach (offices, implementation, and support staff), more than 10 years in business, and implementation experience to ensure success and reduce risk. Being able to see and provide inputs to a business solution road map was a bonus for the organization.

▩ ▩ ▩

The two projects had slightly different challenges, but there were some commonalities of goals and objectives. Cloud computing was seen as a strategic choice for the organizations, and any new business solution implemented would have to conform to that strategy. Elastic and cost-effective scalability and performance were two main drivers of using a public cloud. Automation and agility were seen as side benefits to the IT operations and overall business strategy.

Data collection and consolidation of appropriate data into a demand signal repository (DSR) were vital for the success of the "smart forecasting." The data integration and work flow (e.g., demand-driven forecasting results flowing into demand planning and inventory optimization and replenishment) were other key requirements of improving supply chain management. The business solution provided the data model, advanced analytics, and business insights required, and the cloud provided a viable computing platform to solve challenges of performance, costs, and operations. It was the combination of all areas that provided the required results and benefits.

CHAPTER **6**

Summary

C loud computing has had an evolutionary path, and while there is still room for growth and adoption by organizations and industries worldwide, it is becoming a de facto standard and information technology (IT) operating model. Some organizations are more cautious when it comes to change and adopting new technologies, and this is mainly driven by the type of industry and geographic location they operate in. Large organizations see the risks of security breaches, the location of data, and uncertainty of jurisdiction and resolution mechanisms as the greatest reasons for not using cloud computing (Wauters et al. 2016, 41–45). Legal rules, which can be industry-specific or region-specific such as the European Union's General Data Protection Regulation (GDPR) coming into effect in May 2018, and an organization's level of risk averseness are two other important influencing factors as to whether cloud computing (i.e., public cloud) is leveraged.

There were similar pushback reasons at the initial onset of cloud computing when virtualization of x86 hardware became popular more than a decade ago. During that time period, some organizations were at the forefront of the technology evolution wave, and there were other organizations defined as laggards (slow to adopt) that joined at the end of this technology wave of evolution. Virtualization evolved to virtualization 2.0 (increased automation), and then to a private cloud with further automation and software-defined data centers (SDDCs). Public clouds enhanced automation further and provided reductions in up-front investment outlay.

These public clouds improve the agility required in a dynamic and volatile era of demand and supply of products and services. Elasticity (increasing or decreasing computing, storage, and data processing) is a key benefit of a public cloud, with virtually no boundary or upper limit (in theory at least) of scale and performance. Software applications and related services (e.g., data ingestion, analytics, results) must be cloud-aware to reap the maximum benefits of the cloud. Software applications and processes therefore must be designed accordingly to utilize cloud technologies (e.g., horizontal scaling of computer server nodes, dynamically adding or removing computer server nodes from a cluster of computers, integration of cloud services and data, etc.). Organizations can benefit from the economies of scale that a public cloud provider gains through increased use, leading to decreases in prices and flexible cost models (e.g., PAYG, reserved instances). Prices for cloud services seem to be continuing a downward trend (Rogers, Fellows, and Atelsek 2016, 2), benefiting enterprises.

Organizations across industries have noted that the top five benefits of cloud computing were seen as having faster access to IT infrastructure, greater scalability, high availability, increased speed to market, and improved business continuity (e.g., disaster recovery or prevention) (RightScale 2017, 15). A revenue growth increase of 5 to 9 percent was attributed to the benefits of adopting cloud computing by organizations in Europe (European Commission:, 2014, 41). There is still a high potential of using cloud services and benefiting from such technologies and service and business models in general, as the percentage of enterprises using cloud services is still generally low, though this varies across industries and regions.

In the European Union (EU), for example, an average of 21 percent of enterprises were using cloud services in 2016 (Eurostat , 2017). On the flip side, some of the top reasons for limiting the use or adoption of cloud computing are risks of security breaches, uncertainty of laws and jurisdiction, uncertainty of location of data, and challenges with changing cloud provider (Wauters et al. 2016 b, 42).

The retail and manufacturing sectors have high use and penetration of cloud computing (according to 57 percent and 42 percent of respondents, respectively), with the manufacturing industry benefiting from better production processes, better supply chain management, and better inventory, orders, and distribution (Economist Intelligence Unit 2016, 3). Cloud computing is recognized as an enabler for smart value chains and a smart industry framework (with industry 4.0 at its core) that leverages data and analytics, along with other related technologies such as the Internet of Things (IoT) (European Commission, 2016a, 22–24). In the manufacturing sector, 54 percent of organizations see cloud computing as an important platform for supporting better supply chain management (Economist Intelligence Unit 2016, 6).

Big Data is estimated to lead to €425 billion savings for the top 100 manufacturers in the European Union (EU), and combined with analytics could increase economic growth by 1.9 percent by the year 2020. Such growth would translate to an increase in gross domestic product of €206 billion (European Commission, 2016c, 4). Big Data is estimated to drive almost 403 exabytes of data stored by the year 2021 (Cisco Global Cloud Index 2016–2021, 22). Cloud technology, Internet of Things (IoT), and Big Data with data analytics are three of the top digital technologies adopted by organizations in the EU (European Commission, 2017, 11). There are estimates that data-driven supply chains could improve sales and operations planning (S&OP) processes of European manufacturers — for example, better and faster responses to unexpected events, or increased speed of getting products to market (European Commission 2015, 15).

For organizations in Europe, a benefit-cost ratio (BCR) of 2 was noted for adopting cloud computing, meaning that for every euro a potential organization invests in cloud technologies, it is able to benefit from almost two euros of cost savings (Wauters et al. 2016, 41–45). The overall outcome of adopting cloud technology was rated as favorable by organizations in Europe, with 80 percent of those surveyed reporting positive outcomes (European Commission, 2017, 34).

While private clouds as well as region-, industry-, or government-specific clouds will continue to coexist, the global trend is that data center workloads will be hosted in cloud data centers. Estimates show that almost 94 percent of workloads will be hosted in a cloud data center by the year 2021, with public cloud data centers hosting an estimated 73 percent of workloads (Cisco Global Cloud Index 2016–2021, 14–16). All three cloud service models (IaaS, PaaS, and SaaS) are forecasted to continue growth, with software as a service (SaaS) and platform as a service (PaaS) expected to grow the most over the next few years (Cisco Global Cloud Index 2016–2021, 17–19).

There are two dominant global public cloud vendors at the time of writing, namely Amazon Web Services (AWS) and Microsoft Azure. These two possess the lion's share of the market and continue to grow at exponential rates as more and more organizations across industries and geographies of the world are turning to cloud computing as a strategic choice. Other cloud providers frequently used include VMware vCloud Air, IBM, Google, and Oracle (RightScale 2017, 29). Local cloud operators are servicing local organizations and satisfying special industrial or regulatory requirements (e.g., data must reside in local country, and operation of the cloud must be with local citizens). Germany, for example, is a highly regulated market for cloud computing whereby data must not leave the country or the European Union, and there may also be operational restrictions (e.g., only national citizens can operate the local cloud). The Microsoft Azure cloud offering has responded to such a local challenge by using a glocalization strategy, where it blends global and local practices, and in this example is leveraging a German IT provider (i.e., T-Systems) to provide local cloud data centers and a German trustee for operations and access. The types of services and costs in this example may differ from the global offerings, as providers may have higher costs that they would ultimately pass on to organizations. Enterprises then have more choices in selecting a global, European, or local cloud vendor.

In Europe the top five European public cloud providers based on the European market share are SAP (Germany), T-Systems (Germany), SmartFocus (France/UK), Unit4 (Netherlands), and Cegid (France) in respective order (Wauters et al. 2016, 37). U.S.-headquartered cloud vendors are dominating in terms of the market share they hold from the total revenue of the top 26 to 100 public cloud providers in Europe. U.S. public cloud vendors had a 60.7 percent market share of the total revenue (from the top 26 to 100 public cloud vendors), and European cloud providers had a 34.1 percent market share (Wauters et al. 2016, 40).

Organizations are able to migrate to the cloud in phases to minimize impact, risks, and initial costs to their operations. Once an organization becomes more mature in cloud computing, it can leverage more of the cloud services (e.g., infrastructure as a service, platform as a service, and software as a service) and related subcategories (refer to Chapter 4 for examples of the AWS and Microsoft cloud portfolios). There are various frameworks and methodologies for assessing a cloud vendor and implementing a cloud migration project.

Amazon cloud (AWS) and Microsoft Azure provide similar frameworks for migrating to the cloud, generally referred to as the "R-model." Organizations assess their applications, time, costs, risks, and benefits through the help of such an R-model and can create a migration factory approach to streamline and migrate to the cloud efficiently and in a standardized and repeatable manner. There are system integrators (SIs) and specialist consulting firms that have tools and service offerings to help organizations select the best cloud vendor, cloud services, and cloud strategy and migration approach. Most cloud vendors will also offer tools, services, or recommendations to organizations for migrating to the cloud. A step-by-step or phased approach is most likely to succeed, and organizations typically begin with infrastructure as a service.

Cloud computing and related technologies can assist with goals and objectives of supply chain management. Organizations may follow the philosophy of supply chain management ranging from source of supply to the point of consumption (Werner 2017, 6), but may also follow a more narrow focus. There are different schools of thought (e.g., chain awareness, linkage, information, and integration schools) for defining the range of supply chain management (Werner 2017, 9), and an organization's internal objectives and maturity level of supply chain management will drive the areas of focus. Goals and objectives such as cost reduction, information sharing, and integrated decision and information systems will depend on whether an organization is internally focused (internal value chain processes) or includes extranet activities and systems such as suppliers, production, distribution, and so forth upstream and downstream of the supply chain. In other words, the degree of supply chain management depends on whether the organization's view of the supply chain is only internally focused or also includes a focus on the supply chain network and a holistic perspective.

It is therefore tricky to define an all-encompassing list of objectives of supply chain management that all organizations would wish to follow. Some common goals of supply chain management are the following (Glock 2014, 130):

- Increased product availability
- Efficient uses of resources
- Reduction of lead time/throughput times
- Increased flexibility to handle fluctuations in demand
- Reduction in material and product inventory

Perhaps one of the most common objectives across all schools of thought for supply chain management is to reduce costs, including transaction costs, within an entire supply chain (Werner 2017, 5). Organizations across industries such as automobiles, chemicals, pharmaceuticals, health care, and logistics rate supply chain management as very important (Glock 2014, 131). Digitalization, connected devices, data-driven analytics, connected systems, and connected processes (i.e., internal and external to the organization) involving all of a supply chain network are seen as the most mature level of the supply chain evolutionary phases, and should be the desired state (see Figure 75). The consumer demand for products would be received online, and automatically fed into a connected system to update demand forecasts. This updated demand forecast would then check for constraints (e.g., resources, materials, production capacity, throughput times, inventory, distribution, logistics, lead times, etc.) before placing orders for production or delivery. Information and products would then flow back downstream of the supply chain to fulfill the consumer demand (Werner 2017, 14–15). This may not

Figure 75 Connected Supply Chain Management

have been possible before, but enhancements in technologies such as cloud computing, IoT, Industrial Internet of Things (IIoT; i.e., for smart manufacturing, smart factories, etc.), and data lakes are providing a platform for such a modern supply chain vision.

If there are coordinated communication channels and information systems, and if there is joint planning and execution, then it would be possible to have an all-inclusive (internal to the organization and external to the supply chain (e.g., including partners, suppliers, distribution, etc.) plan and management of a value-added chain (Glock 2014, 131–133). The further the integration of intranet and extranet of the supply chain, the better the demand forecasts, raw material requirements planning, production planning, sequence planning, transport planning, distribution planning, aggregated planning, and strategic supply network planning (Glock 2014, 132–134). This follows the philosophy that in the new era of supply chain competition, the competition is not organization against organization, but supply chain against supply chain (Werner 2017, 11–12). Walmart (the world's largest retailer) estimates reducing costs by approximately 25 percent through supply chain optimization, and other estimates include inventory optimization by 50 to 80 percent through supply chain optimization (Werner 2017, 1). The potential for improvements in supply chain management leading to benefits is therefore very high, and the increase of globalization necessitates closer integration of supply chains (internal and external to the organization) to be successful.

To reap higher benefits from supply chain optimization, an organization should follow a demand-pull philosophy and leverage modern information and communication technologies (ICT) to capture and share data more easily and in a timely manner. Using demand signals as inputs into a demand-driven forecasting process can assist with generating more accurate forecasts, provided that the forecasting techniques used are also appropriate. Generating more accurate forecasts would help organizations avoid producing, stocking, and supplying more stock than demanded. Such demand-driven forecasts would assist with two key objectives of supply chain management, namely, cost reduction and ensuring product availability to consumers (i.e., the right product available in the right quantity and at the right location). Geoff Fisher, Director of Demand and Supply Planning at Nestlé (the world's most prominent food and beverage company) noted that "with SAS, Nestlé are better able to accomplish our goal of right flavor, right time, right store" (SAS Institute 2012). SAS is a software company specializing in advanced analytics and offers a software solution called demand-driven planning and optimization (DDPO) aimed at helping organizations with supply chain optimization challenges (i.e., forecasting, collaborative demand planning, and inventory optimization). (See Figure 76.)

Demand-driven forecasting requires data to drive accurate results, and such data should cover at least two years of history, ideally including other factors (e.g., events, promotions, prices, weather, etc.). Such holistic data could then be fed into a demand signal repository (storage of data for this purpose), and advanced analytics could then be used to identify influencing factors and to forecast demand. For example,

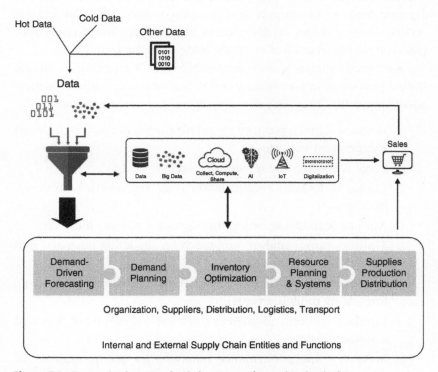

Figure 76 Demand-Driven Supply Chain—Integration and Technologies

the price is a common influencing factor, and price sensitivity analysis could help an organization sense and shape demand for its products.

Demand forecasts should therefore go beyond detecting trends and identify demand signals to help generate more accurate forecasts. This becomes more important as organizations move toward omni-channel forecasting driven by the multiple ways and channels in which consumers operate. The various channels and consumer demographics may have different influencing factors and trends.

Having data available at the right time and location of a connected and integrated supply chain would help organizations to make data-driven and informed decisions (through analytics), and avoid situations such as bullwhip or maverick buying. The bullwhip effect is commonly caused by retailers not having enough local supply of a product and then exaggerating the number of products they order from distributors, who then also exaggerate the number of products ordered from upstream supply chain nodes. This incorrect sensing of demand leads to oversupply and associated costs. Maverick buying occurs when retailers or distributors place orders using guesswork (also referred to as gut feeling or shooting from the hip).

Advanced analytics and demand-driven forecasting solutions should provide advanced features for organizations to reap the highest possible benefits. Examples of such features include the following:

- Demand signal repository model for storing demand signals and independent variables
- Large repository of forecasting models
- Choice of forecast reconciliation (e.g., top-down, bottom-up, middle-out)
- Automatic model selection throughout a product hierarchy
- Multitier causal analysis (approach for modeling push and pull effects of the supply chain)
- Interface for advanced forecaster allowing customizations (e.g., forecasting models, events)
- Interface for demand planner (business-focused work flow and decision aiding)
- Scalability and performance (analytics for a large number of time series in a short time)

Such solution features for demand-driven forecasts and processes should then provide inputs (forecasts) into a collaborative demand planning system and process. Demand planners should be able to review the system-generated forecasts, apply business rules (e.g., top-down or bottom-up allocations), run simulations (e.g., simulate the change in demand if the price is increased), collaborate (e.g., commenting, data entry, and review cycles of teams), and then finalize the demand plan. The demand plan should then feed into other systems for inventory optimization, distribution, production, and materials resource planning (including external suppliers). While there are many forecasting methods ranging from naive methods to neural nets (Mendes 2011, 46; Makridakis 1998), it is also important to note that no single method is universally applicable, and that the forecaster must select the most appropriate method based on the conditions (Mendes 2011, 46; Chatfield 2004).

To improve supply chain performance, the structure within and between members of a supply chain is critical for success, as is moving away from individually managed functions to integrating activities and functions (Mendes 2011, 39; Lambert 2008). Improvement areas in a demand-driven supply chain can be categorized into three key components: demand management, supply and operations management, and product life cycle management (Mendes 2011, 41–42). Demand management in this case includes sensing, shaping, and synchronizing the demand of customers. Supply and operations management concerns itself with matching demand and supply based on actual demand signals and in a cost-efficient way, including procurement, manufacturing flow management, and logistics. Product life cycle management focuses on new product introductions and product sunset (e.g., gradual phaseout), and using historical data of like products for forecasts of new products (Mendes 2011, 41–42). The combination of skills, computers, organizational culture, processes, domain knowledge, and communication skills (interdepartmental and intercompany communication) are key drivers for successful demand planning (Mendes 2011, 46–47; Lapide 2003).

Optimization of the inputs and decisions throughout the supply chain management processes will lead to benefits such as cost savings, higher product availability, and efficient use of resources.

Inventory optimization should include service-level optimization (e.g., simulating the benefit of inventory and product availability versus costs of inventory and distribution), multiechelon analysis (e.g., identifying the best distribution center and supply chain nodes for meeting forecasted demand), economic order quantity, and various buffer stock levels. The cloud as a platform can make current information available where it is needed for all authorized participants of the supply chain such as the enterprise, suppliers, transport, and retailers. This benefit is increased further with global supply chains across geographic regions and time zones (Lehmacher 2016, 186–188). Information sharing and coordination of supply chain activities with members of the supply chain network help reduce demand and supply uncertainties (Mendes 2011, 108; Lee 2002).

Big Data and advanced analytics helped the British supermarket chain Tesco to improve product availability of barbecue products. Inventory data from the previous five years helped identify a spike in demand for barbecue products in at least one weekend of the year. By combining data from other sources (e.g., social media, marketing, websites), Tesco was able to react better and faster in its competitive landscape, reduce costs, and increase sales numbers (Lehmacher 2016, 189). Otto, a German retailer, used Big Data and advanced analytics (e.g., statistics and neural networks) to increase product availability and reduce out-of-stock situations (Lehmacher 2016, 190). Organizations can therefore improve supply chain management through Big Data, advanced analytics (including demand-driven forecasting, inventory optimization, and applying artificial intelligence), and collaboration (e.g., sharing data and processes) with participants of its supply chain.

An estimated 20 percent reduction of inventory could be possible through more accurate forecasts of online sales and applying deep learning, and an estimated 30 percent increase of online sales could be possible by applying dynamic pricing and personalization (Bughin et al. 2017, 24). Cloud computing can act as a scalable and "performant" platform for collecting, computing, and sharing data, enabling authorized participants of a supply chain network to make informed and data-driven decisions and plans at the right time to be the most effective. Benefit, risk, and compliance analysis for encompassing systems and processes must be performed to safeguard sensitive data, especially in light of the General Data Protection Regulation (GDPR) becoming an active regulation in Europe in May 2018.

Technologies such as cloud computing, Big Data, advanced analytics, artificial intelligence, IoT, and digitalization therefore all work together to drive improvements in supply chain management. "Supply Chain Business Today Is Tech Business" (Lehmacher 2016, 191), and a study by the German Federal Association of Logistic concluded that the combination of IT and logistics would provide the greatest future potential for Germany (Hompel, Rehof, and Heistermann 2014, 6). Logistics is an integral part of technological megatrends such as cloud computing, Big Data, industry 4.0, and the Internet of Things (IoT), and these ICT innovation fields will decide the competitiveness of the German industries and sectors (Hompel, Rehof, and Heistermann 2014, 6).

There needs to be legal conformity and data security, an extensive digital high-performance digital infrastructure, interoperability through standardization and standards, and an extension of IT infrastructure up to the inclusion of software and services for industries and countries to be competitive in the future (Hompel, Rehof, and Heistermann 2014, 6).

The chances are that if these technologies would help a developed market and various industries of Germany, then it is very likely that such benefits would apply to other countries and sectors. The top five priorities for supply chain internal to German organizations are business analytics, networking and collaboration, transparency in the value chain, digitalization of business processes, and automation (Kersten et al., 2017, 19). "The supply chain cannot function without ICT," and information technology is an enabler and tool at the same time for the global supply chain (Lehmacher 2016, 192).

In addition to cloud computing, Big Data, and artificial intelligence (also referred to as cognitive computing), IoT, customer journey analytics (e.g., customer awareness, interest, loyalty, purchase), and digitalization are three key areas organizations expect to focus on to increase the potential of improvements in supply chain management (e.g., increased revenue, reduction in costs, increased product availability, etc.). Industrial analytics (IA) is driven by industry 4.0, the Internet of Things, and advanced data analytics, and this type of analytics (IA) collects, analyzes, and uses data generated in industrial operation of organizations manufacturing or selling physical products (Lueth et al. 2016, 11–14).

Organizations wishing to improve their supply chain management can leverage public clouds for cost reductions, and can benefit from scalability and elasticity, especially of computing and storage. Public clouds can also provide a platform for ingesting data (e.g., from IoT), including Big Data, and provide cloud services or building blocks for the advanced analytics (i.e., artificial intelligence). Collaboration, digitalization, and process and data sharing are also made easier through public clouds. The interrelations, benefits, and uses

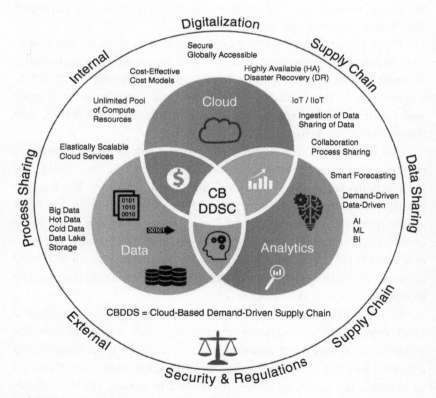

Figure 77 Modern Supply Chain and Technologies

of technologies beneficial to better supply chain management are depicted in Figure 77.

Organizations wishing to improve their supply chain management must leverage information and communication technology (ICT), cloud computing, Big Data, advanced analytics, IoT, and digitalization. Information and communication technology will assist with transparency throughout the supply chain and have information available at a faster rate for timely insights and decisions. With Big Data comes Big Responsibility. Dark Data (unidentified data) (Veritas 2016a) must be avoided in light of the General Data Protection Regulation (GDPR) coming into effect in Europe in 2018. Data should be classified, and organizations should be able to leverage it. Backups and archiving needs (e.g., regulatory) may dictate a certain time period for storage, but to reduce storage costs and possible GDPR penalties organizations must not have any Dark Data.

Organizations should leverage advanced analytics for demand-driven forecasting (including smart forecasting traits), inventory

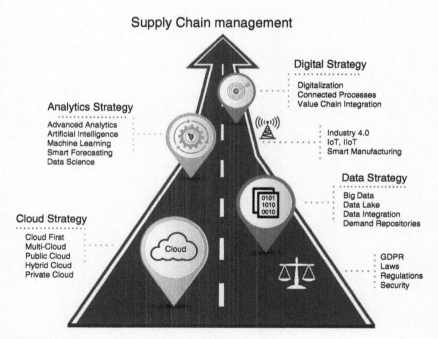

Figure 78   Road to Modern Supply Chain Management

optimization, and supply chain optimization, and be data-driven. Industry 4.0, IoT, and the Industrial Internet of Things (IIoT) will drive data, but can also increase transparency of the supply chain, lead to optimization throughout the value chain, and assist with data-driven decisions in a timely manner. Some organizations will hedge risks by following a multicloud strategy (using several cloud vendors) or utilize a hybrid cloud model (public cloud and on-premises private cloud), but in general utilization of public clouds will continue in the foreseeable future. Strategic categories and key components of modern supply chain management are summarized and depicted in Figure 78. These strategies should also include a focus on three key areas for successful demand-driven supply chain management, namely cloud, data, and advanced analytics (see Figure 21 in Chapter 1).

Glossary

AI Artificial intelligence

BI Business intelligence

CPG Consumer packaged goods

DDSC Demand-driven supply chain

DDSN Demand-driven supply network

DR Disaster recovery

ELT Extract, load, transform

ESP Event stream processing

ETL Extract, transform, load

HA High availability

HDFS Hadoop distributed file system

IaaS Infrastructure as a service

IoT, IIoT Internet of Things, Industrial Internet of Things

IT Information technology

ML Machine learning

NIST National Institute of Standards and Technology

OLAP Online analytical processing

OLTP Online transactional processing

PaaS Platform as a service

S&OP Sales and operations planning

SaaS Software as a service

SDDC Software-defined data center

SCCT Supply chain control tower

References

Alexander, M., P. Brody, J. Chadam, C. Cookson, J. Little, and B. Meadows. 2016. "Digital Supply Chain: It's All about That Data." EYGM.

Amazon Web Services. 2017, April. "Overview of Amazon Web Services."

Aron, D., G. Waller, and L. Weldon. 2014, October; refreshed 2016, September. *Flipping to Digital Leadership: The 2015 CIO Agenda*. Stamford, CT: Gartner.

Barr, J. 2017. "VMware Cloud on AWS—Now Available." AWS News Blog. https://aws.amazon.com/blogs/aws/vmware-cloud-on-aws-now-available/

Barlow, M. 2015. *Learning to Love Data Science: Exploring Predictive Analytics, Machine Learning, Digital Manufacturing, and Supply Chain Optimization*. Sebastopol, CA: O'Reilly Media.

Bartr. 2011, May 3. "Cloud Elasticity—A Real-World Example." Microsoft Developer blog. https://blogs.msdn.microsoft.com/bartr/2011/05/03/cloud-elasticity-a-real-world-example/ (accessed September 9, 2017).

Batty, A., C. Miller, T. Boykin, B. Oswald, M. Quinn, P. Salemme, P. Boykin, B. Dutta, R. Jaganathan, A. Kumar, and J. Varhese. 2017. *The 2017 MHI Annual Industry Report*. Charlotte, NC: MHI.

Bhosle, G., P. Kumar, G. B. Cryan, R. V. Doesberg, M. Sparks, and A. Paton. 2011. *Global Supply Chain Control Towers: Achieving End-to-End Supply Chain Visibility*. London: Capgemini Consulting.

Blue Yonder. 2016. *Six Key Findings on Why Grocers Need to Speed Up Decision-Making*. Karlsruhe, Germany: Blue Yonder.

Briggs, B., and E. Kassner. 2017. *Enterprise Cloud Strategy*. 2nd edition. Seattle, WA: Microsoft Press.

Budd, J., C. Knizek, and B. Tevelson. 2012, May. *The Demand-Driven Supply Chain: Making It Work and Delivering Results*. Boston, MA: Boston Consulting Group.

Bughin, J., E. Hazan, S. Ramaswamy, M. Chui, T. Allas, P. Dahlström, N. Henke, and M. Trench. (2017). "Artificial Intelligence: The Next Digital Frontier?" McKinsey Global Institute.

Cecere L. 2013. *Big Data Handbook: How to Unleash the Big Data Opportunity*. Philadelphia, PA: Supply Chain Insights LLC.

Chase, C. 2013. "Using Demand Sensing and Shaping to Improve Demand Forecasting." *Journal of Business Forecasting* 32 (4): 24–31.

Chatfield, C. 2004. *The Analysis of Time Series: An Introduction*. 6th ed. Boca Raton, FL: Chapman and Hall/CRC.

Chellapa, Ramnath K. 1997. "Intermediaries in Cloud Computing: A New Computing Paradigm." Presented at the INFORMS meeting in Dallas, TX, October 26–29.

Cisco Global Cloud Index. 2015–2020. Cisco Global Cloud Index: Forecast and Methodology 2015–2020. Cisco.

Cisco Global Cloud Index. 2016–2021. Cisco Global Cloud Index: Forecast and Methodology 2016–2021. Cisco.

Croxton, K. L., D. M. Lambert, S. J. Garcia-Dastugue, and D. S. Rogers. 2002. "The Demand Management Process." *International Journal of Logistics Management* 13 (2): 51–66. https://doi.org/10.1108/09574090210806423.

Curran, C., T. Puthiyamadam, J. Sviokla, and G. Verweij. 2015, September. *Lessons from Digital Leaders: 10 Attributes Driving Stronger Performance.* London: PwC.

Daconta, M. 2013. *The Great Cloud Migration: Your Roadmap to Cloud Computing, Big Data and Linked Data.* Denver, CO: Outskirts Press.

Dull, T. 2015. https://blogs.sas.com/content/datamanagement/2015/05/06/analyzing-data-lake/ (accessed March 2, 2017).

Dunning T., and Friedman E. 2014. *Time Series Databases: New Ways to Store and Access Data.* Sebastopol, CA: O'Reilly Media.

Eagle, S. 2017. *Demand-Driven Supply Chain Management.* London: Kogan Page.

Economist Intelligence Unit. 2016. *Ascending Cloud: The Adoption of Cloud Computing in Five Industries.* London: Economist Intelligence Unit.

European Commission. 2013. *Europe's Policy Options for a Dynamic and Trustworthy Development of the Internet of Things.* Luxembourg: Publications Office of the European Union.

European Commission. 2014. *Uptake of Cloud in Europe: Follow-up of IDC Study on Quantitative Estimates of the Demand for Cloud Computing in Europe and the Likely Barriers to Take Up.* Luxembourg: Publications Office of the European Union.

European Commission. 2015. *Digital Transformation of European Industry and Enterprises.* Strategic Policy Forum on Digital Entrepreneurship. Luxembourg: Publications Office of the European Union.

European Commission. 2016a. *Big Data and B2B Digital Platforms: The Next Frontier for Europe's Industry: Recommendations of the Strategic Policy Forum on Digital Entrepreneurship.* Luxembourg: Publications Office of the European Union. Ref. Ares (2016) 4935147 - 02/09/2016.

European Commission. 2016b. *Economic Impact of Cloud Computing in Europe.* Luxembourg: Publications Office of the European Union.

European Commission. 2016c, March. *The EU Data Protection Reform and Big Data Factsheet.* Luxembourg: Publications Office of the European Union.

European Commission. 2017. *Digital Transformation Scoreboard 2017: Evidence of Positive Outcomes and Current Opportunities for EU Businesses*. Luxembourg: Publications Office of the European Union.

Evans, P. C., and M. Annunziata. 2012, November 26. *Industrial Internet: Pushing the Boundaries of Minds and Machines*. Boston, MA: General Electric.

Eurostat. 2017. *Cloud Computing—Statistics on the Use by Enterprises*. http:// ec.europa.eu/eurostat/statistics-explained/index.php/Cloud_computing _-_statistics_on_the_use_by_enterprises

Fildes, R., P. Goodwin, M. Lawrence, and K. Nikopoulus. 2009. "Effective Forecasting and Judgmental Adjustments: An Empirical Evaluation and Strategies for Improvement in Supply-Chain Planning." *International Journal of Forecasing* 25 (1): 3–23.

Fildes, R., and Petropoulos, F. 2015. "How to Improve Forecast Quality: A New Survey. *Foresight: The International Journal of Applied Forecasting* 36: 5–12.

Fischer, S., and C. Winkler. 2017, June. "Datenmassen kanalisieren: Apache-Projekte zur Analyse großer Datenmengen." *iX Magazin fürprofessionelle Informationstechnik S.* 66–70.

Gilliland, M. 2013. "FVA: A Reality Check on Forecasting Practices." *Foresight: The International Journal of Applied Forecasting* 2013 (29): 14–18.

Gilliland, M. 2015. *Forecast Value Added Analysis: Step by Step*. Cary, NC: SAS Institute.

Glock, C. 2014. *Produktion und Supply Chain Management*. Wuerzburg, Germany: B+G Wissenschaftverlag.

Henkes, H. 2016, November. *Cloud Vendor Benchmark 2016 Germany Strategy Paper [Strategiepapier]*. Munich, Germany: Experton Group AG—ISG Business.

Hompel, M. T., J. Rehof, and F. Heistermann. 2014. *Logistik und IT als Innovationstreiber fuer den Wirtschaftsstandort Deutschland: Die neue Fuehrungsrolle der Logistik in der Informationstechnologie*. BVL Bundesvereinigul Logistik. Hamburg, Germany: DVV Media Group.

Izrailevsky, Y. S. Vlaovic, and R. Meshenberg. 2016, February 11. "Completing the Netflix Cloud Migration." Netflix Media Center. https://media.netflix .com/en/company-blog/completing-the-netflix-cloud-migration.

Joss, J., J. Leech, J. Hernandez, B. Peetermans, S. Parker, M. Toon, R. V. D. Heuvel, and A. Mohan. 2016. "Demand-Driven Supply Chain 2.0: A Direct Link to Profitability." 133357-G. KPMG.

Kersten, W., M. Seiter, B. von See, N. Hacklus, and T. Maurer. 2017. *Trends und Strategien in Logistik und Supply Chain Management: Chancen der digitalen Transformation*. BVL Bundervereinigun Logistik. Hamburg, Germany: DVV Media Group.

Kolassa, S., and E. Siemsen. 2016. *Demand Forecasting for Managers*. New York: Business Expert Press.

Kundra, V. 2010. https://obamawhitehouse.archives.gov/blog/2010/05/13/moving-cloud (accessed July 4, 2017) -> Vivek Kundra.

Lambert, D. 2008. *Supply Chain Management: Processes, Partnerships, Performance*. Sarasota, FL: Supply Chain Management Institute.

Lapide, L. 2003. "Organizing the Forecasting Department." *Journal of Business Forecasting Methods & Systems* 22, no. 2 (Summer).

Lawrence, M., M. O'Connor, and B. Edmundson. 2000. "A Field Study of Sales Forecasting Accuracy and Processes." *European Journal of Operational Research* 122:151–160.

Lee, H. 2002. "Aligning Supply Chain Strategies with Product Uncertainties." *California Management Review* 44 (3): 104–119.

Lehmacher, W. 2016. *Globale Supply Chain: Technischer Fortschritt, Transformation und Circular Economy*. Wiesbaden, Germany: Springer Fachmedien Wiesbaden GmbH.

Lueth, L. K., C. Patsioura, Z. D. Williams, and Z. Z. Kermani. 2016. *Industrial Analytics 2016/2017: The Current State of Data Analytics Usage in Industrial Companies*. Hamburg, Germany: IoT Analytics GmbH.

Makridakis, S. 1998. *Forecasting: Methods and Applications*. 3rd edition. New York: Wiley.

Manyika, J., M. Chui, J. Bughin, R. Dobbs, P. Bisson, and A. Marrs. 2013. "Disruptive Technologies: Advances That Will Transform Life, Business, and the Global Economy." McKinsey Global Institute.

Mell P., and Grance, T. 2011. *The NIST Definition of Cloud Computing*. NIST SP 800-145. Gaithersburg, MD: National Institute of Standards and Technology.

Mendes, P. 2011. *Demand Driven Supply Chain: A Structured and Practical Roadmap to Increase Profitability*. Wiesbaden, Germany: Springer Fachmedien Wiesbaden GmbH.

Mentzer, J.T. 1999. "The Impact of Forecasting on Return on Shareholder's Value." *The Journal of Business Forecasting Methods & Systems* 18 (3): 8–10.

Metz, C. 2014, June. "How Facebook Moved 20 Billion Instagram Photos without You Noticing. *Wired*." https://www.wired.com/2014/06/facebook-instagram/ (accessed July 6, 2017).

Microsoft. 2015. *Retail Insights Harnessing the Power of Data*. Seattle, WA: Microsoft.

Mohan, D., L. DuBois, and E. Berggren. 2017. *IDC MarketScape: Worldwide Infrastructure as a Service 2017 Vendor Assessment*. Framingham, MA: IDC.

Muthukrishnan, R., and K. Sullivan. 2012. *Next-Generation Supply Management*. San Jose, CA: Cisco IBSG.

NIST SP 800-145. 2011. https://csrc.nist.gov/publications/detail/sp/800-145/final

Oliver Wight Americas. 2005. CPFR: Collaborative Planning, Forecasting and Replenishment. https://www.oliverwight-americas.com/class_a_glossary_cpfr

RightScale. 2017. "State of the Cloud Report: Public Cloud Adoption Grows as Private Cloud Wanes." RightScale.

RightScale. 2018. "State of the Cloud Report: Data to Navigate Your Multi-Cloud Strategy." RightScale.

Rogers, O., W. Fellows, and J. Atelsek. 2016. Cloud Price Index (2016): Global Pricing Analysis. New York: 451 Research.

Safavi, K., and R. Ratliff. 2015. "Top 5 eHealth Trends: Five Trends Prove That Digital Is Dramatically Influencing the Industry, Today, and Well into Tomorrow." Healthcare IT Vision. Accenture.

SAS Institute. 2012. *Nestlé Drives Bottom-Line Improvements with SAS Demand-Driven Forecasting*. Cary, NC: SAS Institute.

Schindler, H. R., J. Cave, N. Robinson, V. Horvath, P. Hackett, S. Gunashekar, M. Botterman, S. Forge, and H. Graux. 2012. *Europe's Policy Options for a Dynamic and Trustworthy Development of the Internet of Things*. Luxembourg: Publications Office of the European Union. doi:10.2759/22004.

Skyhigh. 2016. *Cloud Adoption & Risk Report*. Santa Clara, CA: Skyhigh Networks.

Spitz, M. 2017. *Daten—das Öl des 21. Jahrhunders?: Nachhaltigkeit im digitalen zeitalter*. Hamburg, Germany: Hoffmann und Campe Verlag.

Synergy Research Group. 2018, February 2. "Cloud Growth Rate Increases; Amazon, Microsoft & Google All Gain Market Share." https://www.srgresearch.com/articles/cloud-growth-rate-increases-amazon-microsoft-google-all-gain-market-share (accessed February 10, 2018).

Veritas. (2016a). *Data Genomics Index: A Report on the True Makeup of Storage Environments from the Experts in Unstructured Data*. Mountain View, CA: Veritas.

Veritas. 2016. *The Databerg Report: See What Others Don't: Identify the Value, Risk, and Cost of Your Data*. Mountain View, CA: Veritas.

Wauters, P., S. V. D. Peijl, V. Cilli, M. Bolchi, P. Janowski, M. Moeremans, H. Graux, G. Taylor, and D. Cocoru. 2016. *Measuring the Economic Impact of Cloud Computing in Europe*. Luxembourg: European Commission, Publications Office of the European Union, doi:10.2759/75071.

Werner, H. 2017. *Supply Chain Management: Grundlagen, Strategien, Instrumente und Controlling*. Wiesbaden, Germany: Springer Fachmedien Wiesbaden GmbH.

Woods, J. 2011. *Five Options for Migrating Applications to the Cloud: Rehost, Refactor, Revise, Rebuild or Replace*. Gartner: The Future of IT Conference: Mexico 2011. Stamford, CA: Gartner.

FURTHER READING

451 Research. 2017. *Can Private Cloud Be Cheaper than Public Cloud?: 41% Said Yes, and the Survey Reveals How.* New York: 451 Research.

Al-Roomi, M., S. Al-Ebrahim, S. Buqrais, and I. Ahmad. 2013. "Cloud Computing Pricing Models: A Survey." *International Journal of Grid and Distributed Computing* 6 (5): 93–106.

Amazon Web Services. 2014. "Total Cost of Ownership (TCO) Comparison." Amazon Web Services.

Amazon Web Services. 2015. "Introduction to AWS Economics: Reducing Costs and Complexity." Amazon Web Services.

Amazon Web Services. 2015. "A Practical Guide to Cloud Migration: Migrating Services to AWS." Amazon Web Services.

Amazon Web Services. 2016. "How AWS Pricing Works." Amazon Web Services.

Amazon Web Services. 2017. "AWS Certifications, Programs, Reports, and Third-Party Attestations." Amazon Web Services.

Amazon Web Services. 2017. "An Overview of the AWS Cloud Adoption Framework: Version 2." Amazon Web Services.

Amazon Web Services. 2017. "10 Considerations for a Cloud Procurement." Amazon Web Services.

Andreessen, M. 2011, August 20. "Why Software Is Eating the World." *Wall Street Journal.*

Avigdor, G., and R. Wintjes. 2015. *Trend Report: Disruptive Innovations and Forward-Looking Policies towards Smart Value Chains.* Luxembourg: Publications Office of the European Union. Ref. Ares (2015) 4619412 - 27/ 10/2015.

Banerjee, A., T. Bandyopadhyay, and P. Acharya. 2013. "Data Analytics: Hyped Up Aspirations or True Potential?" *Journal for Decision Makers, Indian Institute of Management.*

Barnett, T., A. Sumits, S. Jain, U. Andra, and T. Khurana. 2016. Cisco Global Cloud Index 2015–2020: Cisco Knowledge Network (CKN) Session.

Barrett, R., A. Gupta, and K. O'Laughlin. 2014. "Driven by Demand." KPMG.

Batty, A., C. Miller, T. Boykin, B. Oswald, B. Hones, S. Hogikyan, and N. Papageorgiou. 2018. *The 2018 MHI Annual Industry Report: Overcoming Barriers to NextGen Supply Chain Innovation.* Charlotte, NC: MHI.

Baumann, F., G. Cenciza, S. Massicotte, A. Medepalli, and K. Thomas. 2017. *Digital Supply Chain for Dummies: JDA Software Special Edition.* Hoboken, NJ: Wiley.

Bitner, B., and S. Greenlee. 2012. *z/VM: A Brief Review of Its 40 Year History*. Armonk, NY: IBM Corporation.

Blue Ridge. 2015. "How to Supercharge Product Availability without Inflating Inventory." Blue Ridge.

Blue Yonder. 2017. *Kuenstliche Intelligenz rettet den Einzelhandel: Fuenf Wege, um im Haifischbecken zu ueberleben*. Karlsruhe, Germany: Blue Yonder.

Blue Yonder. 2017. *Store Replenishment at Morrisons: How Morrisons Adopted AI Technology to Deliver on Its Promise to Customers and Transform Store Replenishment*. Karlsruhe, Germany: Blue Yonder.

Bradshaw, D., G. Cattaneo, R. Lifonti, and J. Simcox. 2014. *Uptake of Cloud in Europe: Follow-Up of IDC Study on Quantitive Estimates of the Demand for Cloud Computing in Europe and the Likely Barriers to Take-Up*. Luxembourg: European Commission, Publications Office of the European Union, doi:10.2759/791317.

Brook, J. M., S. Field, D. Shackleford, V. Hargrave, L. Jameson, and M. Roza. 2017. "The Treacherous 12: Top Threats to Cloud Computing + Industry Insights." Cloud Security Alliance.

BS Reporter. 2013, October 25. "Excellence Is Not by Accident but Is a Process: Kalam." *Business Standard*. http://www.business-standard.com/article/current-affairs/excellence-is-not-by-accident-but-is-a-process-kalam-113102500516_1.

Burden, A. P., and D. Sauer. 2014. "Accenture Cloud Application Migration Services: A Smarter Way to Get to the Cloud." Accenture.

Cancila, M., D. Toombs, D. A. Waite, and E. Khnaser. 2016, October 13. *2017 Planning Guide for Cloud Computing*. Stamford, CT: Gartner.

Catfield, C. 2004. *The Analysis of Time Series: An Introduction*. 6th edition. Boca Raton, FL: Chapman and Hall/CRC.

Cecere, L. 2012. "Big Data: Go Big or Go Home." Supply Chain Insights.

Cerasis. 2017. *The Digital Supply Chain: The Landscape, Trends, Types, and the Application in Supply Chain Management*. Eagan, MN: Cerasis.

Chappell, D. 2016. *Analytical Scenarios Using the Microsoft Data Platform: A Guide for IT Leaders*. San Francisco, CA: David Chappell & Associates.

Chase, C. 2014. *Intermittent Demand Forecasting and Multi-Tiered Causal Analysis*. Paper SAS036-2014. Cary, NC: SAS Institute.

Chase, C. 2016. *Next Generation Demand Management: People, Process, Analytics, and Technology*. Hoboken, NJ: Wiley.

Chellapa, R. K. 1997. http://www.bus.emory.edu/ram/ (first academic use of term Cloud Computing).

Christopher, M. 2000. "The Agile Supply Chain: Competing in Volatile Markets." *Journal of Industrial Marketing Management* 29 (1): 37–44.

Chui, M., J. Manyika, J. Bughin, B. Brown, J. Danielson, and S. Gupta. 2013. "Ten IT-Enabled Business Trends for the Decade Ahead." McKinsey Global Institute.

CloudEndure. 2017. 2017 *Cloud Migration Survey Report: The Most Up-to-Date Benchmarks, Trends, and Best Practices*. New York: CloudEndure.

Daughert, P. R., and B. Berthon. 2015. "Winning with the Industrial Internet of Things: How to Accelerate the Journey to Productivity and Growth." Accenture.

Davis, M., S. Aronow, J. Barret, S. F. Jacobson, and K. Sterneckert. 2011, July 22. *Demand-Driven Value Networks: Supply Chain Capabilities Road Map for Growth, Agility and Competitive Advantage*. Stamford, CT: Gartner.

Davis, R. A. 2013. *Demand-Driven Inventory Optimization and Replenishment: Creating a More Efficient Supply Chain*. Hoboken, NJ: Wiley.

Demchenko, Y. 2013. *Defining the Big Data Architecture Framework (BDAF): Outcome of the Brainstorming Session at the University of Amsterdam*. Amsterdam, Netherlands: SNE Group, University of Amsterdam.

Dougados, M., and B. Felgendreher. 2016. "The Current and Future State of Digital Supply Chain Transformation: A Cross-Industry Study with 337 Executives in Over 20 Countries Reveals Expectations on Digital Transformation." Capgemini Consulting, GT Nexus.

Duft, N., and L. Fröhlich. 2012. *Cloud Computing im Mittelstand: Wie Unternehmen vom neuen IT-Trend profitieren können*. Berlin: Pierre Audoin Consultants; Bonn: Telekom Deutschland.

Dull, T. 2016. *A Non-Geek's Big Data Playbook: Hadoop and the Enterprise Data Warehouse*. Cary, NC: SAS Institute.

European Commission. 2002. *Life Sciences and Biotechnology: A Strategy for Europe*. Luxembourg: Publications Office of the European Union.

European Commission. 2015. *Monitoring the Digital Economy & Society 2016–2021*. Luxembourg: Publications Office of the European Union.

European Commission. 2016. *Accelerating the Digital Transformation of European Industry and Enterprises: Key Recommendations of the Strategic Policy Forum on Digital Entrepreneurship*. Luxembourg: Publications Office of the European Union. Ref. Ares (2016) 1221351 - 10/03/2016.

European Commission. 2016. *A Digital Compass for Decision Makers: Toolkit on Disruptive Technologies, Impact and Areas for Action: Recommendations of the Strategic Policy Forum on Digital Entrepreneurship*. Luxembourg: Publications Office of the European Union.

European Commission. 2017. *Special Eurobarometer 460: Attitudes towards the Impact of Digitalisation and Automation on Daily Life*. Luxembourg: Publications Office of the European Union.

EY. 2014. "Big Data: Changing the Way Businesses Compete and Operate." EYGM.

Forbes Insights. 2013. *Clearing the Roadblocks to Cloud Computing*. New York: Forbes Insights.

Gartner Press Release. 2012, August 29. Gartner, Stamford, CT. https://www .gartner.com/newsroom/id/2138416 (accessed September 21, 2017).

Gaurav, R., P. Bhatia, and M. Durbha. 2015. *Supply Chain for Dummies: JDA Software Special Edition*. Hoboken, NJ: Wiley.

Ghemawat, S., H. Gobioff, and S. T. Leung. 2003. "The Google File System." SOSP'03, October 19–22. ACM 1-58113-757-5/03/0010.

Gillespie, M. 2017. "Benefits Abound When Moving Analytics to the Cloud." MicroStrategy.

Gilliland, M., L. Tashman, and U. Sglavo. 2016. *Business Forecasting: Practical Problems and Solutions*. Hoboken, NJ: Wiley.

Gomez, J., O. Guzman, M. Leiva, R. Membrila, W. Schuster, P. Soriano, D. Valer, and J. D. Zegarra. 2016. *IDC FutureScape: Worldwide IT Industry 2017 Predictions Latin America Impact*. Framingham, MA: IDC.

Hagerty, J. 2016, October 13. *2017 Planning Guide for Data and Analytics*. Stamford, CT: Gartner.

Hall, P., W. Phan, and K. Whitson. 2016. *The Evolution of Analytics: Opportunities and Challenges for Machine Learning in Business*. Sebastopol, CA: O'Reilly Media.

Hanifan, G. L., C. Newberry, and A. E. Sharma. 2015. "Is Your Supply Chain a Growth Engine?: It Could Be If You Leverage Digital Technologies." Accenture.

Harrington, L. 2016. "The Predictive Enterprise: Where Data Science Meets Supply Chain." DHL Supply Chain.

Harris, J. 2015. https://blogs.sas.com/content/datamanagement/2015/05/06/ analyzing-data-lake/ (accessed March 2, 2017).

Heidkapm, P., and A. Pols. 2017. "Cloud-Monitor 2017: Cyber Security im Fokus—Die Mehrheit vertraut der Cloud." KPMG.

Heppenstall, D., L. Newcombe, and N. Clarke. 2016, February. *Moving to the Cloud—Key Considerations: Key Risk Considerations for Decision Makers*. UK: KPMG.

Hill, A. 2016. *12 Best Practices of Inventory Optimization: Minimize Costs, Maximize Uptime with MRO Inventory Control*. Brisbane: Oniqua.

Hofstraat, H. 2015. "Smart Healthcare Delivery: IT Enabling the Health Continuum." Philips Research.

Hogan, O., S. Mahamed, D. McWilliams, and R. Greenwood. 2010. "The Cloud Dividend: Part One. The Economic Benefits of Cloud Computing to

Business and the Wider EMEA Economy: France, Germany, Italy, Spain and the UK." Centre for Economics and Business Research, CEBR.

Hompel, M. T. 2014. "Logistik und IT als Innovationstreiber: Wie wir mit modernen Informationstechnologien unsere Welt aendern." Deutscher Logistikkongress. Fraunhofer IML.

Hubbard, T. 2015. *Big Data in Health Care—Challenges, Innovations and Imple-mentations.* 3rd International Systems Biomedicines Symposium. London: King's College London.

Hugos, H. 2011. *Essentials of Supply Chain Management.* 3rd edition. Hoboken, NJ: Wiley.

Intel IT Center. 2016. *Big Data in the Cloud: Converging Technologies—How to Create Competive Advantage Using Cloud-Based Big Data Analytics.* Santa Clara, CA: Intel.

iX Magazin. 2017, June. Pages 66-70. https://www.heise.de/ix/, https://www.heise-gruppe.de/. Heise Medien.

Jahn, M. 2017. *Industrie 4.0 konkret: Ein Wegweiser in die Praxis.* Wiesbaden, Germany: Springer Fachmedien Wiesbaden GmbH.

Jaucot, F., V. D. M. Poel, D. K. Coster, P. A. Billiet, and S. Vanhout. 2017. "Are You Ready for Connected Retail?" PwC Belgium.

Jayachandran, J. 2017. "Cloud Migration Methodology." Aspire Systems.

JDA Software. 2017. *The Digitalization of Grocery: The Impact of Shifting Consumer Behaviors.* Scottsdale, AZ: JDA Software Group.

Keese, C. 2017. *Silicon Germany: Wie wir die digitale Transformation schaffen.* Munich, Germany: Albrecht Knaus Verlag.

Kepes, B. 2013. "Cloud Adoption—Barriers, Roadblocks and Belligerence: Learn about the Hurdles You'll Encounter When Promoting Cloud Tech-nologies in Your Company . . . and How to Jump over Them." Diversity Limited.

Kleemann, F. C., and A. H. Glas. 2017. *Einkauf 4.0: Digitale Transformation der Beschaffung.* Wiesbaden, Germany: Springer Fachmedien Wiesbaden GmbH.

Lyons, A., A. Coronado Mondragon, F. Piller, and R. Poler. 2012. *Customer-Driven Supply Chains: From Glass Pipelines to Open Innovation Networks.* Wiesbaden, Germany: Springer Fachmedien Wiesbaden GmbH.

Manenti, P., W. Lee, and L. Veronesi. 2014. *The Future of Manufacturing.* Framingham, MA: IDC.

Manssila, E. M. 2016. *Accelerating the Digital Transformation of European Compa-nies.* Global Forum 2016. Eindhoven, Netherlands: European Commission.

McDivitt, C., D. E. Veer, and B. Pivar. 2014. "Demand-Driven Supply Chain: Capgemini's Demand-Driven Supply Chain Approach Helps Consumer

Products and Retail Companies Create a Pull Supply Chain Driven by Consumer Demand." Capgemini.

McFedries, P. 2012. *Cloud Computing: Beyond the Hype*. San Francisco, CA: HP Press.

Mell, P., and T. Grance. 2011. *The NIST Definition of Cloud Computing: Recommendations of the National Institute of Standards and Technology*. Special Publication 800-145. Gaithersburg, MD: National Institute of Standards and Technology.

Mensah, A. 2015. *From Geonomics to Population Health: Accelerating the Evolution of Human Care*. Redwood City, CA: Oracle.

Microsoft Press. 2017. https://news.microsoft.com/features/microsoft-facebook-telxius-complete-highest-capacity-subsea-cable-cross-atlantic/ (accessed September 23, 2017).

Mishra, D. 2014, July. "Cloud Computing: The Era of Virtual World Opportunities and Risks Involved." *International Journal of Computer Science Engineering* 3 (4): 204–209.

Morley, M. 2017. *Supply Chain Analytics for Dummies: OpenText Special Edition*. Hoboken, NJ: Wiley.

Namless. 2015. "Ignited Quotes of Dr. APJ Abdul Kalam." CreateSpace Independent Publishing Platform.

Nanda, M. 2011. *Designing a Lean-Based Supply Chain Using Demand Pull*. Bangalore, India: Wipro Consulting.

National Institute of Standards and Technology. 2015a. *NIST Big Data Interoperability Framework*. Vol. 5, *Security and Privacy*. NIST Special Publication 1500-5. Gaithersburg, MD: National Institute of Standards and Technology.

National Institute of Standards and Technology. 2015b. *NIST Big Data Interoperability Framework*. Vol. 6, *Reference Architecture*. NIST Special Publication 1500-6. Gaithersburg, MD: National Institute of Standards and Technology.

National Institute of Standards and Technology. 2015c. *NIST Big Data Interoperability Framework*. Vol. 7, *Standards Roadmap*. NIST Special Publication 1500-7. Gaithersburg, MD: National Institute of Standards and Technology.

Nichols, K., and K. Sprague. 2011. "Getting Ahead in the Cloud." McKinsey & Company.

OECD. 2014. *Data-Driven Innovation for Growth and Well-Being*. Paris: OECD Publications.

OECD. 2017. Health at a Glance 2017: OECD Indicators. Paris: OECD Publishing. https://dx.doi.org/10.1787/health_glance-2017-en.

Offersen, D. 2016. *The Power of Inventory: How to Simplify, Course Correct, and Use Inventory as a Strategic Advantage*. Offersen Publishing.

Pardo, J., A. Flavin, and M. Rose. 2016. "2016 Top Markets Report: Cloud Computing." U.S. Department of Commerce: International Trade Administration: Industry & Analysis (I&A).

Probst, L., B. Pedersen, O. K. Lonkeu, M. Diaz, L. N. Araujo, D. Klitou, J. Conrads, and M. Rasmussen. 2017. *Digital Transformation Scoreboard 2017: Evidence of Positive Outcomes and Current Opportunities for EU Businesses*. Luxembourg: Publications Office of the European Union.

Raab, M., and B. Griffin-Cryan. 2011. "Digital Transformations of Supply Chains: Creating Value—When Digital Meets Physical." Capgemini Consulting.

Raskino, M. 2015, April 10. *Highlights of the 2015 CEO Survey: Business Leaders Are Betting on Tech*. Stamford, CT: Gartner.

Rogers, D. S., and S. Simmerman. 2017. *Warehouse of the Future*. Scottsdale, AZ: JDA Software Group.

Rogers O., and J. Atelsek. 2016. *451 Research: Voice of the Enterprise (2016). Quarterly Advisory Report: Workloads and Projects Cloud*. New York: 451 Research.

Said, M. R. 2015. "Big Data: An Opportunity or a Distraction? Signal or Noise?" 3rd International Systems Biomedicine Symposium, Luxembourg.

Sandiford, T. 2013. "Inventory Optimization." Capgemini.

SAS Institute. 2009. *How Can Finance and Operations Work Together to Maximize Inventory Provisions While Minimizing Working Capital Costs?* Cary, NC: SAS Institute.

SAS Institute. 2014. *SAS for Demand-Driven Planning and Optimization: Listen to Customers, Focus on the Market and Respond to Demand in Near-Real Time*. Cary, NC: SAS Institute.

SAS Institute. 2017. *Data Visualization Techniques: From Basics to Big Data with SAS Visual Analytics*. Cary, NC: SAS Institute.

SAS Institute. 2017. *The Enterprise Artificial Intelligence (AI) Promise: Path to Value*. Cary, NC: SAS Institute.

SAS Institute. 2017. *How Any Size Organization Can Supersize Results with Data Visualization*. Cary, NC: SAS Institute.

SAS Institute. 2017. *SAS Forecast Analyst Workbench*. Cary, NC: SAS Institute.

Schrauf, S., and P. Berttram. 2016. "Industry 4.0: How Digitalization Makes the Supply Chain More Efficient, Agile, and Customer-Focused." PwC.

Shepard, D. 2012. "Collaborative Demand and Supply Planning between Partners: Best Practices for Effective Planning." Supply Chain Acuity.

Shevenell, M., and T. Diep. 2015. "Managing the Software Defined World: Managing Your Infrastructure in the Highly Agile World of Software Defined Networks." CA Technologies.

Simorjay, F. 2017. "Shared Responsibilities for Cloud Computing." Microsoft.

Skyhigh. 2017. *Custom Applications and IaaS Trends*. Santa Clara, CA: Skyhigh Networks.

Snyder, L. 2008. *Multi-Echelon Inventory Optimization: An Overview*. Center for Value Chain Research. PA: Lehigh University.

Stanton, D. 2019. *Supply Chain Management for Dummies*. Hoboken, NJ: Wiley.

Telekom Deutschland. 2013. *Datenschutz und Datensicherheit beim Cloud Computing*. Bonn, Germany: Telekom Deutschland.

Terrill, S., and S. Purba. 2015. *Data-Driven Business Transformation: Driving Performance, Strategy and Decision Making*. Canada: KPMG.

Tompkins, B., and C. Ferrell. 2012. *Finished Goods Inventory Management: Presenting Growth & Adaption Through Metrics*. Raleigh, NC: Tompkins Supply Chain Consortium.

Toolingu. 2014. *Manufacturing Insights Report: Winning Practices of World-Class Companies*. Cleveland, OH: Toolingu.

Tulloch, M. 2013. *Introducing Windows Azure for IT Professionals*. Seattle, WA: Microsoft Press.

Tyndall, G. 2012. *Demand-Driven Supply Chains: Gitting It Right for True Value*. Raleigh, NC: Tompkins International.

Usie, W., L. Gill, G. Ceniza, and V. Fayen. 2016. *Profitable Omni-Channel for Dummies: JDA Software Special Edition*. Hoboken, NJ: Wiley.

Varia, J. 2012. "The Total Cost of (Non) Ownership of Web Applications in the Cloud." Amazon Web Services.

Veritas. 2015. *The Databerg Report: The State of Information Management*. Mountain View, CA: Veritas.

Veritas. 2017. *2017 Truth in Cloud Report: The Rise of Multi-Cloud: Combatting Misconceptions and Realigning Data Management Responsibilities*. Mountain View, CA: Veritas.

VMware. 2006. *Reducing Server Total Cost of Ownership with VMware Virtualization Software*. Palo Alto, CA: VMware.

VMware. 2014. *Do You Believe the Myths around Virtualization?* Palo Alto, CA: VMware.

VMware. 2017. *VMware TCO Comparison Calculator Report*. Palo Alto, CA: VMware.

Vogt, A. 2016. *Cloud Vendor Benchmark 2016: Datenintegration—Die Herausforderung in der Cloud*. Munich, Germany: Experton Group—ISB Business.

White, D. 2013. *Visualization: Set Your Analytics Users Free*. Boston, MA: Aberdeen Group.

Yeoh, J., and F. Guanco. 2015. "How Cloud Is Being Used in the Financial Sector: Survey Report." Cloud Security Alliance.

WEBSITES

http://analytics-magazine.org/value-added-analysis-business-forecasting-
    effectiveness/ (accessed August 12, 2017).
http://appsso.eurostat.ec.europa.eu/nui/show.do?dataset=isoc_cicce_use&
    lang=en (accessed October 7, 2017).
http://bigdata2015.uni.lu/bigdata2015_%20/content/download/480/2213/
    version/1/file/Dirk_Evers_BigData2015.pdf (accessed December 23, 2017).
http://bigdata2015.uni.lu/bigdata2015_%20/content/download/483/2225/
    version/1/file/MSaid_InternationalSystemsBiomedicineSymposium_
    28Oct15_vf.pdf (accessed December 23, 2017).
http://bigdata2015.uni.lu/eng/Presentation (accessed December 23, 2017).
http://bigdata2015.uni.lu/eng/Presentation HEALTH CARE and BIG DATA
    and ANALYTICS (accessed December 23, 2017).
http://cdn.ey.com/echannel/gl/en/services/advisory/envision/ey-trusted-
    cloud-migration.pdf (accessed November 11, 2017).
http://cloud-readiness-check.com/ Cloud READINESS (accessed November 5,
    2017).
http://d0.awsstatic.com/whitepapers/Big_Data_Analytics_Options_on_AWS
    .pdf (accessed November 11, 2017).
http://database.guide/what-is-a-document-store-database/ (accessed Decem-
    ber 22, 2017).
http://datagenomicsproject.org/data-genomics-report-2016.html (accessed
    September 21, 2017).
http://demand-planning.com/2014/11/24/new-ibf-blog-series-forecast-value-
    added-fva/ (accessed August 12, 2017).
http://download.microsoft.com/download/0/4/3/0430CF1B-0E7B-44E0-
    BAF4-23C03E12F065/The_Digital_Business_Divide_white_paper.pdf
    (accessed September 16, 2017).
http://dtucalculator.azurewebsites.net/ DTU calculator (accessed December
    22, 2017).
https://dx.doi.org/10.6028/NIST.SP.1500-1 (accessed September 16, 2017).
http://ec.europa.eu/DocsRoom/documents/17924 (accessed September 16,
    2017).
http://ec.europa.eu/DocsRoom/documents/18503 (accessed September 16,
    2017).
http://ec.europa.eu/DocsRoom/documents/21501 (accessed December 24,
    2017).
http://ec.europa.eu/DocsRoom/documents/21501 (accessed September 16,
    2017).

http://ec.europa.eu/eurostat/cache/infographs/ict/bloc-3b.html (accessed October 7, 2017).

http://ec.europa.eu/eurostat/statistics-explained/index.php/Cloud_computing_-_statistics_on_the_use_by_enterprises (accessed July 12, 2017).

http://ec.europa.eu/eurostat/statistics-explained/index.php/Cloud_computing_-_statistics_on_the_use_by_enterprises (accessed December 25, 2017).

http://ec.europa.eu/eurostat/statistics-explained/index.php/Digital_economy_and_society_statistics_-_enterprises (accessed November 18, 2017).

http://ec.europa.eu/eurostat/statistics-explained/index.php/File:V1_Use_of_cloud_computing_services,_2014_and_2016_(%25_of_enterprises).png (accessed November 18, 2017).

http://ec.europa.eu/eurostat/web/products-eurostat-news/-/DDN-20170330-1 (accessed November 18, 2017).

http://ec.europa.eu/growth/content/fourth-trend-report-%E2%80%98 disruptive-innovations-and-forward-looking-policies-towards-smart-value_en (accessed September 16, 2017).

http://ec.europa.eu/growth/publications_en (accessed September 16, 2017).

http://go.rackspace.com/costofexpertise-TY.html?aliId=193108446#form (accessed June 17, 2017).

http://google-file-system.wikispaces.asu.edu/ (accessed July 4 and 6, 2017).

http://government-2020.dupress.com/driver/cloud-computing/ (accessed October 7, 2017).

http://info.totaltraxinc.com/blog/demand-driven-supply-network-are-you-meeting-the-demands (accessed October 14, 2017).

http://issuu.com/supplydemandchainfoodlogistics/docs/flog0817?e=16809 490/52223226 (accessed September 16, 2017).

http://journals.sagepub.com/doi/pdf/10.1177/0256090920130401 (accessed September 21, 2017).

http://muddassirism.com/importance-of-demand-forecasting-in-supply-chain/ (accessed September 21, 2017).

http://nvlpubs.nist.gov/nistpubs/Legacy/SP/nistspecialpublication800-145.pdf -> NIST definition of Cloud (accessed July 4, 2017).

http://research.isg-one.de/research/studien/cloud-vendor-benchmark-2016/ergebnisse-ch.html (accessed September 23, 2017).

http://research.isg-one.de/research/studien/cloud-vendor-benchmark-2016/anbieter.html (accessed September 23, 2017).

http://s354933259.onlinehome.us/mhi-blog/7-ways-iiot-making-supply-chain-smarter-sustainable/ (accessed October 14, 2017).

http://searchcloudcomputing.techtarget.com/feature/Cloud-computing-timeline-illustrates-clouds-past-predicts-its-future (accessed July 4, 2017).

http://supplychaininsights.com/research-reports/big-data/ (accessed August 11, 2017).

http://supplychaininsights.com/wp-content/uploads/2012/07/Big_Data _Report_16_JULY_2012.pdf (accessed August 5, 2017).

http://uk.businessinsider.com/microsoft-stay-top-enterprise-it-market-share-battle-chart-2017-7?utm_source=feedburner&utm_medium=feed&utm _campaign=Feed%3A+typepad%2Falleyinsider%2Fsilicon_alley_insider+ %28Silicon+Alley+Insider%29&r=US&IR=T (accessed July 17, 2017).

http://usblogs.pwc.com/emerging-technology/data-lakes-and-the-promise-of-unsiloed-data/ (accessed October 14, 2017).

http://viewer.zmags.com/publication/a02dd3b8 (accessed September 24, 2017).

http://whatiscloud.com/origins_and_influences/a_brief_history (accessed July 4, 2017) -> 1961 John McCarty.

http://www.annese.com/blog/roadblocks-to-cloud-adoption-in-the-financial-sector (accessed May 17, 2017).

http://www.bmc.com/blogs/saas-vs-paas-vs-iaas-whats-the-difference-and-how-to-choose/ (accessed October 28, 2017).

http://www.computerweekly.com/answer/Star-schema-vs-snowflake-schema-Which-is-better (accessed October 14, 2017).

http://www.computerweekly.com/feature/A-history-of-cloud-computing (accessed November 4, 2017).

http://www.computerweekly.com/tutorial/Star-schema-in-database-Guide-to-construction-and-composition (accessed October 14, 2017).

http://www.coolheadtech.com/blog/vanson-bournes-business-impact-of-the-cloud (accessed September 23, 2017).

http://www.cs.cornell.edu/courses/cs614/2004sp/papers/gfs.pdf (accessed July 4, 2017).

http://www.data-profits.com/resources/blog/proof-improving-forecast-accuracy-delivers-high-roi/ (accessed September 21, 2017).

http://www.dataversity.net/brief-history-cloud-computing/ (accessed July 4, 2017).

http://www.diversity.net.nz/wp-content/uploads/2013/03/Whitepaper _SCREEN.pdf (accessed May 17, 2017) ROADBLOCKS to CLOUD.

http://www.dummies.com/programming/big-data/big-data-for-dummies-cheat-sheet/ (accessed October 14, 2017).

http://www.ebnonline.com/author.asp?section_id=4033 (accessed September 16, 2017).

http://www.eugdpr.org/gdpr-faqs.html (accessed August 5, 2017).

http://www.eugdpr.org/key-changes.html (accessed August 5, 2017).

http://www.forecastpro.com/Trends/forecasting101January2009.html (accessed October 14, 2017).

http://www.gtnexus.com/resources/blog-posts/digital-supply-chain-transformation-infographic (accessed August 5, 2017).

http://www.icc-usa.com/back-to-basics-what-is-virtualization.html (accessed July 6, 2017).

http://www.inspirage.com/2015/11/the-history-of-cloud-computing-some-key-moments/ (accessed July 4, 2017).

http://www.jamesserra.com/archive/2015/04/what-is-a-data-lake/ (accessed September 16, 2017).

http://www.jamesserra.com/archive/2015/07/what-is-polyglot-persistence/ (accessed September 16, 2017).

http://www.jamesserra.com/archive/2016/08/what-is-the-lambda-architecture/ (accessed September 16, 2017).

http://www.nytimes.com/2012/02/12/sunday-review/big-datas-impact-in-the-world.html?_r=0 (accessed September 16, 2017).

http://www.oecd.org/els/health-systems/health-data.htm (accessed December 22, 2017).

http://www.oecd.org/els/health-systems/health-statistics.htm (accessed December 22, 2017).

http://www.oecd.org/health/health-systems/health-at-a-glance-19991312.htm OECD Data (accessed December 23, 2017).

http://www.oecd-ilibrary.org/docserver/download/8117301e.pdf?expires=1515316946&id=id&accname=guest&checksum=68E21B89BB9DDFCF73FB6F6C7240B31A (accessed December 22, 2017).

http://www.referenceforbusiness.com/history2/84/salesforce-com-Inc.html (accessed July 4, 2017).

http://www.sandia.gov/news/publications/labnews/archive/14-22-08.html (accessed September 21, 2017).

http://www.sas.com/images/landingpage/docs/Nestle_Customer_Story.pdf (accessed December 22, 2017).

http://www.scmfocus.com/demandplanning/2011/05/a-better-way-of-importing-data-into-forecasting-and-analytic-systems/ (accessed October 14, 2017).

http://www.sfisaca.org/images/FC12Presentations/D1_2.pdf (accessed October 30, 2017).

http://www.supplychain247.com/article/new_perspectives_on_the_value_of_demand_sensing (accessed September 21, 2017).

http://www.supplychaindigital.com/logistics/how-demand-driven-forecasting-paid-nestle (accessed September 24, 2017).

http://www.supplychaindigital.com/technology/ibm-and-maersk-establish-blockchain-based-supply-chain-company BLOCKCHAIN (accessed January 20, 2018).

http://www.supplychaindigital.com/top-10/seven-reasons-why-you-need-forecast-supply-chain (accessed September 21, 2017).

http://www.supplychainopz.com/2013/01/is-apple-supply-chain-really-no-1-case.html (accessed August 5, 2017).

http://www.supplychainquarterly.com/topics/Strategy/20170626-making-the-journey-to-a-multimodal-segmented-supply-chain/ (accessed September 16, 2017).

http://www.supplychainquarterly.com/topics/Technology/20141230-machine-learning-a-new-tool-for-better-forecasting/?__hssc=180668984.5.15055 541773636.__hstc=180668984.9a83839a2855b779a56709652eed5fbf.15 05550204337.1505550204337.1505554177363.26.__hsfp=177514101086 hsCtaTracking=412ceaca-8e7b-4615-a730-290bc54a0e31%7C845ad2bf-171b-478d-a549-4300f91b0eab (accessed September 16, 2017).

http://www.supplychainshaman.com/demand/demanddriven/demand-driven-can-we-sidestep-religious-arguments/ (accessed October 14, 2017).

http://www.supplychainshaman.com/demand/demanddriven/what-happened-to-the-concept-of-demand-driven/ (accessed October 14, 2017).

http://www.telegraph.co.uk/news/obituaries/8851410/John-McCarthy.html (accessed November 11, 2017).

http://www.tomsitpro.com/articles/azure-vs-aws-cloud-comparison,2-870-2.html (accessed October 28, 2017).

http://www.tomsitpro.com/articles/azure-vs-aws-cloud-comparison,2-870-2.html AWS vs Azure comparison of service (accessed December 21, 2017).

http://www.vanguardsw.com/2017/06/demand-data-key-supply-chain-management/ (accessed September 21, 2017).

http://www.vcloudnews.com/every-day-big-data-statistics-2-5-quintillion-bytes-of-data-created-daily/ (accessed November 16, 2017).

http://www.vldb.org/pvldb/1/1454166.pdf (accessed September 21, 2017).

http://www.zdnet.com/article/microsoft-aws-and-google-may-have-just-started-the-next-cloud-computing-price-war/ (accessed July 17, 2017).

http://www3.weforum.org/docs/WEF_TC_MFS_BigDataBigImpact_Briefing _2012.pdf (accessed May 5, 2017).

https://451research.com/cloud-price-index-overview (accessed July 6, 2017).

https://451research.com/images/Marketing/productsheets/CPI_Tearsheet_06 _13_2017.pdf (accessed November 10, 2017).

https://assets.kpmg.com/content/dam/kpmg/pdf/2016/05/demand-driven-supply-chain.pdf (accessed July 5, 2017).

https://assets.kpmg.com/content/dam/kpmg/pdf/2016/06/co-cm-4-driven-by-demand.pdf (accessed July 5, 2017).

https://aws.amazon.com/about-aws/ (accessed July 4, 2017).

https://aws.amazon.com/about-aws/global-infrastructure/ (accessed October 30, 2017).

https://aws.amazon.com/about-aws/global-infrastructure/regional-product-services/ (accessed December 21, 2017).

https://aws.amazon.com/architecture/ (accessed August 11, 2017).

https://aws.amazon.com/big-data/ (accessed November 11, 2017).

https://aws.amazon.com/blogs/aws/vmware-cloud-on-aws-now-available/ (accessed August 29, 2017).

https://aws.amazon.com/compliance/shared-responsibility-model/ (accessed October 28, 2017).

https://aws.amazon.com/ec2/pricing/ AWS PRICING (accessed October 30, 2017).

https://aws.amazon.com/ec2/pricing/on-demand/ AWS PRICING (accessed October 30, 2017).

https://aws.amazon.com/emr/details/ (accessed August 11, 2017).

https://aws.amazon.com/iot-platform/ (accessed November 11, 2017).

https://aws.amazon.com/pricing/ (accessed October 28, 2017).

https://aws.amazon.com/solutions/case-studies/all/ (accessed December 21, 2017)

https://aws.amazon.com/solutions/case-studies/yelp/ (accessed November 11, 2017).

https://aws.amazon.com/whitepapers/ (accessed October 30, 2017).

https://aws.amazon.com/whitepapers/overview-of-amazon-web-services/ (accessed October 30, 2017).

https://awstcocalculator.com/ (accessed October 28, 2017).

https://azure.microsoft.com/en-gb/ (accessed December 21, 2017).

https://azure.microsoft.com/en-gb/blog/microsoft-azure-germany-now-available-via-first-of-its-kind-cloud-for-europe/ (accessed October 30, 2017).

https://azure.microsoft.com/en-gb/overview/azure-vs-aws/ (accessed July 4, 2017).

https://azure.microsoft.com/en-gb/overview/cortana-intelligence/ (accessed September 21, 2017).

https://azure.microsoft.com/en-gb/overview/datacenters/ (accessed December 21, 2017).

https://azure.microsoft.com/en-gb/overview/what-is-paas/ (accessed September 23, 2017).

https://azure.microsoft.com/en-gb/pricing/ (accessed October 28, 2017).

https://azure.microsoft.com/en-gb/pricing/calculator/?service=cost-management (accessed October 28, 2017).

https://azure.microsoft.com/en-gb/pricing/details/batch/ (accessed October 28, 2017).

https://azure.microsoft.com/en-gb/resources/451-research-economics-serverless-cloud-computing/en-us/ (accessed July 4, 2017).

https://azure.microsoft.com/en-gb/resources/forrester-economic-impact-azure-iaas/en-us/ (accessed July 4, 2017).

https://azure.microsoft.com/en-gb/resources/whitepapers/ (accessed July 4, 2017).

https://azure.microsoft.com/en-gb/services/data-catalog/ (accessed September 21, 2017).

https://azure.microsoft.com/en-gb/services/data-factory/ (accessed September 21, 2017).

https://azure.microsoft.com/en-gb/services/event-hubs/ (accessed September 21, 2017).

https://azure.microsoft.com/en-gb/status/ (accessed July 4, 2017).

https://azure.microsoft.com/en-us/blog/behind-the-scenes-of-azure-data-lake-bringing-microsoft-s-big-data-experience-to-hadoop/ (accessed September 21, 2017).

https://azure.microsoft.com/en-us/pricing/ PRICING (accessed December 21, 2017).

https://azure.microsoft.com/en-us/pricing/calculator/ (accessed October 28, 2017).

https://azure.microsoft.com/en-us/pricing/details/mysql (accessed December 22, 2017).

https://azure.microsoft.com/en-us/pricing/details/virtual-machines/linux/ (accessed December 21, 2017).

https://azure.microsoft.com/en-us/pricing/hybrid-benefit/ (accessed December 21, 2017).

https://azure.microsoft.com/en-us/pricing/reserved-vm-instances/ (accessed December 21, 2017).

https://azure.microsoft.com/en-us/regions/ Azure REGIONS (accessed December 21, 2017).

https://azure.microsoft.com/en-us/regions/services/ AZURE PRODUCTS BY REGION (accessed December 21, 2017).

https://azure.microsoft.com/en-us/services/ (accessed December 21, 2017).

https://azure.microsoft.com/en-us/services/?filter=cognitive-services (accessed December 22, 2017).

https://azure.microsoft.com/en-us/services/?filter=compute (accessed
    December 21, 2017).

https://azure.microsoft.com/en-us/services/?filter=iot (accessed December 23,
    2017).

https://azure.microsoft.com/en-us/services/active-directory/ (accessed
    December 23, 2017).

https://azure.microsoft.com/en-us/services/active-directory-b2c/ (accessed
    December 23, 2017).

https://azure.microsoft.com/en-us/services/active-directory-ds/ (accessed
    December 23, 2017).

https://azure.microsoft.com/en-us/services/api-management/ (accessed
    December 22, 2017).

https://azure.microsoft.com/en-us/services/api-management/ (accessed
    December 23, 2017).

https://azure.microsoft.com/en-us/services/app-center/ (accessed December
    23, 2017).

https://azure.microsoft.com/en-us/services/application-gateway/ (accessed
    December 21, 2017).

https://azure.microsoft.com/en-us/services/application-insights/ (accessed
    December 23, 2017).

https://azure.microsoft.com/en-us/services/app-service/ (accessed December
    21 and 22, 2017).

https://azure.microsoft.com/en-us/services/app-service/api/ (accessed
    December 22, 2017).

https://azure.microsoft.com/en-us/services/app-service/mobile/ (accessed
    December 22, 2017).

https://azure.microsoft.com/en-us/services/app-service/web/ (accessed
    December 22, 2017).

https://azure.microsoft.com/en-us/services/backup/ (accessed December 21,
    2017).

https://azure.microsoft.com/en-us/services/batch/ (accessed December 21 and
    22, 2017).

https://azure.microsoft.com/en-us/services/bot-service/ (accessed December
    22, 2017).

https://azure.microsoft.com/en-us/services/cache/ (accessed December 22,
    2017).

https://azure.microsoft.com/en-us/services/cdn/ (accessed December 21,
    2017).

https://azure.microsoft.com/en-us/services/cloud-services/ (accessed Decem-
    ber 21, 2017).

https://azure.microsoft.com/en-us/services/cognitive-services/text-analytics/
(accessed December 22, 2017).

https://azure.microsoft.com/en-us/services/container-instances/ (accessed
December 21, 2017).

https://azure.microsoft.com/en-us/services/container-service/ (accessed
December 21, 2017).

https://azure.microsoft.com/en-us/services/cosmos-db/ (accessed December
22, 2017).

https://azure.microsoft.com/en-us/services/data-catalog/ (accessed December
22, 2017).

https://azure.microsoft.com/en-us/services/data-factory/ (accessed December
22, 2017).

https://azure.microsoft.com/en-us/services/data-lake-analytics/ (accessed
December 22, 2017).

https://azure.microsoft.com/en-us/services/data-lake-store/ (accessed December 21, 2017).

https://azure.microsoft.com/en-us/services/devtest-lab/ (accessed December
23, 2017).

https://azure.microsoft.com/en-us/services/dns/ (accessed December 21, 2017).

https://azure.microsoft.com/en-us/services/event-grid/ (accessed December
23, 2017).

https://azure.microsoft.com/en-us/services/event-hubs/ (accessed December
22, 2017).

https://azure.microsoft.com/en-us/services/event-hubs/ (accessed December
23, 2017).

https://azure.microsoft.com/en-us/services/expressroute/ (accessed December
21, 2017)

https://azure.microsoft.com/en-us/services/genomics/ (accessed December
22, 2017).

https://azure.microsoft.com/en-us/services/hdinsight/ (accessed December
22, 2017).

https://azure.microsoft.com/en-us/services/hdinsight/apache-spark/
(accessed December 22, 2017).

https://azure.microsoft.com/en-us/services/hockeyapp/ (accessed December
23, 2017).

https://azure.microsoft.com/en-us/services/iot-edge/ (accessed December 23,
2017).

https://azure.microsoft.com/en-us/services/iot-hub/ (accessed December 23,
2017).

https://azure.microsoft.com/en-us/services/key-vault/ (accessed December 23, 2017).

https://azure.microsoft.com/en-us/services/load-balancer/ (accessed December 21, 2017).

https://azure.microsoft.com/en-us/services/location-based-services/ (accessed December 23, 2017).

https://azure.microsoft.com/en-us/services/log-analytics/ (accessed December 22, 2017).

https://azure.microsoft.com/en-us/services/logic-apps/ (accessed December 22 and 23, 2017).

https://azure.microsoft.com/en-us/services/machine-learning-studio/ (accessed December 23, 2017).

https://azure.microsoft.com/en-us/services/media-services/ (accessed December 22, 2017).

https://azure.microsoft.com/en-us/services/media-services/content-protection/ (accessed December 22, 2017).

https://azure.microsoft.com/en-us/services/media-services/media-analytics/ (accessed December 22, 2017).

https://azure.microsoft.com/en-us/services/media-services/media-player/ (accessed December 22, 2017).

https://azure.microsoft.com/en-us/services/multi-factor-authentication/ (accessed December 23, 2017).

https://azure.microsoft.com/en-us/services/mysql/ (accessed December 22, 2017).

https://azure.microsoft.com/en-us/services/network-watcher/ (accessed December 21, 2017).

https://azure.microsoft.com/en-us/services/notification-hubs/ (accessed December 22 and 23, 2017).

https://azure.microsoft.com/en-us/services/postgresql/ (accessed December 22, 2017).

https://azure.microsoft.com/en-us/services/power-bi-embedded/ (accessed December 22, 2017).

https://azure.microsoft.com/en-us/services/search/ (accessed December 22, 2017).

https://azure.microsoft.com/en-us/services/security-center/ (accessed December 23, 2017).

https://azure.microsoft.com/en-us/services/service-bus/ (accessed December 23, 2017).

https://azure.microsoft.com/en-us/services/service-fabric/ (accessed December 21, 2017).

https://azure.microsoft.com/en-us/services/site-recovery/ (accessed December 21, 2017).

https://azure.microsoft.com/en-us/services/sql-database/ (accessed December 22, 2017).

https://azure.microsoft.com/en-us/services/sql-server-stretch-database/ (accessed December 22, 2017).

https://azure.microsoft.com/en-us/services/storage/ (accessed December 21, 2017).

https://azure.microsoft.com/en-us/services/storage/blobs/ (accessed December 21, 2017).

https://azure.microsoft.com/en-us/services/storage/files/ (accessed December 21, 2017).

https://azure.microsoft.com/en-us/services/storage/queues/ (accessed December 21, 2017).

https://azure.microsoft.com/en-us/services/storage/unmanaged-disks/ (accessed December 21, 2017).

https://azure.microsoft.com/en-us/services/storsimple/ (accessed December 21, 2017).

https://azure.microsoft.com/en-us/services/stream-analytics/ (accessed December 22, 2017).

https://azure.microsoft.com/en-us/services/time-series-insights/ (accessed December 23, 2017).

https://azure.microsoft.com/en-us/services/traffic-manager/ (accessed December 21, 2017).

https://azure.microsoft.com/en-us/services/virtual-machines/ (accessed December 21, 2017).

https://azure.microsoft.com/en-us/services/virtual-machine-scale-sets/ (accessed December 21, 2017).

https://azure.microsoft.com/en-us/services/virtual-network/ (accessed December 21, 2017).

https://azure.microsoft.com/en-us/services/visual-studio-team-services/ (accessed December 23, 2017).

https://azure.microsoft.com/en-us/services/vpn-gateway/ (accessed December 21, 2017).

https://azure.microsoft.com/en-us/solutions/architecture/personalized-marketing/ (accessed September 21, 2017).

https://azure.microsoft.com/en-us/status/ Azure STATUS Dashboard (accessed December 21, 2017).

https://azure.microsoft.com/en-us/status/ STATUS of AZURE (accessed December 21, 2017).

https://azure-costs.com/ (accessed November 18, 2017).

https://azuremarketplace.microsoft.com/en-us/marketplace/apps/category/networking

https://bi-survey.com/benefits-business-intelligence (accessed October 14, 2017).

https://bi-survey.com/data-driven-decision-making-business (accessed October 14, 2017).

https://blog.blue-yonder.com/de/2016/09/19/in-sechs-schritten-zur-optimalen-customer-experience (accessed October 15, 2017).

https://blog.blue-yonder.com/en/7-ways-retailers-benefit-from-ai (accessed October 14, 2017).

https://blog.blue-yonder.com/en/enabling-smarter-decisions-in-retail-with-artificial-intelligence (accessed October 14, 2017).

https://blog.toolsgroup.com/en/a-shift-in-supply-chain-planning-priorities?_ga=2.169251810.259407702.1505550204-1822606399.1505550204 (accessed September 16, 2017).

https://blog.toolsgroup.com/en/coming-now-the-age-of-advanced-demand-analytics (accessed September 16, 2017).

https://blog.toolsgroup.com/en/five-things-you-need-to-know-about-machine-learning-for-supply-chain-planning (accessed September 16, 2017).

https://blog.toolsgroup.com/en/five-ways-machine-learning-can-improve-demand-forecasting (accessed September 16, 2017).

https://blog.toolsgroup.com/en/four-prerequisites-for-demand-sensing-success (accessed December 24, 2017).

https://blog.toolsgroup.com/en/the-seven-key-capabilities-of-demand-sensing (accessed September 24, 2017).

https://blogs.cisco.com/datacenter/the-5-ps-of-cloud-computing (accessed July 4, 2017).

https://blogs.msdn.microsoft.com/azuredatalake/2016/10/12/understanding-adl-analytics-unit/ AU - ANALYTICS UNIT (accessed December 22, 2017).

https://blogs.msdn.microsoft.com/azuresecurity/2016/04/18/what-does-shared-responsibility-in-the-cloud-mean/ (accessed October 28, 2017).

https://blogs.sas.com/content/datamanagement/2015/05/06/analyzing-data-lake/ (accessed March 2, 2017).

https://blogs.sas.com/content/subconsciousmusings/2017/10/17/online-learning-machine-learnings-secret-big-data/?lipi=urn%3Ali%3Apage%3Ad_flagship3_feed%3BamoGkrZ%2BS7%2BS1f8aq1NLLQ%3D%3D (accessed October 15, 2017).

https://blogs.vmware.com/management/2017/07/private-vs-public-cloud-costs-surprising-451-research-results.html (accessed August 10, 2017).

https://businessintelligence.com/bi-insights/the-four-vs-of-big-data-infographic/attachment/ibm-big-data/ (accessed August 11, 2017),

https://calculator.s3.amazonaws.com/index.html (accessed October 28, 2017).

https://cloudsecurityalliance.org/download/ (accessed October 7, 2017).

https://community.spiceworks.com/topic/1295652-infographic-virtualization-history-why-everyone-s-gone-virtual -> 5 Benefits of virtualization (accessed July 6, 2017).

https://connect.cloudspectator.com/2017-top-european-cloud-providers-report (accessed January 25, 2018).

https://consumergoods.com/nestle-drives-better-demand -> 2012 (accessed December 22, 2017).

https://customers.microsoft.com/en-us/story/big-data-solution-transforms-healthcare-with-faster-a2 (accessed September 16, 2017).

https://customers.microsoft.com/en-us/story/kotahi (accessed December 24, 2017).

https://d0.awsstatic.com/analyst-reports/Experton%20Group%20AWS%20White%20Paper%2007.12.16.pdf (accessed October 30, 2017).

https://d0.awsstatic.com/whitepapers/aws_cloud_adoption_framework.pdfAWS 6R (accessed October 30, 2017).

https://data.oecd.org/gdp/gdp-long-term-forecast.htm (accessed October 14, 2017).

https://docs.microsoft.com/en-us/azure/analysis-services/analysis-services-overview (accessed December 22, 2017).

https://docs.microsoft.com/en-us/azure/architecture/guide/technology-choices/data-store-overview (accessed December 22, 2017).

https://docs.microsoft.com/en-us/azure/cosmos-db/introduction (accessed September 21, 2017).

https://docs.microsoft.com/en-us/azure/cosmos-db/modeling-data (accessed December 22, 2017).

https://docs.microsoft.com/en-us/azure/cosmos-db/use-cases (accessed December 22, 2017).

https://docs.microsoft.com/en-us/azure/cost-management/overview (accessed November 18, 2017).

https://docs.microsoft.com/en-us/azure/data-catalog/data-catalog-what-is-data-catalog (accessed September 21, 2017).

https://docs.microsoft.com/en-us/azure/data-factory/introduction (accessed September 21, 2017).

https://docs.microsoft.com/en-us/azure/event-hubs/event-hubs-capture-overview (accessed September 21, 2017).

https://docs.microsoft.com/en-us/azure/event-hubs/event-hubs-what-is-event-hubs (accessed September 21, 2017).

https://docs.microsoft.com/en-us/azure/sql-database/sql-database-technical-overview (accessed December 22, 2017).

https://docs.microsoft.com/en-us/azure/sql-database/sql-database-service-tiers (accessed December 22, 2017).

https://docs.microsoft.com/en-us/azure/sql-database/sql-database-in-memory (accessed December 22, 2017).

https://docs.microsoft.com/en-us/azure/sql-database/sql-database-what-is-a-dtu (accessed December 22, 2017).

https://docs.microsoft.com/en-us/sql/relational-databases/indexes/columnstore-indexes-overview (accessed December 22, 2017).

https://dupress.deloitte.com/dup-us-en/focus/industry-4-0.html (accessed October 7, 2017).

https://dupress.deloitte.com/dup-us-en/focus/industry-4-0/digital-twin-technology-smart-factory.html (accessed October 7, 2017) INDUSTRY 4.0.

https://dupress.deloitte.com/dup-us-en/focus/industry-4-0/digital-transformation-in-supply-chain.html (accessed October 7, 2017) DIGITAL SUPPLY CHAIN.

https://dupress.deloitte.com/dup-us-en/topics/analytics/five-types-of-analytics-of-things.html (accessed September 21, 2017).

https://dzone.com/articles/5-key-events-history-cloud (accessed November 4, 2017).

https://dzone.com/articles/lambda-architecture-with-apache-spark (accessed September 16, 2017).

https://ec.europa.eu/digital-single-market/en/%20european-cloud-initiative (accessed July 9, 2017).

https://ec.europa.eu/digital-single-market/en/cloud (accessed July 9, 2017).

https://ec.europa.eu/digital-single-market/en/european-cloud-computing-strategy (accessed July 9, 2017).

https://ec.europa.eu/digital-single-market/en/news/cloud-standards-coordination-final-report (accessed July 9, 2017).

https://ec.europa.eu/digital-single-market/en/news/european-cloud-strategy-0 (accessed July 9, 2017).

https://ec.europa.eu/digital-single-market/en/news/measuring-economic-impact-cloud-computing-europe (accessed July 9, 2017).

https://ec.europa.eu/digital-single-market/en/policies/building-european-data-economy.

https://ec.europa.eu/digital-single-market/en/policies/cloud-computing.

https://en.wikipedia.org/wiki/Demand_chain_management (accessed October 14, 2017).

https://en.wikipedia.org/wiki/Google_File_System (accessed July 4, 2017).

https://gallery.azure.ai/Solution/Demand-Forecasting-for-Shipping-and-Distribution-2 (accessed December 24, 2017).

https://gallery.cortanaintelligence.com/solution/513038e359b7464390be575513043ef3 (accessed September 21, 2017).

https://github.com/Azure/cortana-intelligence-price-optimization/blob/master/Automated%20Deployment%20Guide/Post%20Deployment%20Instructions.md (accessed September 21, 2017).

https://hbr.org/2013/12/analytics-30 (accessed October 15, 2017).

https://hbr.org/2014/05/an-introduction-to-data-driven-decisions-for-managers-who-dont-like-math (accessed October 15, 2017).

https://home.kpmg.com/content/dam/kpmg/pdf/2016/04/moving-to-the-cloud-key-risk-considerations.pd (accessed November 5, 2017).

https://home.kpmg.com/de/de/home/themen/2017/05/cloud-monitor-2017-interaktiv.html (Accessed November 5, 2017).

https://info.cloudendure.com/rs/094-DCS-290/images/2017-Cloud-Migration-Survey_Feb20.pdf (accessed November 11, 2017).

https://internethalloffame.org/inductees/jcr-licklider (accessed July 4, 2017).

https://iot-analytics.com/industrial-analytics-report-20162017-download/ (accessed February 2, 2018).

https://ir.netflix.com/index.cfm (accessed October 30, 2017).

https://media.netflix.com/en/company-blog/completing-the-netflix-cloud-migration (accessed October 30, 2017).

https://medium.com/aws-enterprise-collection/6-strategies-for-migrating-applications-to-the-cloud-eb4e85c412b4 (accessed June 7, 2017) MIGRATING to CLOUD.

https://medium.com/aws-enterprise-collection/6-strategies-for-migrating-applications-to-the-cloud-eb4e85c412b4 6 Rs of Cloud Migration (accessed November 5, 2017).

https://msdn.microsoft.com/en-gb/magazine/hh547103.aspx (accessed December 22, 2017).

https://news.microsoft.com/2009/11/17/microsoft-cloud-services-vision-becomes-reality-with-launch-of-windows-azure-platform/ (accessed July 4, 2017).

https://news.microsoft.com/facts-about-microsoft/ (accessed December 21, 2017).

https://news.microsoft.com/features/microsoft-facebook-telxius-complete-highest-capacity-subsea-cable-cross-atlantic/ (accessed September 23, 2017).

https://newsroom.cisco.com/focus/2017/oct/health-and-technology (accessed December 24, 2017).

https://newsroom.cisco.com/focus/2017/sept/ar-and-vr (accessed December 24, 2017).

https://research.google.com/archive/gfs.html (accessed July 4, 2017).

https://resources.toolsgroup.com/ai-supply-chain-planning-software-release-optimized-for-the-cloud?_ga=2.168834146.259407702.1505550204-1822606399.1505550204 (accessed September 16, 2017).

https://sourcingjournalonline.com/push-pull-supply-chain-management-zara/ (accessed December 26, 2017).

https://static.ibmserviceengage.com/TIW14162USEN.PDF (accessed September 21, 2017).

https://storageservers.wordpress.com/2013/07/17/facts-and-stats-of-worlds-largest-data-centers/ (accessed August 19, 2017).

https://virtualizationreview.com/articles/2014/10/14/7-layer-virtualization-model.aspx (accessed July 6, 2017).

https://visualrsoftware.com/advantages-data-visualization/ (accessed October 15, 2017).

https://www.accenture.com/_acnmedia/Accenture/Conversion-Assets/Microsites/Documents20/Accenture-Healthcare-Technology-Vision-2015-Infographic.pdf (accessed December 23, 2017).

https://www.accenture.com/t00010101T000000Z__w__/at-de/_acnmedia/Accenture/Conversion-Assets/DotCom/Documents/Global/PDF/Dualpub_11/Accenture-Industrial-Internet-of-Things-Positioning-Paper-Report-2015.ashx (accessed December 21, 2017).

https://www.accenture.com/t20170524T014807__w__/us-en/_acnmedia/PDF-49/Accenture-Digital-Health-Technology-Vision-2017-Infographic.pdf (accessed December 23, 2017).

https://www.accenture.com/t20170925T085436Z__w__/us-en/_acnmedia/Accenture/Conversion-Assets/DotCom/Documents/Global/PDF/Technology_9/Accenture-Cloud-Application-Migration-Services.pdf (accessed November 11, 2017).

https://www.apache.org/ -> Definitions of HADOOP ecosystem (accessed July 12, 2017).

https://www.aspiresys.com/WhitePapers/Cloud-Migration-Methodology.pdf (accessed November 11, 2017).

https://www.backblaze.com/blog/hard-drive-cost-per-gigabyte/ (accessed July 27, 2017).

https://www.bcg.com/publications/2014/supply-chain-management-retail-demand-forecasting-the-key-to-better-supply-chain-performance.aspx (accessed October 14, 2017).

https://www.bcg.com/publications/2015/infrastructure-needs-of-the-digital-economy.aspx (accessed October 14, 2017).

https://www.bcg.com/publications/2015/technology-digital-making-big-data-work-supply-chain-management.aspx (accessed October 14, 2017).

https://www.bcg.com/publications/2016/big-data-energy-cooper-rehal-changing-game-data-lake.aspx (accessed October 14, 2017).

https://www.bcg.com/publications/2016/three-paths-to-advantage-with-digital-supply-chains.aspx (accessed October 14, 2017).

https://www.bcg.com/publications/2017/digital-transformation-transformation-data-driven-transformation.aspx (accessed October 14, 2017).

https://www.bcgperspectives.com/content/articles/supply_chain_management_sourcing_procurement_demand_driven_supply_chain/?chapter=2 (accessed October 14, 2017).

https://www.blue-granite.com/blog/azure-data-lake-analytics-holds-a-unique-spot-in-the-modern-data-architecture (accessed September 16, 2017).

https://www.blue-granite.com/blog/bid/402596/top-five-differences-between-data-lakes-and-data-warehouses (accessed October 14, 2017).

https://www.blue-yonder.com/sites/default/files/neue_studie-lebensmittel handler_mussen_schnellere_entscheidungen_treffen.pdf (accessed October 15, 2017).

https://www.bundesdruckerei.de/de/beratung Cloud READINESS (Accessed November 5, 2017).

https://www.bvl.de/files/1951/1988/2128/Trends_und_Strategien_in_Logistik _und_Supply_Chain_Management_-_Kersten_von_See_Hackius_Maurer .pdf (accessed December 28, 2017).

https://www.bvl.de/misc/filePush.php?id=26066&name=BVL14_Positions papier_Logistik_IT.pdf (accessed December 28, 2017).

https://www.bvl.de/schriften (accessed December 28, 2017).

https://www.cbi.eu/market-information/outsourcing-bpo-ito/cloud-computing/europe/ (accessed December 25, 2017).

https://www.channele2e.com/channel-partners/csps/cloud-market-share-2017-amazon-microsoft-ibm-google/ (accessed October 30, 2017).

https://www.cips.org/en-gb/knowledge/procurement-topics-and-skills/ developing-and-managing-contracts/demand-management1/demand _driven-supply-chain/ (accessed October 14, 2017).

https://www.cisco.com/c/m/en_us/solutions/data-center/offers/Digital-Readiness-Assessment/index.html Cloud READINESS (accessed November 5, 2017).

https://www.cloudatoz.com/6-rs-of-cloud-migration/ 6 Rs of Cloud Migration (accessed November 5, 2017).

https://www.crisp-research.com/cloud-trends-2016/ (accessed October 7, 2017).

https://www.datamation.com/storage/enterprises-are-hoarding-dark-data-veritas.html (accessed September 21, 2017).

https://www.datapine.com/blog/data-driven-decision-making-in-businesses/ (accessed October 15, 2017).

https://www.demanddriveninstitute.com/the-facts (accessed October 14, 2017).

https://www.demanddriveninstitute.com/the-facts - ARM Research - The DDSN (accessed October 14, 2017).

https://www.domo.com/learn/data-never-sleeps-5?aid=ogsm072517_1&sf10 0871281=1 (accessed November 16, 2017).

https://www.ec2instances.info/AWS PRICING (accessed October 30, 2017).

https://www.emc.com/leadership/digital-universe/2014iview/executive-summary.htm (accessed July 17, 2017).

https://www.entrepreneur.com/article/290553 (accessed November 4, 2017).

https://www.entrepreneur.com/article/303901 (accessed November 4, 2017) -> CLOUD Infographic - History Very NICE.

https://www.eugdpr.org/ GDPR (accessed December 22, 2017).

https://www.forbes.com/sites/kevinomarah/2017/07/13/your-roadmap-to-a-digital-supply-chain/3/#6ffe4eb07f9e (accessed October 14, 2017).

https://www.forbes.com/sites/louiscolumbus/2016/03/13/roundup-of-cloud-computing-forecasts-and-market-estimates-2016/#7189c1892187 (accessed September 23, 2017).

https://www.ft.com/content/76cffe96-db1b-11e0-bbf4-00144feabdc0 (accessed September 21, 2017) Benefits of Demand Forecasting.

https://www.ft.com/content/76cffe96-db1b-11e0-bbf4-00144feabdc0 (accessed September/ 21, 2017).

https://www.gartner.com/binaries/content/assets/events/keywords/catalyst/ catus8/2017_planning_guide_for_data_analytics.pdf (accessed September 21, 2017).

https://www.gartner.com/binaries/content/assets/events/keywords/catalyst/catus8/2017_planning_guide_for_cloud.pdf (October 2016) (accessed June 19, 2017).

https://www.gartner.com/doc/3728317?srcId=1-8729325372 (May 2017) (accessed October 14, 2017).

https://www.gartner.com/it-glossary/big-data (accessed September 16, 2017).

https://www.gartner.com/it-glossary/demand-driven-value-network-ddvn (accessed June 24, 2017).

https://www.gartner.com/newsroom/id/1684114 (May 2011) (accessed June 14, 2017).

https://www.gartner.com/newsroom/id/1684114 5-Rs of Cloud Migration (May 2011) (accessed November 5, 2017).

https://www.gartner.com/newsroom/id/2138416 (August 2012) (accessed June 24, 2017).

https://www.gartner.com/newsroom/id/3143718 (October 2015) (accessed May 6, 2017).

https://www.gartner.com/newsroom/id/3384720 (July 2016) (accessed October 7, 2017).

https://www.gartner.com/newsroom/id/3616417 (February 2017) (accessed May 15, 2017).

https://www.gartner.com/smarterwithgartner/gartner-predicts-our-digital-future/ (October 2015) (accessed September 2, 2017).

https://www.gartner.com/smarterwithgartner/how-to-build-a-business-case-for-demand-management-investment/ (May 2017) (accessed December 24, 2017).

https://www.gartner.com/technology/supply-chain/top25.jsp

https://www.ge.com/digital/industrial-internet (accessed December 21, 2017).

https://www.ge.com/docs/chapters/Industrial_Internet.pdf (accessed December 21, 2017).

https://www.ibm.com/blogs/cloud-computing/2014/03/a-brief-history-of-cloud-computing-3/ (accessed July 4, 2017).

https://www.idc.com/getdoc.jsp?containerId=prUS43196617 (accessed November 16, 2017).

https://www.isixsigma.com/tools-templates/graphical-analysis-charts/making-sense-time-series-forecasting/ (accessed December 24, 2017).

https://www.kdnuggets.com/2015/09/data-lake-vs-data-warehouse-key-differences.html (accessed September 16, 2017).

https://www.linkedin.com/pulse/20140602173917-185626188-the-history-of-cloud-computing-and-cloud-storage (accessed July 4, 2017).

https://www.linkedin.com/pulse/importance-accurate-sales-forecasting-stephen-p-crane-cscp (accessed September 21, 2017).

https://www.linkedin.com/pulse/marketers-ask-hadoop-enterprise-ready-tamara-dull (accessed September 16, 2017).

https://www.linkedin.com/pulse/marketers-ask-isnt-data-lake-just-warehouse-revisited-tamara-dull (accessed August 16, 2017).

https://www.linkedin.com/pulse/marketers-ask-what-can-hadoop-do-my-data-warehouse-cant-tamara-dull (accessed September 16, 2017).

https://www.linkedin.com/pulse/marketers-ask-why-do-we-need-hadoop-were-doing-big-data-tamara-dull (accessed September 16, 2017).

https://www.mckinsey.com/~/media/McKinsey/Industries/Advanced%20Electronics/Our%20Insights/How%20artificial%20intelligence%20can%20deliver%20real%20value%20to%20companies/MGI-Artificial-Intelligence-Discussion-paper.ashx (accessed December 27, 2017).

https://www.mckinsey.com/business-functions/digital-mckinsey/our-insights/disruptive-technologies (accessed May 4, 2017).

https://www.mckinsey.com/business-functions/digital-mckinsey/our-insights/leaders-and-laggards-in-enterprise-cloud-infrastructure-adoption (accessed October 7, 2017).

https://www.mckinsey.com/business-functions/digital-mckinsey/our-insights/the-case-for-digital-reinvention (accessed December 24, 2017).

https://www.mckinsey.com/business-functions/operations/our-insights/how-three-external-challenges-made-nokias-supply-chain-stronger (accessed December 21, 2017).

https://www.mckinsey.com/business-functions/organization/our-insights/six-building-blocks-for-creating-a-high-performing-digital-enterprise (accessed November 5, 2017).

https://www.microsoft.com/en-gb/cloud-platform/what-is-cortana-intelligence (accessed September 21, 2017).

https://www.mittelstand-nachrichten.de/verschiedenes/52-prozent-der-fuehrungskraefte-im-deutschen-lebensmittelhandel-entscheiden-warendisposition-nach-gefuehl/ (accessed August 15, 2017).

https://www.nist.gov/el/cyber-physical-systems/big-data-pwg (accessed September 16, 2017).

https://www.predictiveanalyticstoday.com/bigdata-platforms-bigdata-analytics-software/ (accessed August 11, 2017).

https://www.pwc.com/gx/en/advisory-services/digital-iq-survey-2015/campaign-site/digital-iq-survey-2015.pdf (accessed September 16, 2017).

https://www.quora.com/What-is-the-history-of-Hadoop -> history of HADOOP and GFS Google File System (accessed July 4, 2017).

https://www.sas.com/content/dam/SAS/en_us/doc/overviewbrochure/sas-for-demand-driven-planning-optimization-107293.pdf (accessed August 5, 2017).

https://www.sas.com/content/dam/SAS/en_us/doc/whitepaper1/forecast-value-added-analysis-106186.pdf (accessed August 12, 2017).

https://www.sas.com/de_ch/news/press-releases/2017/oktober/2017-10-12-nestle-enhances-demand-forecast-with-sas-analysis-solutions.html (accessed October 14, 2017).

https://www.sas.com/en_au/customers/forecasting-supply-chain-nestle.html (accessed October 14, 2017).

https://www.sas.com/en_au/customers/forecasting-supply-chain-nestle.html# (accessed October 14, 2017).

https://www.sas.com/en_us/offers/sem/demand-signal-analytics-107229.html?gclid=EAIaIQobChMIiOidkfCn1wIV4bztCh1sxgU6EAAYAyAAEg J0dvD_BwE (accessed September 21, 2017).

https://www.sitepoint.com/a-side-by-side-comparison-of-aws-google-cloud-and-azure/ (accessed August 11 and October 28, 2017).

https://www.skyhighnetworks.com/cloud-security-blog/11-advantages-of-cloud-computing-and-how-your-business-can-benefit-from-them/ (accessed September 23, 2017).

https://www.skyhighnetworks.com/cloud-security-blog/microsoft-azure-closes-iaas-adoption-gap-with-amazon-aws/ (accessed July 11 and 17, 2017).

https://www.slideshare.net/cranesp/A-Roadmap-To-World-Class-Forecasting-AccuracyIBFFinal (accessed September 21, 2017).

https://www.srgresearch.com/articles/cloud-market-keeps-growing-over-40-amazon-still-increases-share (accessed November 4, 2017).

https://www.srgresearch.com/articles/leading-cloud-providers-continue-run-away-market (accessed July 29, 2017).

https://www.srgresearch.com/articles/microsoft-google-and-ibm-charge-public-cloud-expense-smaller-providers (accessed October 30, 2017).

https://www.srgresearch.com/articles/microsoft-leads-saas-market-salesforce-adobe-oracle-and-sap-follow (accessed September 2, 2017).

https://www.statista.com/statistics/477277/cloud-infrastructure-services-market-share/ (accessed October 30, 2017).

https://www.strategyand.pwc.com/reports/industry4.0 (accessed October 14, 2017).

https://www.timetoast.com/timelines/cloud-computing-history (accessed November 4, 2017).

https://www.tompkinsinc.com/en-us/Insight/Tompkins-Blog/what-digital-components-are-affecting-your-supply-chain (accessed September 21, 2017).

https://www.toolsgroup.com/solutions/demand-sensing/ (accessed September 24, 2017).

https://www.vansonbourne.com/research-report/state-of-enterprise-it-2018 (accessed September 23, 2017).

https://www.vansonbourne.com/StateOfIT2018Reports/cloud-computing (accessed December 2, 2017).

https://www.veritas.com/dark-data (accessed December 28, 2017).

https://www.veritas.com/news-releases/2016-03-15-veritas-global-databerg-report-finds-85-percent-of-stored-data (accessed September 21, 2017).

https://www.veritas.com/news-releases/2016-03-15-veritas-global-databerg-report-finds-85-percent-of-stored-data (accessed December 28, 2017).

https://www.veritas.com/product/information-governance/global-databerg.html (accessed September 21, 2017).

https://www.vmware.com/go/tcocalculator/?src=WWW_US_HP_generic_TCOCalculator_R2C4_D_NA_TryNow (accessed July 6, 2017).

https://www.vmware.com/pdf/TCO.pdf -> TCO of physical servers versus VMWare (accessed July 6, 2017).

https://www.vmware.com/uk/products/cloud-foundation.html?cid=7013400
0001CUFs&src=ps_5919df50a6e29&kw=%2Bamazon%20%2Bvmware&mt=b&k_clickid=87087314-ccb5-4196-a2b4-f9037ffddeac (accessed August 29, 2017).

https://www.vmware.com/uk/solutions/virtualization.html (accessed July 6, 2017).

https://www.weforum.org/reports/big-data-big-impact-new-possibilities-international-development (accessed September 16, 2017).

https://www-01.ibm.com/common/ssi/cgi-bin/ssialias?htmlfid=ZZL03134 USEN (accessed October 14, 2017).

https://www-935.ibm.com/industries/uk-en/retail/supply-chain/?S_PKG=AW&cm_mmc=Search_Google-_-Consumer_Retail-_-UK_UKI-_-+demand++forecasting_Broad_AW&cm_mmca1=000023LB&cm_mmca2=10005782&cm_mmca7=9046107&cm_mmca8=kwd-3115615 19697&cm_mmca9=41966e4e-e2e4-45a6-95dc-8fb25a47daa9&cm_mmca10=222444828947&cm_mmca11=b&mkwid=41966e4e-e2e4-45a6-95dc-8fb25a47daa9|1185|501&cvosrc=ppc.google.%2Bdemand %20%2Bforecasting&cvo_campaign=000023LB&cvo_crid=22244482 8947&Matchtype=b (accessed September 24, 2017).

About the Author

Vinit Sharma (Berkshire, UK) is a cloud solutions architect at Microsoft focusing on the Microsoft data platform and artificial intelligence. Before his current role, he was a principal technical architect in a global position for advanced analytics at SAS Institute, specializing in a solution suite called Demand-Driven Planning and Optimization for supply chain optimization. Vinit has an MBA, a postgraduate diploma in management, and two degrees in business administration (one from the UK and one from Germany). In addition to these academic qualifications, he also has or held many industry qualifications, such as AWS Certified Solutions Architect, VCP, MCDBA, MCTS, OCP Developer, MCSE, BEA Administrator, a Chargeback and Activity-Based Cost Management certification from the IT Financial Management Association (ITFMA), and ITIL Foundation. He has more than 15 years of IT and industry experience working in various roles and fields (e.g., cloud computing, supply chain optimization, SAS, and virtualization).

Index

3-E test. *See* Effective, efficient, and economical

5Rs. *See* Retire Replace Retain and wrap Re-host Re-envision

6Rs. *See* Retire Retain Re-host Re-platform Re-purchase Re-factor

A

Access control lists (ACLs), 173, 194

Active Directory Lightweight Directory Services, 141

Active geo-replication (availability feature), 184

AD. *See* Amazon Microsoft Active Directory

Adaptability, 82

ADF. *See* Azure Data Factory

ADLS. *See* Azure Data Lake Store

Advanced analytics, 226, 246
  cloud/data, combination, 39f
  leverage, 251–252
  machine learning/artificial intelligence, leveraging, 41
  usage, 248

AES 256-bit encryption, usage, 171

AKS. *See* Azure Container Service

Amazon API Gateway, 151–152

Amazon AppStream 2.0, 154, 155

Amazon Athena, 144

Amazon Aurora, 128–129, 132

Amazon Certificate Manager, 140, 142

Amazon Chime, 153, 154

Amazon Cloud Directory, 140, 141

Amazon CloudFormation, 137, 138

Amazon CloudFront, 133, 134

Amazon CloudHSM, 140, 142

Amazon CloudSearch, 144, 145

Amazon cloud service, response values, 138

Amazon CloudTrail, 137, 138, 143

Amazon CloudWatch, 137

Amazon CodeBuild, 136

Amazon CodeCommit, 136

Amazon CodeDeploy, 136

Amazon CodePipeline, 136

Amazon Cognito, 149–150

Amazon Config, 137, 139

Amazon Dash, button (usage), 158

Amazon Data Pipeline, 144, 146–147

Amazon Device Farm, 149, 150

Amazon Direct Connect, 134, 135

Amazon Directory Service, 140, 142

Amazon DynamoDB, 128, 130–131, 144–145, 150, 157

Amazon Elasticache, 128, 131

Amazon Elastic Beanstalk, 124

Amazon Elastic Block Store (EBS), 125, 126–127

Amazon Elastic Compute Cloud
(EC2), 118, 119–122
instances, 135, 136
on-demand pricing, examples,
121f, 123
Systems Manager, 137,
138
Amazon Elastic Compute
Container Registry (ECR),
118, 122
Amazon Elastic Compute
Container Service (ECS),
118, 122
Amazon Elastic File System
(EFS), 125, 127
Amazon Elastic Load Balancers,
143
Amazon Elastic Load Balancing
(ELB), 134, 135
Amazon Elastic Map Reduce
(EMR), 144–146
Amazon Elasticsearch Service,
144, 145
Amazon Elastic Transcoder, 151,
152
Amazon GameLift, 158
Amazon Glacier, 125, 127
Amazon Glue, 144, 147
Amazon Greengrass, 157
Amazon Identity and Access
Management (IAM), 140,
141
Amazon Inspector, 140, 142
Amazon IoT Button, 157, 158
Amazon IoT Platform, 157
Amazon Key Management
Service (KMS), 140, 143
Amazon Kinesis, 144–146, 157
Amazon Lambda, 118, 124, 146,
150, 157
Amazon Lex, 147, 148
Amazon Lightsail, 118, 124
Amazon Lumberyard, 158

Amazon Machine Learning (ML),
147, 150, 157
Amazon-managed cloud service,
136
Amazon Managed Services, 137
Amazon Management Console,
138
Amazon Microsoft Active
Directory (AD), 142
Amazon Microsoft SQL Server
instances, 142
Amazon Mobile Analytics,
149–151
Amazon Mobile Hub, 149
Amazon Mobile SDK, 149, 150
Amazon OpsWorks, 137, 139
Amazon Organizations, 141, 143
Amazon Personal Health
Dashboard, 137
Amazon Pinpoint, 149, 150
Amazon Polly, 147, 148
Amazon Prime Photos, 148
Amazon QuickSight, 144, 146
Amazon Redshift, 132, 144, 145,
151
Amazon Rekognition, 147,
148
Amazon Relational Database
Service (RDS), 128, 129
Amazon Route 53, 134, 135
Amazon S3, 144–145, 150, 151,
153, 157
Amazon Service Catalogue, 137,
139
Amazon Shield, 141, 143
Amazon Simple Email Service
(SES), 152
Amazon Simple Notification
Service (SNS), 151, 152
Amazon Simple Queue Service
(SQS), 151, 152
Amazon Simple Storage Service
(S3), 125, 126, 135

Amazon Simple Workflow
(SWF), 151, 152
Amazon Step Functions, 151
Amazon Storage Gateway, 125,
127–128
Amazon Trusted Advisor, 137,
139–140
Amazon Virtual Private Cloud
(VPC), 133, 134, 142
Amazon Web Application
Firewall (WAF), 141, 143
Amazon Web Services (AWS),
118, 225
6Rs, 100–101
Application Discovery, 131,
132
Cloud Adoption Framework
(CAF), 101, 103t
cloud migration (6Rs), 102f
compute classification,
118–125
cost calculation, example,
69t
Database Migration Service,
131, 132
EMR, 146
global regions, 125f
joint partnership, 52
Server Migration Service
(SMS), 131, 132
shared responsibility model,
72f
SLA commitment, provision,
120
Snowball, 131, 133
Snowball Edge, 131, 133
Snowball Mobile, 131
Snowmobile, 133
spot instances, 68
Amazon Web Services (AWS)
cloud
framework approach, 101
portfolio categories, 119f

provider, 54, 61
service portfolio, 159f
Amazon WorkDocs, 153–154
Amazon WorkMail, 153, 154
Amazon Workspaces, 154
Amazon X-Ray, 136, 137
AML. *See* Azure Machine
Learning
Analytics, 144–147, 181
benefits, 41
types/maturity, 22f
usage, 9, 21–29, 41
Analytics unit (AU), 194
Android
applications, 213, 214
mobile application usage, 150
tablets, usage, 154
Apache Accumulo, 60
Apache Ambari, 55
Apache Apex, 58
Apache Avro, 57
Apache Beam, 59
Apache Calcite, 59
Apache Cassandra, 58
Apache Falcon, 57
Apache Flink, 56
Apache Flume, 59
Apache GraphX (graph
computation), 196
Apache Hadoop, 57
Apache Hama, 59
Apache HBase, 58
Apache Hive, 58
Apache Kafka, 56
Apache MapReduce, 57
Apache Mesos, 56, 180–181
Apache MLlib (machine
learning), 196
Apache Oozie, 57
Apache ORC, 60
Apache Parquet, 60–61
Apache Phoenix, 60
Apache Pig, 58

Apache REEF, 59
Apache Samza, 56
Apache Spark, 56–57
Apache Spark SQL, 196
Apache Squoop, 56
Apache Storm, 56
Apache Tajo, 59
Apache Tez, 58
Apache YARN, 57, 193
Apache Zeppelin, 60
Apache Zookeeper, 60
API. *See* Application
    programming interface
APN. *See* Apple Push Notification
Append Blob, 171
Apple macOS, usage, 154
Apple Push Notification (APN),
    178, 207
Application
  analytics, 149
  application-level provided
    information, 135
  content delivery, 149
  services, 151–152
  streaming, 154–155
Application programming
    interface (API)
  Amazon design, 119
  calls, usage, 138, 152
  Gateway, usage, 151–152
  request, person/service
    identification, 138
  support, 187
  usage, 103
Archiving needs, impact, 251
ARIMA, usage, 217
ARM. *See* Azure Resource
    Manager
Artificial intelligence (AI),
    147–151, 161, 191–200,
    203
  cognitive services, relationship,
    200–203

example, 24f
leveraging, 41
AS2, 207
ASR. *See* Automating speech
    recognition
At-least-once processing, 153
AU. *See* Analytics unit
Australian InfoSec Registered
    Assessors Program, 160
Authentication capabilities,
    179
Automatic backups (availability
    feature), 184
Automating speech recognition
    (ASR), 148
Availability Zones (AZs), 118,
    126
Aviva, 167
Azure, 61, 159
  cloud platform, 203
  low-priority VMs, 68
  portal screenshot, 73f, 74f
  SQL Server 2016 Tabular
    Models, deployment, 198
Azure Active Directory (AAD)
    (AD), 179, 195, 210–212
Azure Advisor, 215
Azure AI and Cognitive Services,
    200–201
Azure Analysis Services, 192,
    198–199
Azure Apache Spark (for Azure
    Insight), 192, 196–197
Azure API Management, 175,
    177–178, 213, 214
Azure Application Gateway, 164,
    167, 168
Azure Application Insights, 213,
    214, 215
Azure App Service, 162,
    164–165, 175–176, 178, 179
Azure Archive Storage, 170
Azure Automation, 215

Azure Automation and Control, 215

Azure Autoscale, 164

Azure Backup, 171, 174, 215

Azure Batch, 162, 166, 178, 179, 201

Azure Blob Storage, 170, 171, 217

Azure Bot Service, 191, 193, 200

Azure Cloud Service, 162, 165–166

Azure Cloud Shell, 215

Azure Cognitive Services, 201

Azure Container Instances, 162, 165–166, 178

Azure Container Registry, 166, 178–180

Azure Container Service (AKS), 162, 165, 180–181

Azure Content Delivery Network (CDN), 167, 168–169, 175, 176

Azure Cosmos DB, 181, 186–190, 204, 206
  consistency levels, 189
  NoSQL database support, 187

Azure Cost Management, 215

Azure Custom Speech Service, 192, 199

Azure Database
  Migration Service, 181, 191
  usage, 181, 185

Azure Data Catalog, 192, 196

Azure Data Factory (ADF), 186, 191, 195, 200, 217

Azure Data Lake Analytics, 191, 193–194

Azure Data Lake Store (ADLS), 171, 172–173, 194–195

Azure DDoS Protection, 167, 170

Azure DevTest Labos, 213, 214

Azure Disk Storage, 170, 172

Azure Domain Name System (Azure DNS), 167, 168

Azure Event Grid, 204, 206–207

Azure Event Hubs, 192, 193, 199, 204, 207–208

Azure ExpressRoute, 167, 169–170

Azure File Storage, 170, 172

Azure Functions, 162, 165

Azure Government,
  ExpressRoute circuit (creation), 170

Azure HDInsight, 100, 173, 186, 191, 192, 194, 196

Azure HockeyApp, 213, 214

Azure Hybrid, 164

Azure Insight, 192, 215

Azure IoT Edge, 193, 203, 205

Azure IoT Hub, 203, 204, 205

Azure Key Vault, 173, 210, 211

Azure Load Balancer, 164, 167, 168

Azure Location-Based Services, 204, 208

Azure Log Analytics, 192, 196, 215

Azure Logic Apps, 204, 207

Azure Machine Learning (AML) (ML), 196, 213, 217
  Services, 200
  Studio, 200, 203, 206

Azure Managed Applications, 215

Azure Marketplace, 167

Azure Media Services, 175, 176–177

Azure Migrate, 215

Azure Mobile app, 215

Azure Monitor, 215

Azure Multi-Factor
Authentication, 210,
212–213
Azure Network Watcher, 167,
170, 215
Azure Notification Hubs, 175,
178, 204, 207
Azure Portal, 215
Azure Power BI Embedded, 191,
195
Azure Protection and Recovery,
215
Azure Queue Storage, 170, 172
Azure Redis Cache, 181, 190–191
Azure Reserved Virtual Machines
Instances, 162, 164
Azure Resource Manager (ARM),
198, 215
Azure Scheduler, 215
Azure Search, 175, 177
Azure Security Center, 210–211
Azure Security & Compliance,
215
Azure Service Fabric, 162, 166,
178, 180
Azure Service Health, 215
Azure Site Recovery, 171, 174,
215
Azure SQL
Database, 181–185,
192–199–200, 218
Data Warehouse, 181,
185–186, 200
Server, 217
Stretch Database, 181, 186
Azure Storage, 170, 171
Azure StorSimple, 171, 173–174
Azure Stream Analytics, 191,
192–193, 203, 205–206
Azure Text Analytics API, 192,
197
Azure Time Series Insights, 204,
206

Azure Traffic Manager, 167, 169,
215
Azure Virtual Machines (VMs),
161–164
Azure Virtual Network, 167, 191
Azure VPN Gateway, 167, 168

B
Back-end resources, operation
requirement, 136
Back-end systems, 152, 207
Bar codes, 202
BCR. *See* Benefit-cost ratio
Benefit-cost ratio (BCR), 240
Bidirectional communication,
possibility, 204
Big Data, 47, 52, 181, 203
3-Vs, 172, 194
analysis, 41
challenges, 191
Hadoop framework, 186, 200
impact, 54f
NIST definition, 16–17
open source ecosystem, 55f
philosophy, 218
platforms, usage, 173, 194
presence, 145
query, 196
scalable framework, 144–145
usage, 248
volume/variety/velocity/
variability, 17–18
Binary large object (BLOB)
format, 187
types, 171
Block Blob, 171
Business
insights, improvement, 31
productivity, 153–154
solution, 229
Business intelligence (BI), 195,
205
reporting tool, usage, 174

C

C173DX, 188

Capital expenditure, costs (shift), 81

CCM. *See* Cloud Controls Matrix

CDN. *See* Azure Content Delivery Network

Cegid, 241

Central processing unit (CPU)
  intensiveness, 152
  number, decrease, 119
  usage, 137

Chef (IT platform), 139

Chellapa, Ramnath, 44

CI/CD. *See* Continuous integration and continuous development

Cisco Global Cloud Index, 78f, 80f, 240

Citrix, integration, 211

CJIS. *See* Criminal Justice Information Services

Classic Load Balancer, 135

Cloud
  adoption, impact, 88t
  approach, steps, 93f
  benefits, 40–41, 81–89, 82f, 83f
  business reasons, identification, 94–96
  challenges, 85f, 87f
  characteristics, 61–70
  Cisco global cloud index, 78f
  cloud-managed service, 207–208
  cloud-native database, 186
  computing facilities, impact, 155, 157
  data, 39f, 41
  deployment models, 77f
  economies, impact, 41
  edge, 205
  enterprise use, prevention (factors), 95f

logic, 149
  management tools, 137–140
  maturity, increase, 87f
  price index, 70f
  providers, 40, 109
  public cloud, private cloud (contrast), 80f
  readiness checks, 96–99, 97t–98t
  readiness results, example, 98f
  R framework, migration (example), 100f
  scalability, 40
  services, 160–161, 190–191
  solutions, company adoption (percentage), 85t
  sovereign clouds, 77
  type, identification, 94, 107–113
  users, costs/benefits, 89f
  vendor, 107–113, 112f

Cloud Adoption Framework (CAF). *See* Amazon Web Services

Cloud-based demand-driven supply chain (CBDDS), 39f, 40

Cloud computing (CC), 44
  economic impact, 95f
  impact, 242
  IT benefits, 87f
  NIST definition, 61
  onset, 238
  time line, 45f–46f
  usage, prevention (factors), 95f

Cloud Controls Matrix (CCM), 160

Cloudera, 173, 194

Cloud migration, 106f
  decisions, KPMG considerations, 104
  factory, 108f, 114f

Cloud Security Alliance (CSA),
160
Cloud service, 145, 192
consumer options, 64
economic return, ranking, 109t
identification, 107–113
integration, 238–239
models, 71f, 75f
provider, selection, 110t, 111t
public providers, EU market
shares, 113t
types, availability, 109
Cognitive computing, 249
Cognitive services, 161, 200–203
Cold data, analysis, 41
Collaboration, usage, 9, 29–41
Collaborative approach, usage,
29–41
Columnar store (data storage),
130
Column family data model,
example, 189f
Common Criteria EAL4+ security
standards, usage, 211
Complex event process (CEP)
pipelines, 193
Compliance certification, 187
Compute category, 161–167
Computing resources, usage, 40
Connected devices, usage, 243
Connected supply chain
management, 243f
Consumer packaged goods
(CPGs), 10
Containers, 178–181
Content delivery network (CDN),
Amazon provision, 134
Content, end-user requests, 134
Continuous integration and
continuous development
(CI/CD), 164, 179
Conversation bots, 149
Cookie-based sessions, 168

Cookie, storage, 168
CPGs. *See* Consumer packaged
goods
Criminal Justice Information
Services (CJIS), 160
Cron job syntax, usage, 165
Cryptographic keys, storage, 211
CSA. *See* Cloud Security Alliance
CustomerID, sequence
(example), 188
Customer journey analytics, 249
Customer satisfaction,
improvement, 31

D
Dark Data
avoidance, 251
databerg, relationship, 32f
Dark Lake phenomenon,
avoidance, 196
Data, 9–21, 41, 246
analytics, 109
centers, 49f, 53f, 118
cloud/advanced analytics,
combination, 39f
consistency, 187
creation, 41
data-driven analytics, usage,
243
data-driven approach, 150
data-driven decisions, 248–249
dimensions, 218
encryption, 173
flow, 12f, 195f
generation, Cisco GCI estimate,
155
intelligence, 191–200
lakes, 17f, 41
leveraging, 41
models, 187, 224
services scale, organizational
needs, 41
sources, 192

warehouse, MPP architecture design (usage), 199–200
Database administrators (DBAs), usage, 129
Databases, 128–133
engines, Amazon RDS cloud service support, 129
RDS support, 128
Databerg, dark data (relationship), 32f
Data transaction units (DTUs), 183. *See also* Elastic data transaction units
DC/OS, 165, 178, 180
DDPO. *See* SAS Demand-Driven Planning and Optimization
Dedicated hosts, 120
Dell, 167
Demand
demand-driven insights, 41
forecasts, usage, 246
management, 247
planner, interface, 246
sensing, 28
shaping, 28–29, 29f
Demand-driven forecasting, 202, 231
IoT, relationship, 25f
solutions, 246
Demand-driven supply chain (DDSC), 30, 30f, 203
advantages, 31
benefits, 40f
integration/technologies, 245f
Demand forecasting
Azure Cloud, usage, 216–218
data, usage, 17f
Demand signal repository (DSR), 36, 223, 224, 228, 235
Deployment models, 75–81
Descriptive Diagnostic Predictive Prescriptive (DDPP) model, 21, 22f

Desktop streaming, 154–155
Developer tools, 136–137, 161, 213–214
DevOps, 104, 182, 214
Digital infrastructure, impact, 249
Digitalization, 243
Digital supply chain, interconnection, 5f
Disaster recovery (DR), 82, 110
Discounted unit prices, 68
Distributed denial of service (DDoS) attacks, protection services, 143
Distribution planning, 244
Docker Hub, 164, 166, 178, 179
Docker Swarm, 179–180
Document data model, example, 190t
Document store (data storage), 130
Domain name system (DNS), 124, 135
Downstream consumers, recommendations, 41
DPM. *See* Microsoft
DR. *See* Disaster recovery
Drag-and-drop interface, usage, 138
DSR. *See* Demand signal repository
DTUs. *See* Data transaction units
Dynamic capabilities, leverage, 234
Dynamic data masking, usage, 184

E
EBS. *See* Amazon Elastic Block Store
EC2. *See* Amazon Elastic Compute Cloud
Economic return, 109t

Economies of scale, 40, 238–239
ECR. *See* Amazon Elastic
Compute Container Registry
ECS. *See* Amazon Elastic
Compute Container Registry
Edge locations, 134
EDIFACT, 207
eDTUs. *See* Elastic data
transaction units
Effective, efficient, and
economical (3-E test),
105
EFS. *See* Amazon Elastic File
System
Elastic data transaction units
(eDTUs), 183
Elasticity, leverage, 234
Elastic pools, usage, 183
ELB. *See* Amazon Elastic Load
Balancing
Electronic data interchange
(EDI), support, 207
EMR. *See* Amazon Elastic Map
Reduce
End-user devices, 154
End-user requests, 134
Enterprise-grade cloud service,
requirement, 154
Enterprise integration, 161,
208–210
Enterprise resource planning
(ERP) systems, 195
Enterprise SaaS growth, market
leaders, 76f
Enterprises, cloud computing
usage (prevention), 95f
ETL. *See* Extract, transform, and
load
European Union (EU) cloud
provider market, 111
service, 113t, 239
Europe, cloud computing
(economic impact), 95f

Evaluation metrics, 229
Event-driven applications,
development, 206–207
Event stream processing (ESP),
13–14
Exponential smoothing, usage,
217
ExpressRoute circuit, creation,
170
Extract, transform, and load
(ETL) data, usage, 147

F
Facebook, 149, 212
Facebook Messenger, 193
Failover, 169, 184
Federal Risk and Authorization
Management Program
(FedRAMP), 160, 187
FireOS, mobile application usage,
150
First-in, first-out (FIFO)
processing, 153
Forecasting, 9, 251
demand-driven forecasting, IoT
(relationship), 25f
Forecast reconciliation, 246
Forecast value added, example,
34–35
Front-end applications, interface,
152

G
Games, development, 158–159
GCM. *See* Google Cloud
Messaging
GDPR. *See* General Data
Protection Regulation
General availability (GA), 150
General Data Protection
Regulation (GDPR), 196,
238, 251
alteration, 38

launch, 105
regulations, impact, 94
Genomics, 200, 201
Germany
cloud vendor benchmark
(2016), 112f
IT provider, leverage, 241
GitHub, 164, 179, 214
Git, usage, 178, 214
Google, 200, 207, 240
Google+, 212
Google Chromebooks, 154
Google Cloud Messaging (GCM),
178, 207
Graph database (data storage),
130
Graphics processing units
(GPUs), 152

H
H.265 video, conversion, 152
Hadoop, 144–145, 192
Hadoop framework (HDFS), 173,
186, 194, 200
Hard disk drives (HDDs)
memory, usage, 131
organization selection, 126
selection, 146
Hardware security module
(HSM), 142, 173, 194, 211
Hash key, 188
Health Information Trust
Alliance (HITRUST), 187
Health Insurance Portability and
Accountability Act (HIPAA),
160, 187
High-level lambda architecture
design, 18f
High-performance computing
(HPC), 166, 179
HIPAA. *See* Health Insurance
Portability and
Accountability Act

HITRUST. *See* Health Information
Trust Alliance
Hortonworks, 173, 194
Hot data, analysis, 41
HSM. *See* Amazon CloudHSM;
Hardware security module
HTML 5 compatibility, 155
Hybrid data flow, supply chain
analytics, 20f
Hypertext transfer protocol
(HTTP), 165, 168
Hyper-V virtual machines. *See*
Microsoft

I
IA. *See* Industrial analytics
IAM. *See* Amazon Identity and
Access Management
IDE. *See* Integrated development
environment
Identity, 140–143
Image recognition, usage, 202
Implementation partners,
availability, 110
Industrial analytics (IA), 250
Industrial Internet Data Loop,
203, 204f
Industrial Internet economic
potential, 156f
Industrial Internet of Things
(IIoT), 192, 203, 205, 252
Information communication
technology (ICT), 81, 249
Information, recording, 138
Information technology (IT), 2,
44, 81, 118
architecture design, ability, 224
Big Data, impact, 54f
cloud computing, impact, 87f
operating model, 238
Infrastructure as a Service (IaaS),
70–72, 107, 159, 225, 240
example, 73f

Infrastructure as a Service (IaaS)
(*Continued*)
    platforms, public cloud, 81f
    virtualization/usage, 234
In-memory analytics, 226
In-memory OLTP, usage, 181
Input/output (I/O), usage, 172
Inputs, optimization, 247–248
Integrated development
    environment (IDE), 164,
    179, 197
IntelliJ IDEA, 197
Internal Revenue Service (IRS)
    1075, 160
International Traffic in Arms
    Regulations (ITAR), 160
Internet of Things (IoT), 6, 13,
    109, 155–158, 192, 194,
    203–208
    demand-driven forecasting,
        relationship, 25f
    demand sensing, example, 28
    devices, usage, 199
    earning potential, 155
    time-series data, 206
Internet Protocol (IP), 124, 138
    defining, organizational
        control, 134
    IPSec VPNs, support, 168
Inventory, 243
    costs, reduction, 31
    optimization, 231–235
    reduction, possibility, 248–249
iOS, mobile application usage,
    150, 154, 178, 207, 212–213
iPad, usage, 154
iPhone X, Hello feature, 202
IRS. *See* Internal Revenue Service
ISG cloud readiness
    check, example, 96, 97t–98t
    results, example, 98t
ITAR. *See* International Traffic in
    Arms Regulations

J
Java Database Connectivity
    (JDBC), 147
JavaScript, 165
JavaScript Object Notation
    (JSON), 130, 181, 189
Java, support, 197
Jupyter notebooks, support, 197

K
Kafka platform, 192
Key-value, 130, 187, 188t
KMS. *See* Amazon Key
    Management Service
KPMG, cloud migration
    considerations, 104
Kubernetes, 165, 180, 181
Kundra, Vivek, 44

L
Lambda architecture design, 18f
Latency-based routing,
    configuration, 135
Lead time, 242, 243
Lift and shift, 103–104
Lightweight Directory Access
    Protocol (LDAP), 141, 213
Linux VMs, 164
Low-priority VMs, 68
Lua scripting language, support,
    190

M
Machine learning (ML), 41, 147,
    200, 203, 226
macOS applications, 213, 214
MAD. *See* Mean absolute
    deviation
Management, 215–219
MAPE. *See* Mean absolute
    percentage error
MapR, 173, 194
MariaDB, 128, 129

Market share/reputation, 110
Massive parallel processing (MPP), 146, 185–186, 199–200
Material inventory, reduction, 242
Material requirements planning, 244
Mean absolute deviation (MAD), 223
Mean absolute percentage error (MAPE), 223, 229
Memcached, 131
Mesophere, 165, 178, 180, 181
Messaging services, 152–153
Metadata tagging, 202
MHI 2018 survey results, 8f
Microservices-based design, usage, 104
Microsoft (MS), 24f, 25f
  Azure. *See* Azure.
  Bing, usage, 200
  cloud, 54, 101, 103–104, 241
  Exchange, 174
  Genomics, 200, 201
  hypervisor virtualization technology, 174
  hyper-V virtual machines, 174
  Office 365, 207
  Power BI. *See* Power BI.
  R Server, integration, 197
  SharePoint, 174
  Skype, 193
  System Center Data Protection Manager (DPM), 174
  Teams, 193
  Visual Studio, 164, 182, 198, 213–214
  Windows, usage, 154, 178
  Xbox game console, 159
Microsoft Dynamics, 159
Microsoft Office, 159

Microsoft Push Notification Service (MPNS), 178
Microsoft SQL Server, 129, 132, 159, 174, 181
  databases, 186
  Stretch Database, 186
Migration, 131–133
  factory, 94, 113–115, 132
ML. *See* Amazon Machine Learning; Azure Machine Learning; Machine Learning
Mobile cloud services, 175–178
Mobile services, 148–151
Monitoring, 215–219
Monolithic design, usage, 104
MPEG2 video, conversion, 152
MPNS. *See* Microsoft Push Notification Service
MPP. *See* Massive parallel processing
MTCS. *See* Singapore Multi-Tier Cloud Security
Multifactor authentication, 173, 194
Multimodel data storage, 130
Multimodel support, 187
Multitier causal analysis, 246
MyDay, integration, 211
MySQL, 128, 129
  Azure Database, usage, 181, 185

N
National Institute of Standards Technology (NIST) definitions, 17, 61
Natural language understanding (NLU), 148
Netflix, case study, 115
Networking, 133–135, 167–170
Networks
  network-level provided information, 135
  topology, visualization, 170

News and media company, case
study, 222–229
Node.js, 164, 185, 207, 214
NoSQL database, 149, 186
management, 206
types, evolution, 130

O
OAuth 2.0, protocol, 212
Oil and energy company, case
study, 230–235
OLAP. *See* Online analytical
processing
Omni-channel demand insights,
31
On-demand instances, 120
On-demand services, 134
On-demand video-streaming
services, 152
One-time passcode (OTP), 212
Online analytical processing
(OLAP), 130, 181
Online retailers, websites, 134
Online shopping, example, 28–29
Online transactional processing
(OLTP), 130, 181
On-premises sources, 146–147
OpenID Connect, protocol, 212
Open source
ecosystem, 55f
Redis cache engine, basis, 190
Operating expenditure, costs
(shift), 81
Operating systems (OSs), choices,
119–120
Operational databases, 41
Oracle, 128, 129, 240
Oracle to Oracle, 132
OTP. *See* One-time passcode

P
Page Blob, 171
Parallel computing, 234

Parallel workloads, usage, 166
Passwords, storage, 211
Pay-as-you-go (PAYG), 239
business model, 120
cost model, 68, 134
financial model, 36, 41, 229
model, 164
priority, 179
Payment Card Industry (PCI),
187
People, collaborative approach
(usage), 29–41
Performance tests, settings, 228
Performant platform, 206,
248–249
Personalized recommendations,
28–29, 29f
PHP, 164, 179, 207
Platform as a service (PaaS), 40,
71–74, 107, 128
example, 74f
usage, 159, 164, 225, 240
Point-in-time restore (availability
feature), 184
Point of sale (POS) scanners,
usage, 199, 202, 208
POSIX-based access control lists
(ACLs), 173, 194
PostgreSQL, 36, 128, 129
Azure Database, usage, 181,
185
Power BI, 195, 197, 217, 2001
PowerShell, 165, 178, 214
Price-to-value ratio, 110
Private cloud, public cloud
(contrast), 80f
Processes, collaborative approach
(usage), 29–41
Product availability, increase, 242
Product dimension hierarchy, 10f
Product inventory, reduction,
242
Production capacity, 243

Product management, 227, 234
Public cloud, 81f, 238–239
  AWS global regions, 125f
  leadership, race, 112f
  private cloud, contrast, 80f
Push and pull, 4
Push notifications, 149
Python, 164, 167, 179, 185, 193, 206, 214

Q
QlikView, 197
QR codes, 202
Query processing unit (QPU), 198

R
R (platform), 192, 206
Radius, 213
Random-access memory (RAM), amount (decrease), 119
Random walk, forecast (example), 34f
RDS. *See* Amazon Relational Database Service
Real-time analytics, usage, 169
Recovery point objective (RPO), 182
Redhat, usage, 120
Redis, 131
Relational databases, 130
Representational State Transfer (REST)
  APIs, usage, 172, 178, 214
  web protocol, 171
Research and development (R&D), 227, 234
Reserved instances (RI), 68, 120, 164, 179, 239
REST. *See* Representational State Transfer
Retainable evaluator execution framework (REEF), 59

Retire Replace Retain and wrap Re-host Re-envision (5Rs), 101, 103–104
Retire Retain Re-host Re-platform Re-purchase Re-factor (6 Rs), 100–101, 102f
Revenue growth, cloud adoption (impact), 88t, 239
R framework, 99–107, 100f
RLS. *See* Row-level security
R-model, 92, 94, 99–100, 107, 241
Rockwell Automation, cloud service leverage, 204
Row-based storage, usage, 182
Row-level security (RLS), 184–185
RPO. *See* Recovery point objective
R Server, integration, 197

S
S3. *See* Amazon Simple Storage Service
SaaS. *See* Software as a service
Sales
  opportunities, increase, 31
  random walk, forecast (example), 35f
  revenue, increase, 31
Sales and operations planning (S&OP) processes, 240
Sales and operations process, 4f
Salesforce (SFDC), 207
SAML. *See* Security Assertion Markup Language 2.0
SAP, 241
  ASE, 132
  Business Objects Lumira, 197
  enterprise resource planning (ERP), 195
SAS, 36, 245

SAS Demand-Driven Planning and Optimization (DDPO), 37f
software solution suite, 36
Scalability, 40, 82
Scala, support, 197
SCCTs. *See* Supply chain control towers
Schema, defining, 141
Schema-on-write approach, relational database usage, 130
SDK. *See* Software Development Kit
Seasonal random walk, forecast (example), 35f
Secure socket layer (SSL)
leverage, 129, 142
offloading, 168
Security, 140–143
Security Assertion Markup Language 2.0 (SAML 2.0), 211, 212
Server Message Block (SMB) protocol, 172
Server Migration Service (SMS), 131, 132, 212–213
Servers, virtualization, 48f
Server virtual machine, 228
Service
levels, 31, 110
models, 70–75
tiers, 198
type, identification, 94
Service-level agreements (SLAs), 105, 120, 182, 194
absence, 191
Service Organization Control (SOC), 160
SES. *See* Amazon Simple Email Service
Shared responsibility model, 71

Singapore Multi-Tier Cloud Security (MTSC), 160
Single sign-on (SSO), 173, 179, 194
SmartFocus, 241
SMS. *See* Amazon Web Services
SNS. *See* Amazon Simple Notification Service
SOC. *See* Service Organization Control
Software as a service (SaaS), 40, 71, 107, 159, 225, 240
applications, 26, 103
consumer options, 64
growth, market leaders, 76f
service models, 70
Software-defined data centers (SDDCs), 71, 76, 238
Software Development Kit (SDK), 138, 213
Software tool/components, 55–61
Software vendor, strategic partnership, 227
Solid state disk (SSD)
memory, usage, 131
selection, 126, 146
storage, 124
throughput provision, 172
S&OP. *See* Sales and operations planning
Sovereign clouds, 77
Spark platform, 192
Spark Streaming, 196
Speech recognition, 202
Spot instances (AWS), 68, 120
SQL. *See* Structured Query Language
SQL Server Analysis Services (SSAS), 198
SQS. *See* Amazon Simple Queue Service

SSAS. *See* SQL Server Analysis
 Services
Star schema, forecast
 dimensions, 12f
Static Internet Protocol (IP)
 address, 124
Storage, 109, 125–128,
 170–174
Storm platform, 192
Strategic supply network
 planning, 244
Structured Query Language
 (SQL), 57, 144, 146
 Management Studio, usage,
 182
 Server Data Tools, usage,
 198
 U-SQL, 193
Supply chain
 agility, enhancement, 31
 analytics, 12f, 20f
 business, 224
 control tower, 7f
 demand-driven supply chain
 (DDSC), 30, 30f, 40f
 management, 242, 243f,
 247–248, 251f
 optimization, 232f, 244–245
 performance, improvement,
 247
 technologies, 250f
Supply chain control towers
 (SCCTs), 6–8
SUSE, usage, 120
SWF. *See* Amazon Simple
 Workflow
System integrators (SIs), usage,
 242

T
Tableau, 197
Tabular Model Scripting
 Language (TMSL), 198

Tabular Object Model (TOM),
 SSAS support, 198
Tasks, automation/outsourcing,
 82
TDE. *See* Transparent data
 encryption
Temporal logic, implementation,
 205
Tesco, Big Data/advanced
 analytics (usage), 248
Text-to-voice functionality, 147
Third-party networking,
 leverage, 167
Throughput times, 242, 243
ThyssenKrupp, cloud service
 leverage, 204
Time efficiencies, 82
Time horizon, defining, 228
Time stamp, 138
TMSL. *See* Tabular Model
 Scripting Language
TOM. *See* Tabular Object Model
Traffic routing methods, 169
Transactional data, usage,
 183–184
Transcoding processes, CPU
 intensiveness, 152
Transparent data encryption
 (TDE), 184
Transport layer security (TLS),
 leverage, 142
T-Systems, 241
Twitter (identity provider), 149
Two-tier deployment
 architecture, 228

U
Ubuntu, usage, 120
UK G-Cloud, 160
Uniform resource identifier
 (URI), 131
Unique selling point (USP), 205
Unit4, 241

UPS, Azure/bots/cognitive
    services usage, 193
Uptime, cloud vendor selection
    factor, 110
User authentication/
    management, 150
User data storage, 149
User sign-in, 149
USP. *See* Unique selling point
U-SQL, 193

V
Value-added chain,
    plan/management, 244
Variability, 18
Variety, 17
Velocity, 18
Vending machine, IoT demand
    sensing (example), 28
Vendor
    ecosystem, 110
    knowledge/experience/
        know-how, 110
    lock-in, 86
    market comparison, 111t
    type, identification, 94
Video streaming services, 134
Virtual CPUs/RAM, performance
    baseline, 120
Virtual desktop infrastructure
    (VDI) solutions, 154
Virtual infrastructure, 138
Virtualization, 47–52, 174
Virtual local area networks
    (vLANs), 135
Virtual machines (VMs), 138. *See
    also* Azure Virtual Machines;
    Linux VMs; Low-priority
    VMs; Microsoft; Windows
    VMs
    containers, comparison, 50f

form, 119
low-priority VMs, 68
operating system, 47–48
running, 168
shutdown, 120
types, 163
usage, 103–104
VMware-based virtual
    machines, 174
Virtual private networks (VPNs),
    134, 213
    leverage, 129
    tunnel, 167
vLANs. *See* Virtual local area
    networks
VMs. *See* Virtual machines
    (VMs)
VMware, usage, 47, 174
VMware vCloud Air, 240
Voice/image recognition, 147
Volume, 17
Volume Variety Velocity
    Variability (4 Vs), 17–18
VPC. *See* Amazon Virtual Private
    Cloud
VPNs. *See* Virtual private
    networks

W
WAF. *See* Amazon Web
    Application Firewall
Web cloud services, 175–178
Weighted round robin, 135,
    169
Windows Push Notification
    Service (WNS), 178, 207
Windows Store, technology
    leverage, 187
Windows VMs, 164
WNS. *See* Windows Push
    Notification Service

Wrappers, addition, 103
WS-Federation, 211

X
X12, 207
x86 hardware, virtualization, 238
Xamarin, 214

Xbox Live gaming services, technology leverage, 187
XML data, usage, 181

Y
Yet another resource negotiator (YARN), 193